# CVC Storybooks
## 15 Emergent Readers

Set 1

# Student Workbook

Stories and Pictures
by
Mark Linley

bartlebysbox.com

Dedicated to all teachers
   and to the children in their care

ISBN  978-0-9977255-7-5

Copyright © 2020 by Mark Linley
All rights reserved by author.

# CONTENTS

| | | |
|---|---|---|
| Welcome | ............ | i |
| Student Workbook & Teacher Edition | ............ | ii |
| How to Use CVC Storybooks | ............ | iii |
| Sequence of Instruction | ............ | iv |
| Student Directions | ............ | v |
| Book 1 RAT | ............ | 1 |
| Book 2 FED | ............ | 13 |
| Book 3 HIT IT | ............ | 25 |
| Book 4 MOM | ............ | 37 |
| Book 5 SUN | ............ | 49 |
| Book 6 HAT | ............ | 61 |
| Book 7 WET | ............ | 73 |
| Book 8 PIG DIGS | ............ | 85 |
| Book 9 DOG JOGS | ............ | 97 |
| Book 10 HUG | ............ | 109 |
| Book 11 FAT RAT | ............ | 121 |
| Book 12 WET PET | ............ | 133 |
| Book 13 BIG DIG | ............ | 145 |
| Book 14 HOP | ............ | 157 |
| Book 15 GUM | ............ | 169 |

# Welcome

Dear Teachers, Parents, Tutors, and Caregivers,

Hello! My name is Mark Linley. I am a veteran teacher in the primary grades and the author of these and many other high quality educational materials. The **CVC Storybooks** series is a thoughtfully developed, rigorous set of early literacy minibooks for teaching consonant-vowel-consonant (CVC) words to children. It was created to teach students in classroom settings the fundamentals of CVC decoding, blending, segmenting, and word recognition. It is now available in Workbook format, for use in class and at home.

I personally use these CVC Storybooks as a teaching tool in my own kindergarten classroom as part of an extensive and fully developed systematic early literacy program which I have pieced together and refined over the course of twenty years as an educator in the primary grades. This Student Workbook is for children from four to six years of age, and for older students who are struggling to learn how to read. It can be used independendently and without the aid of the Teacher Edition.

I originally wrote and illustrated the stories in the **CVC Storybooks** series to fill a gap I saw in the available literature, to use with my own students. I had students who needed to learn how to blend simple words and I could not find the right books - *story*books written with CVC words only. Many students get confused and frustrated by beginner books with sentences that contain both CVC words and sight words together. They don't know if a word should be sounded out or recognized iconically as a sight word. Many kids learn the alphabet and are then are passed too quickly on to emergent readers that combine CVC and sight words. Many children struggle at this juncture.

With this series the children you teach will be able read entire books without the frustrating experience of guessing whether to sound out a word or to remember it iconically as a sight word - every word in this series can be sounded out. Children feel a sense of accomplishment when they are able to read a book by themselves all the way to the end. They feel proud when they are able to successfully read a page and then turn the page because they've read it correctly.

These books will help you to navigate your little student(s) through the very beginning stages of reading. **CVC Storybooks** will help you teach your kids to read.

Enjoy!

# Student Workbook & Teacher Edition
## *A Comparison*
### ~~~

## Student Workbook

This **Student Workbook** contains the same stories as the Teacher Edition, but it does not require the Teacher Edition for use: **Student Workbooks can be used on their own.** The **Student Workbook** is a companion to the Teacher Edition, but it is not necessary to use them in conjunction with one another. Teachers, schools, and school districts may choose to purchase the Workbooks to eliminate teacher labor at the photocopy machine and to give teachers a resource that's a simple Grab and Go. Parents can simply buy the workbook alone and have what is needed to get their child beginning to read.

## Teacher Edition

The **Teacher Edition** is designed for use by teachers who have access to a photocopy machine and who will then put the minibooks together to make class sets. It is published in a special format which allows teachers to staple together mini-books for each title: teachers photocopy, cut, fold, and staple each storybook into class sets of 12 page booklets.

The **Teacher Edition** of **CVC Storybooks** contains Comprehension Questions for each page, which provide a check for understanding as well as provide plenty of room for discussion. The Teacher Edition also contains reproducible Independent Worksheets that are meant to be photocopied and used as a follow-up for students who need it.

# How to Use **CVC Storybooks** to Teach Reading

~~~

***CVC Storybooks*** are designed specifically to target one of the earliest stages of reading acquisition. After most of the sounds have been taught, students are taught how to decode Consonant-Vowel-Consonant (CVC) words.

***CVC Storybooks*** contain only CVC words. They do not contain sight words, which can confuse students and should at first be taught separately. With these books, students concentrate on the singular skill of reading words sound by sound as they blend sounds together to form whole words.

Effective teachers of early reading use the following time-honored and efficient long term instructional plan to get their students to read.

1. Teach the ABCs, their names and the sounds associated with them.
2. Introduce CVC decoding: "sounding out" words sound by sound and then blending the sounds together to form a word.
3. Introduce sight-word recognition. Lists of sight words can be easily found. Search for Dolch and Fry high frequency word lists.
4. Continue to review ABC names and sounds, CVC decoding processes, and sight words throughout the year, adding new sight words and introducing more advanced emergent readers with complete sentences as children progress.

***CVC Storybooks*** specifically target the second phase of the above instructional progression. Consider following the Sequence of Instruction to help you to use ***CVC Storybooks*** to teach CVC decoding to your student(s).

# Sequence of Instruction

### TEACH *the ABCs first*

**CVC Storybooks** are especially useful once children are acquainted with the ABCs, particularly the sounds the letters make, though it is not necessary for all letter sounds to be known for **CVC Storybooks** to be effective.

### READ TOGETHER

SEAT your student in front of his or her own copy of the book.
READ each page, chorally sounding out the words together.

### DEMONSTRATE blending, sound by sound

BLEND each word with the child or students, sound by sound.
  *Point* to each letter and enunciate each sound: /c/ - /a/ - /t/.
  *Point* to the first two letters and enunciate the first two phonemes blended together, followed by the final consonant: /ca/ - /t/.
  Alternatively, point to the first letter and enunciate the first phoneme, then the medial vowel and final consonant together: /c/ - /at/.
  *Swipe* your finger under the word and blend the entire word: 'cat'.

USE the following script(optional)
  Teacher: *Put your finger under the first letter. Ready begin.*
  Teacher and student: /c/ - /a/ - /t/, /ca/ - /t/, or: /c/ - /a/ - /t/, /c/ - /at/
  Teacher: *What's the word?*
  Teacher and student: 'cat'

### TALK as you read together

TALK about the story, making connections to other areas of life and knowledge as you read along. Use this, and frankly, any other opportunity to talk about things with your child. Help your child through any difficulties he or she may be having.
ENCOURAGE your child to look at the pictures and make comments.
CONTINUE reading the story.

### WRITE each word

TRACE and WRITE the page's word in the workbook.
FOLLOW the stroke order indicated on each page by the arrows.
WRITE as the book is being read, page by page *or* READ the story first and write the words afterwards.

### COLOR the pictures (Optional)

USE crayons and colored pencils. Wide crayons help develop early fine motor skills. Colored pencils give students more pencil practice which translates later into faster success in letter formation, word writing, and sentence writing.

## Student Directions

- Look carefully at each picture
- Think about what is happening in each story
- Sound out each word
- Read all of the words on every page
- Trace and write the words in both upper case and lower case letters
- Review the words on the last page of the story
- Color the pictures

RAT

1 rat

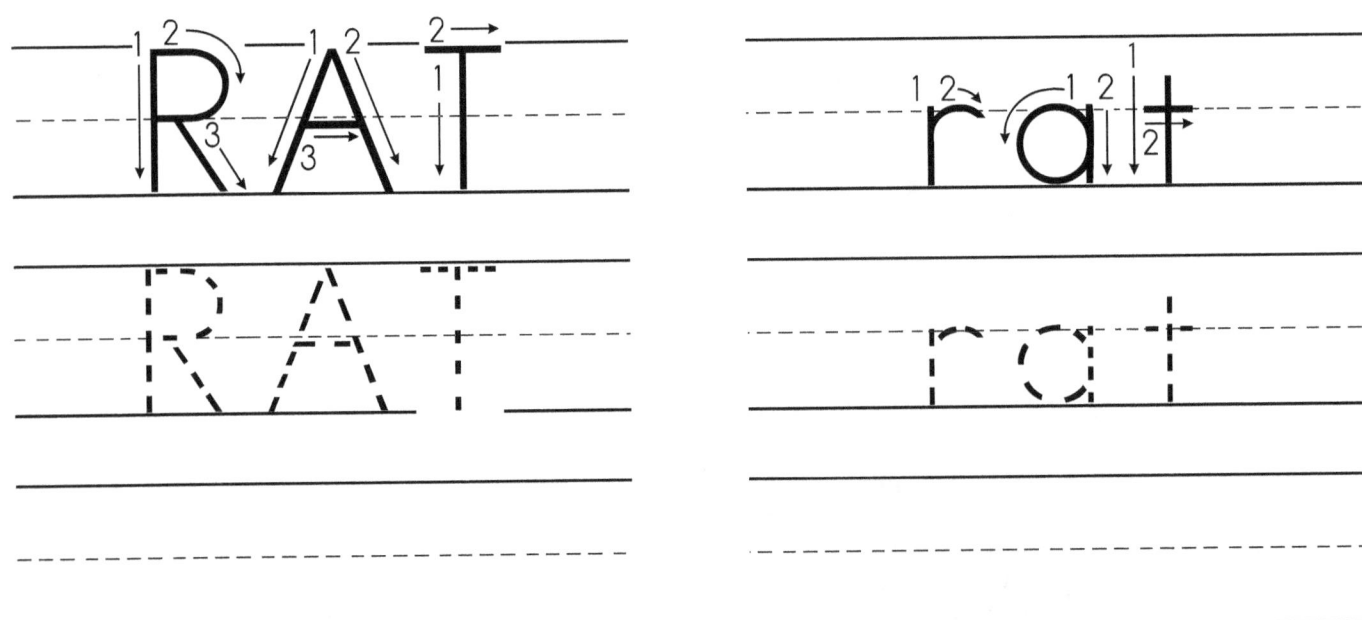

HAT

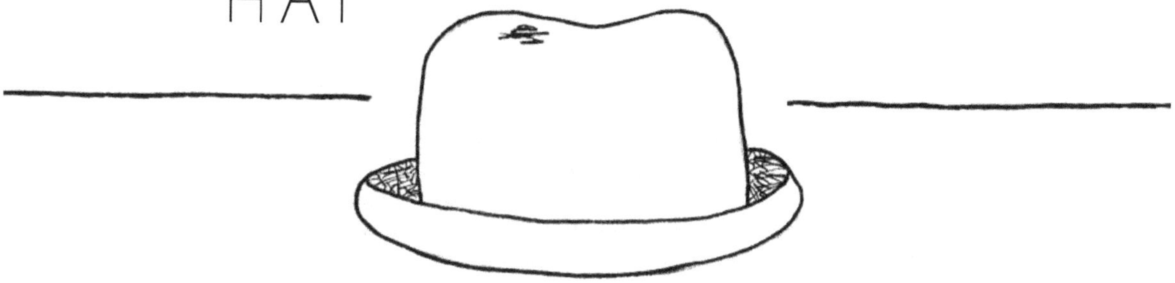

hat   2

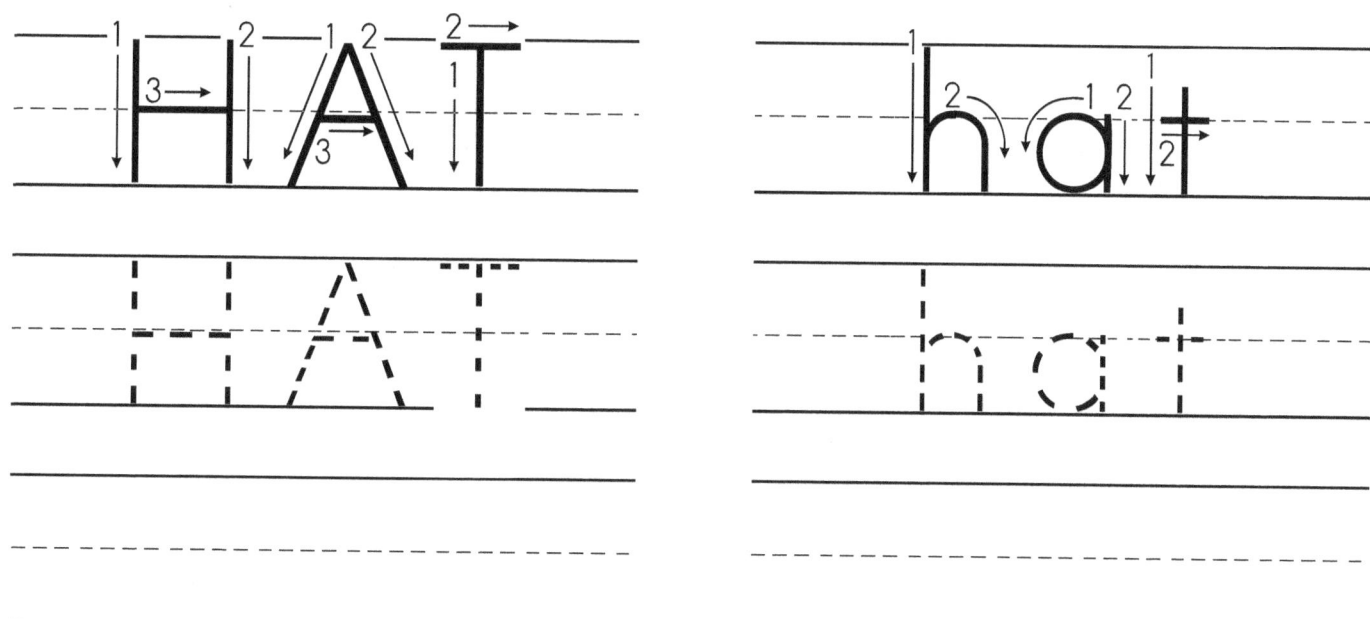

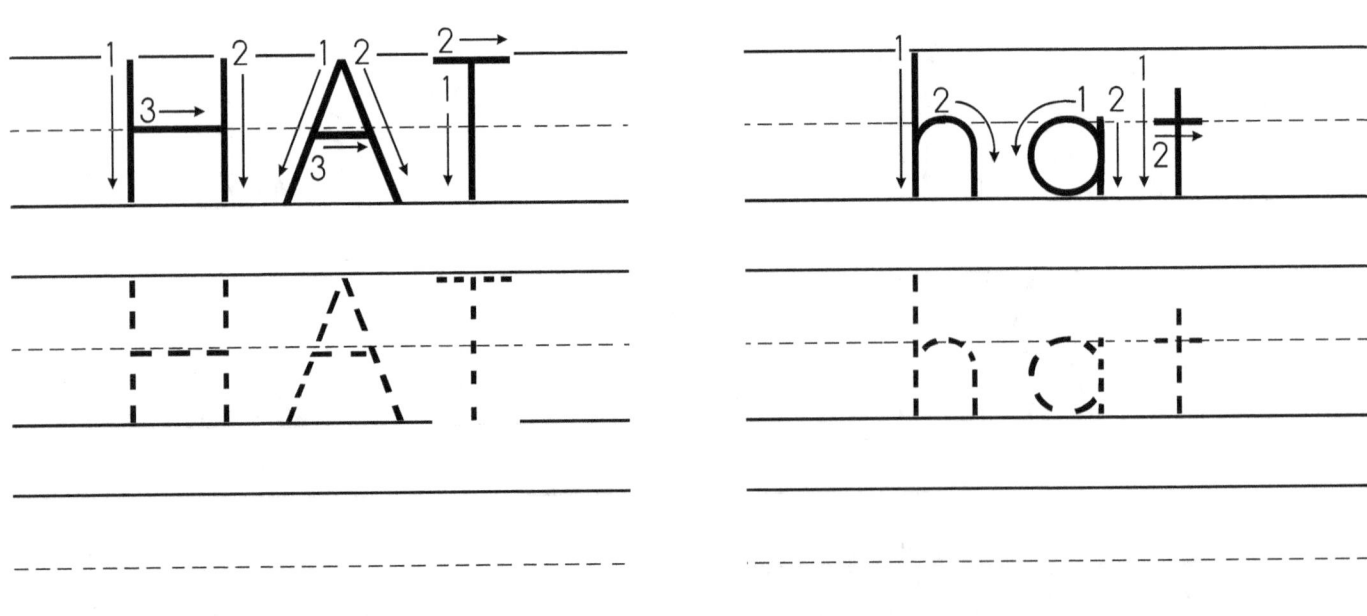

3  hat

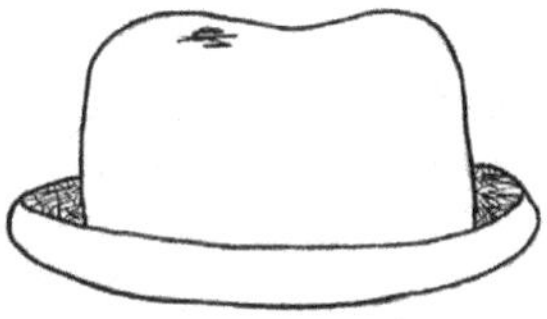

HAT

hat

4

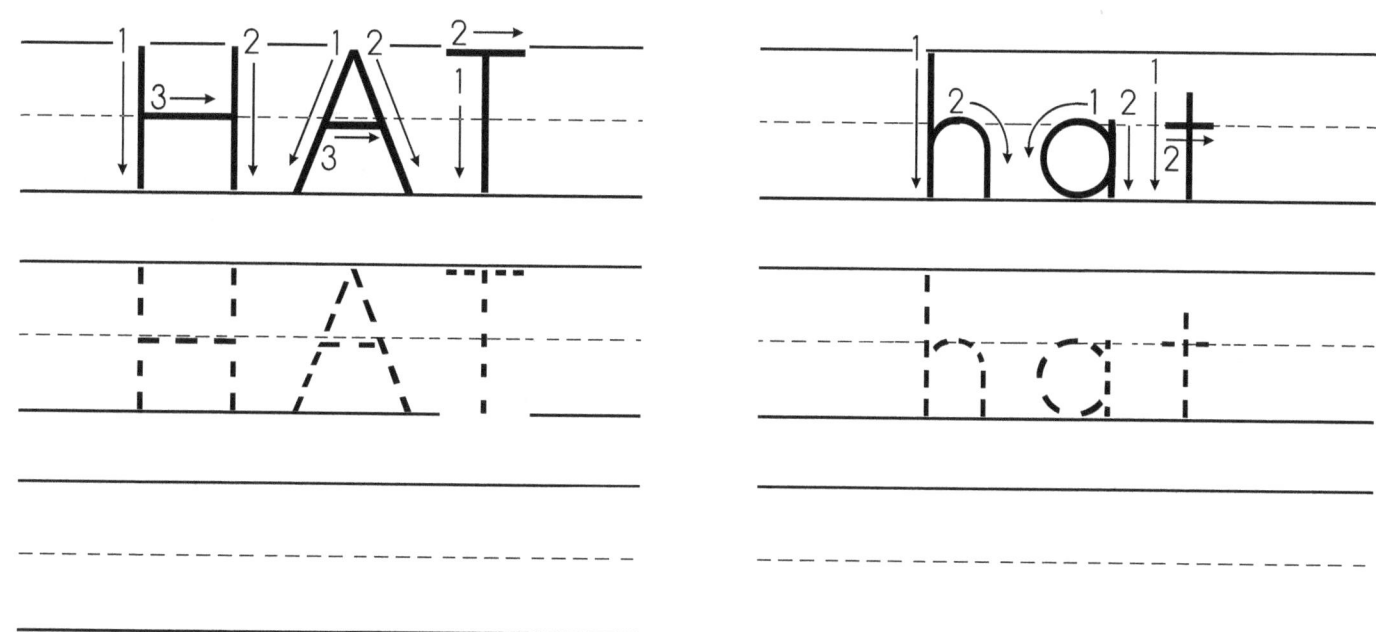

RAT

5 rat

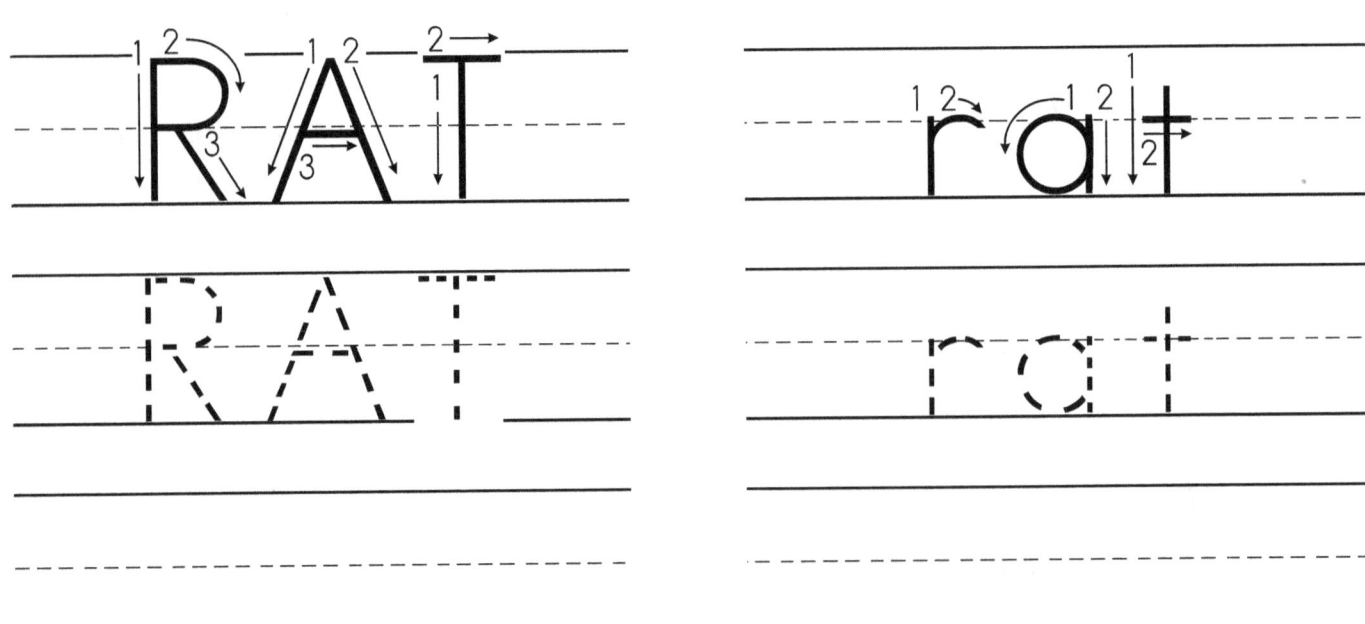

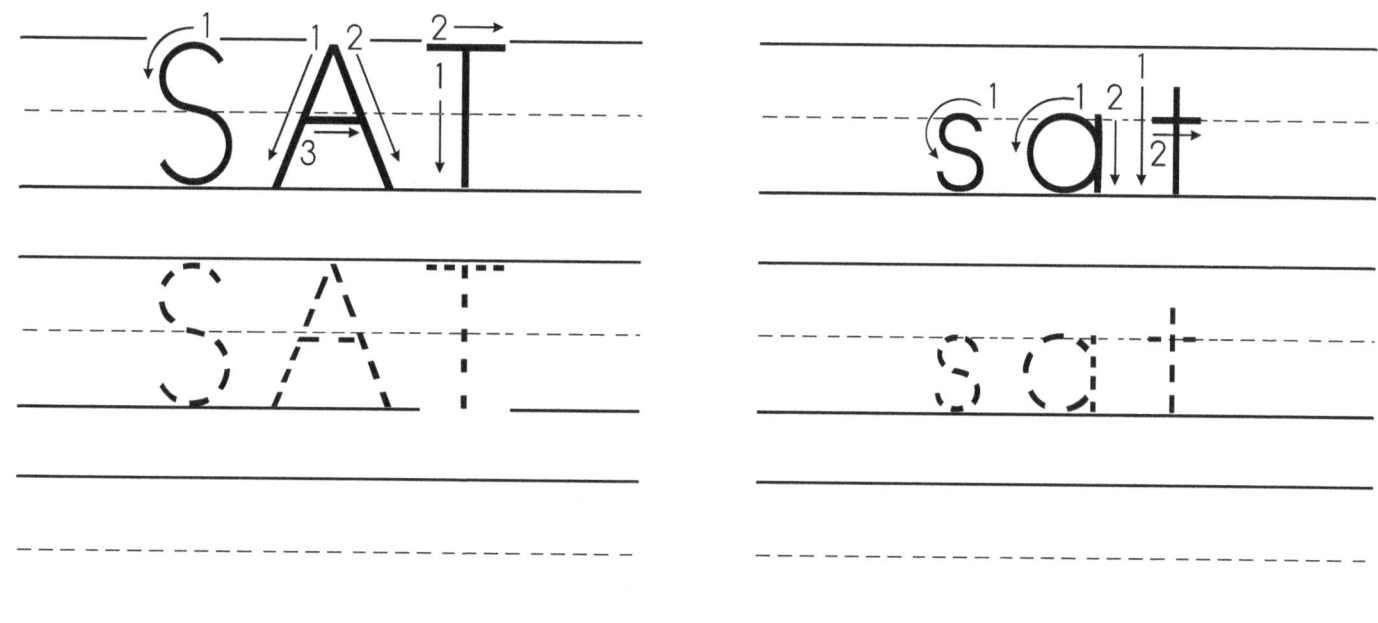

HAT

7 | hat

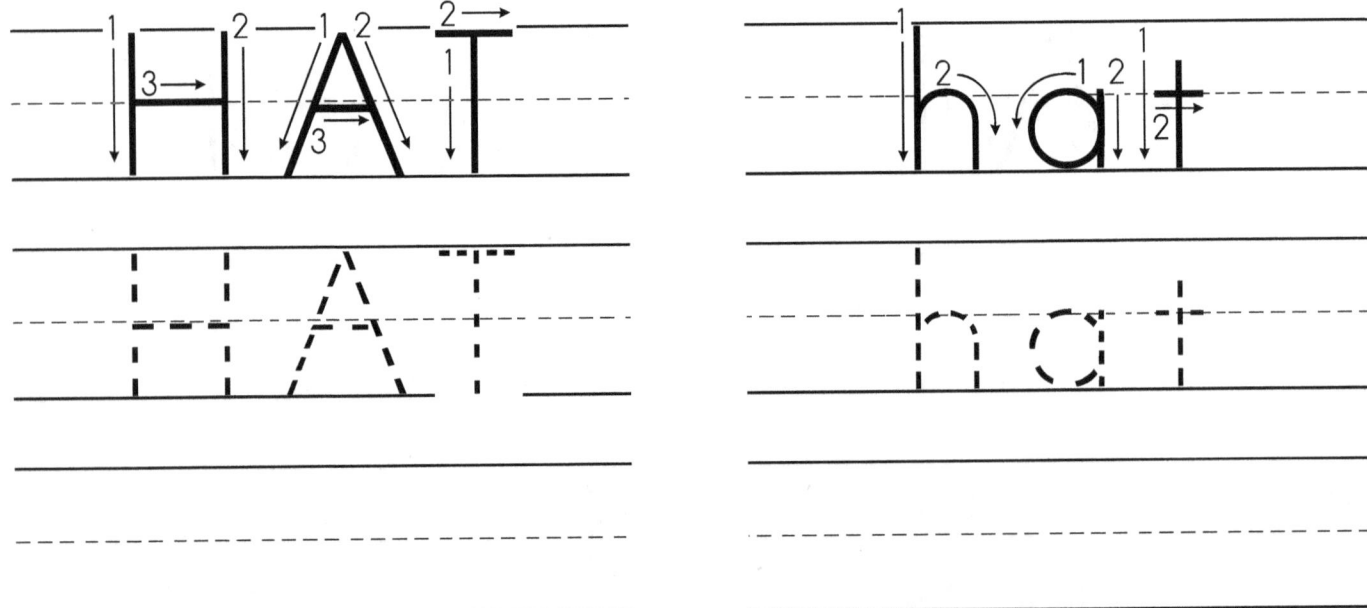

HAT

hat  8

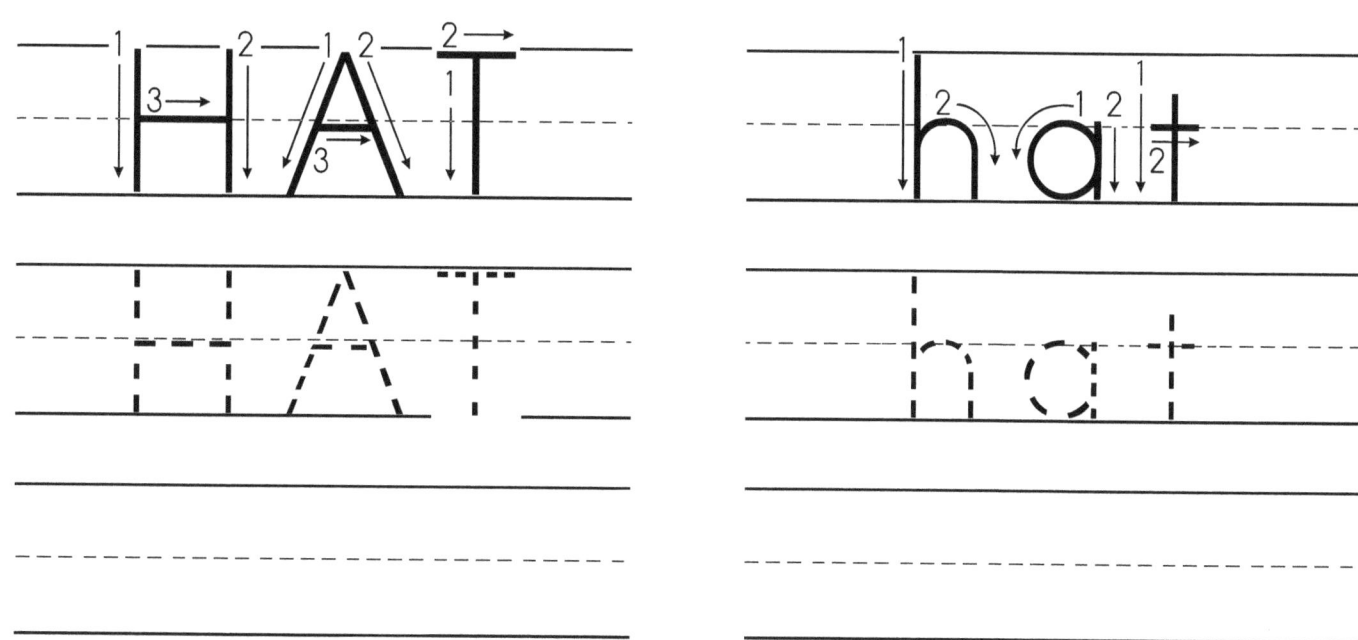

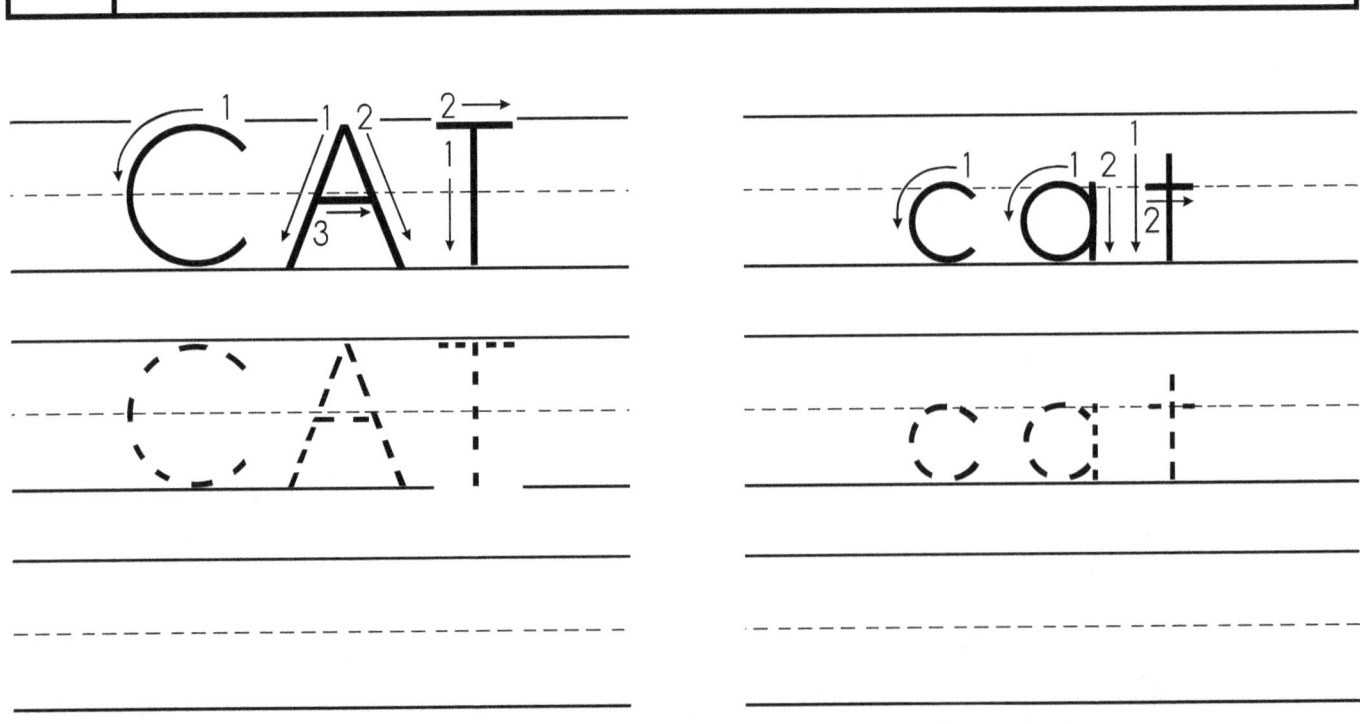

9 cat

hat

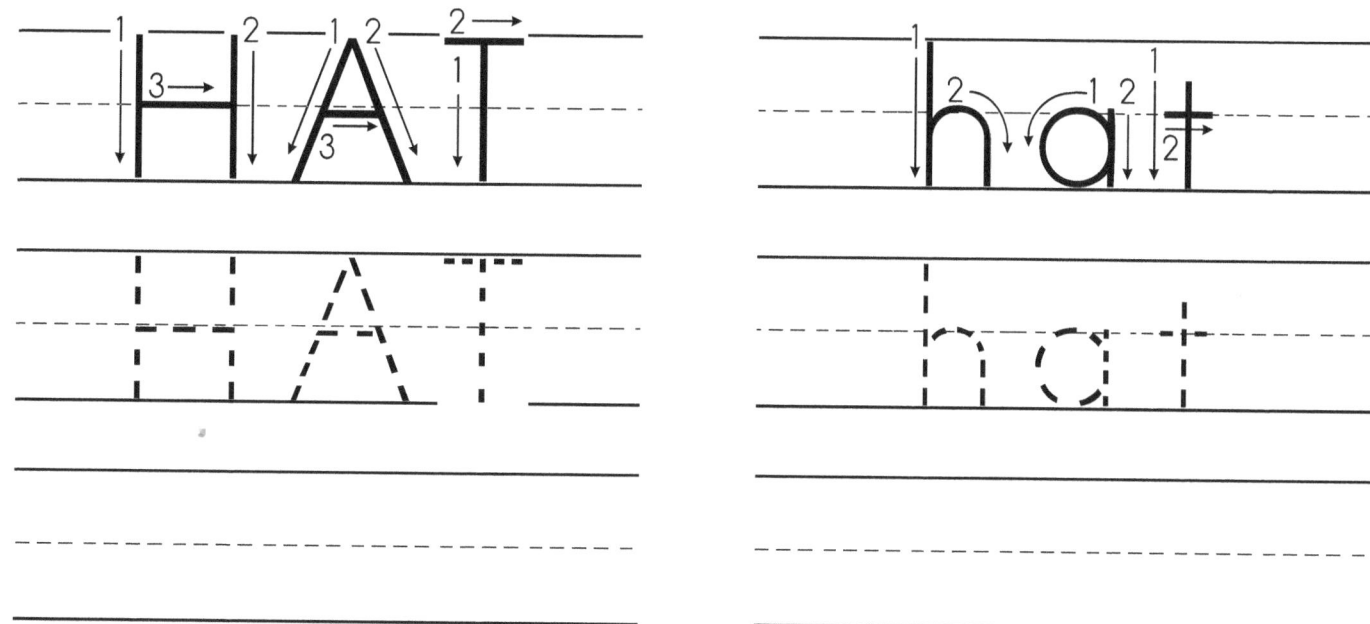

# RAT

rat    sat

hat    cat

Got it!

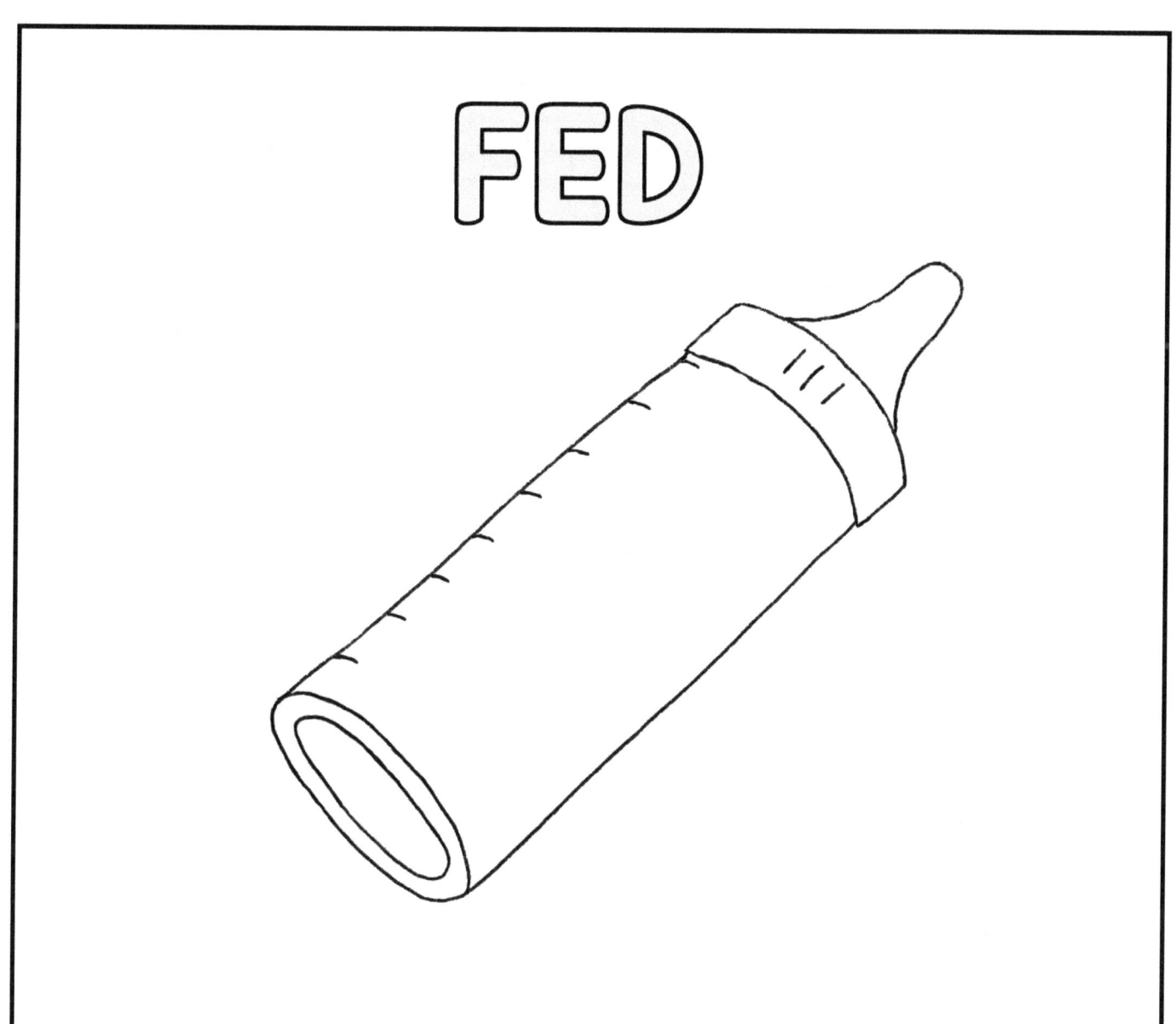

TED

**1** Ted

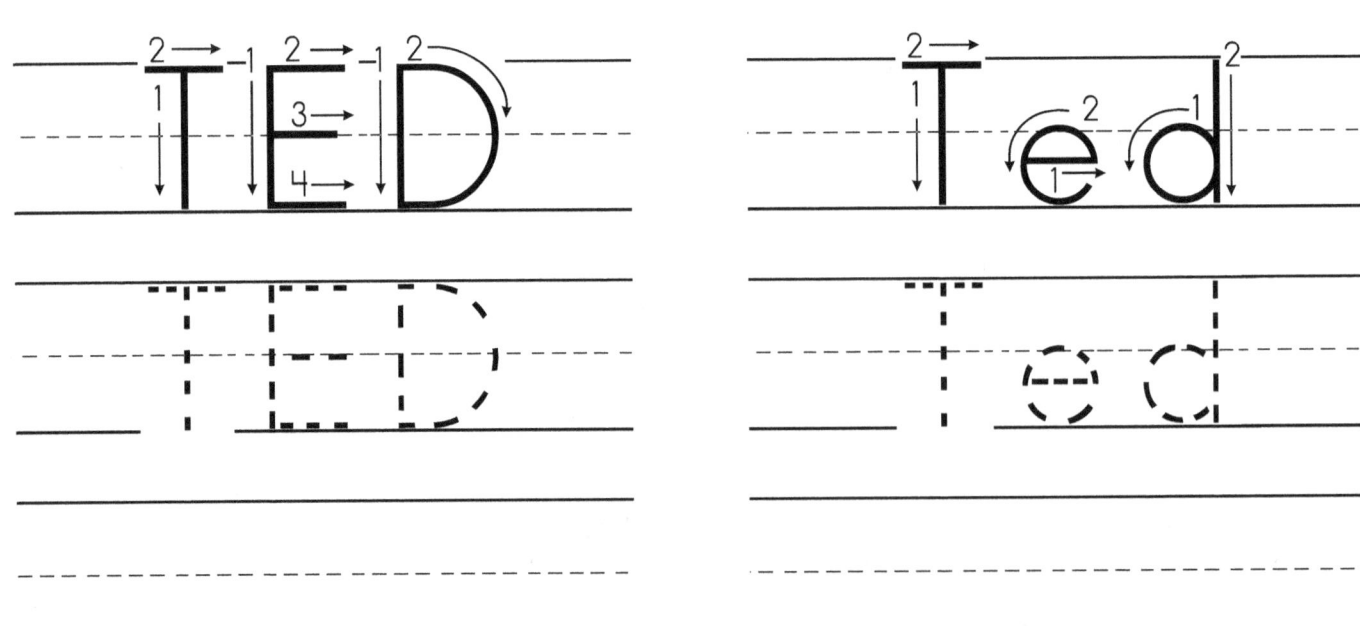

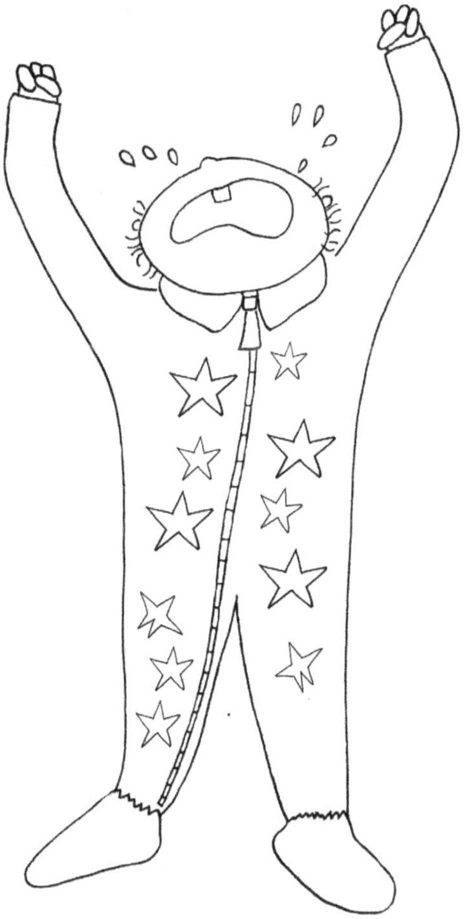

NED

# Ned

2

ED

3 | Ed

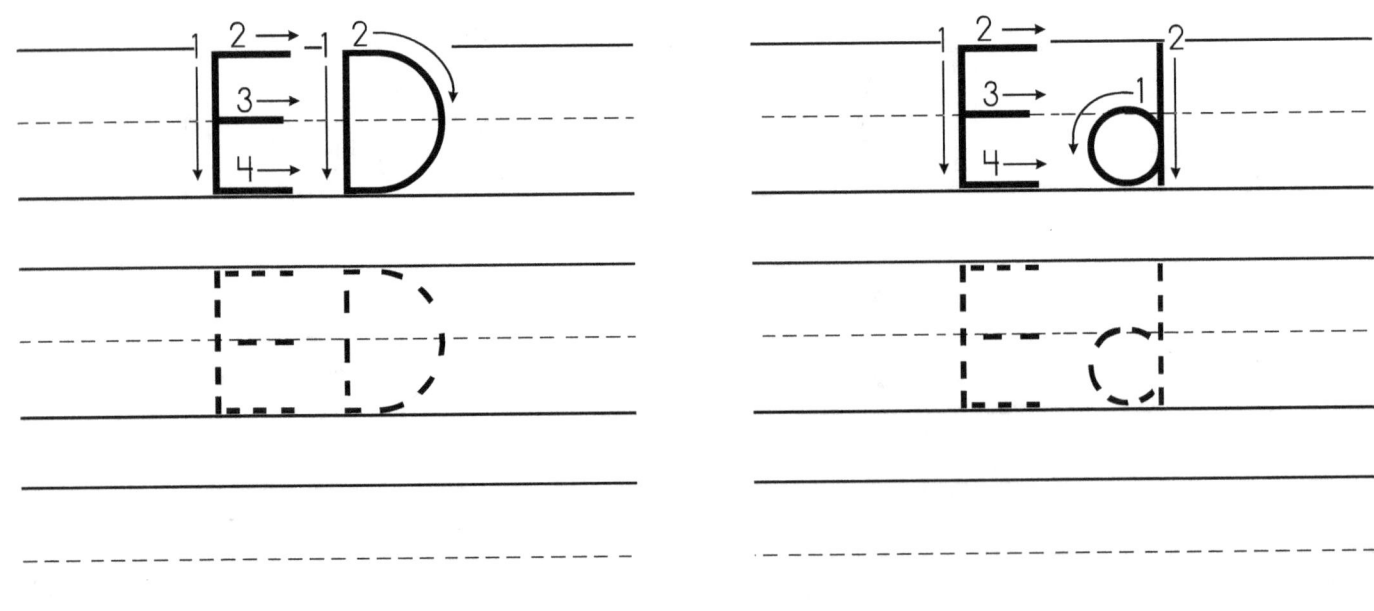

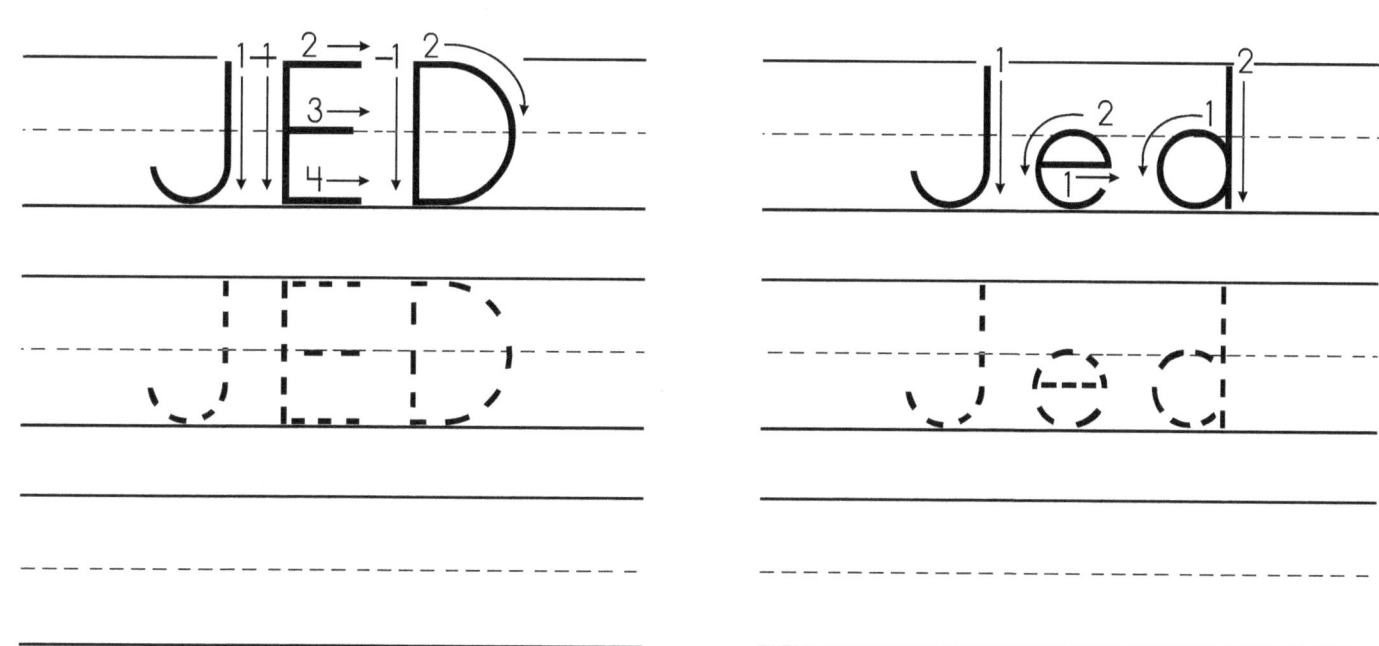

JED

Jed 4

TED

**5** Ted

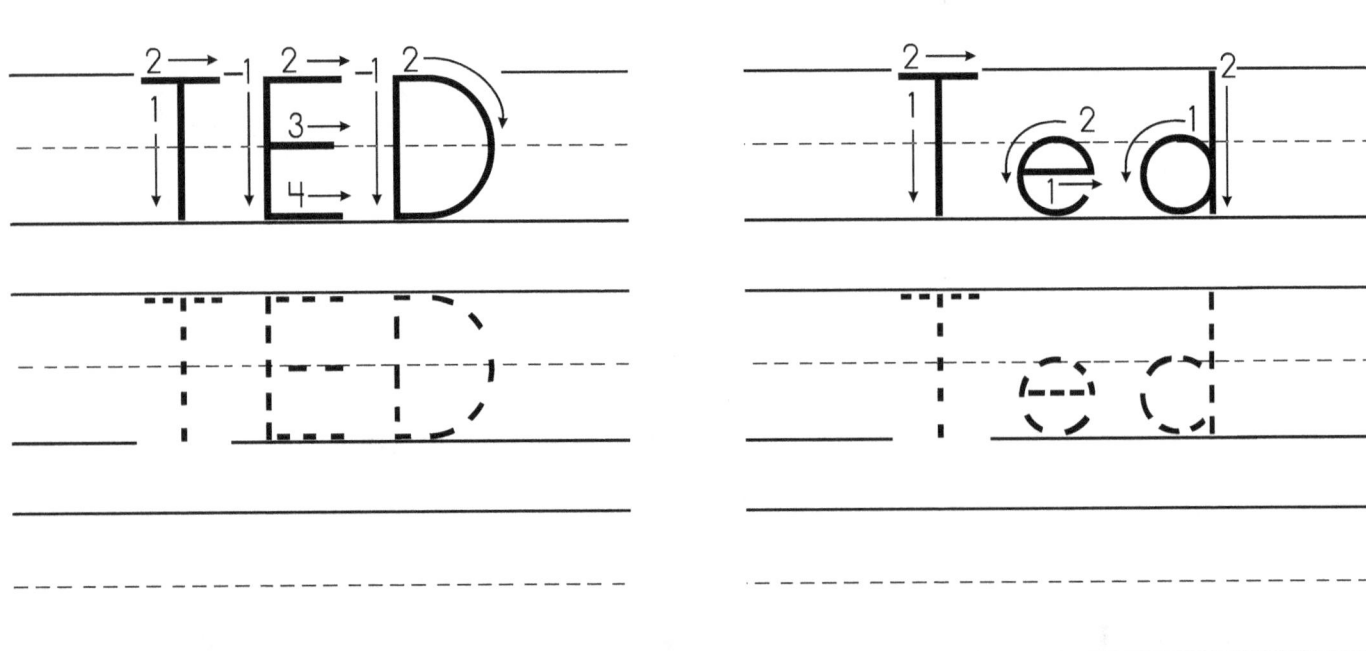

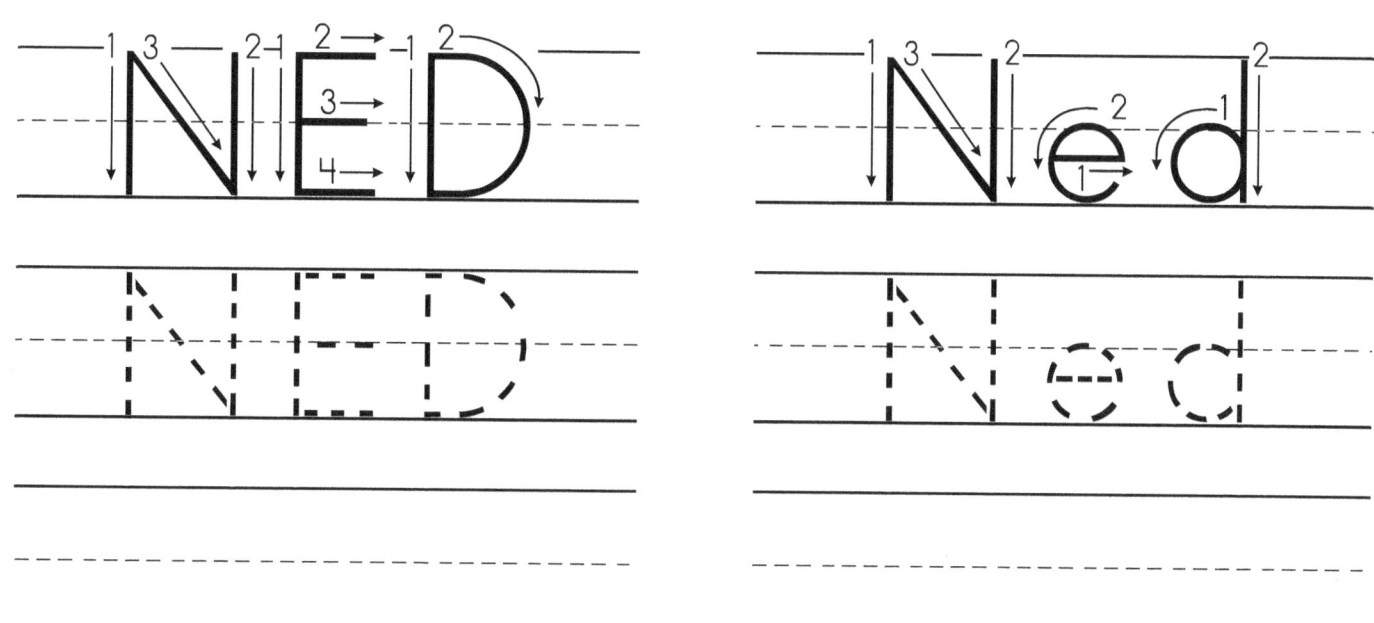

NED

# Ned

6

ED

# Ed

7

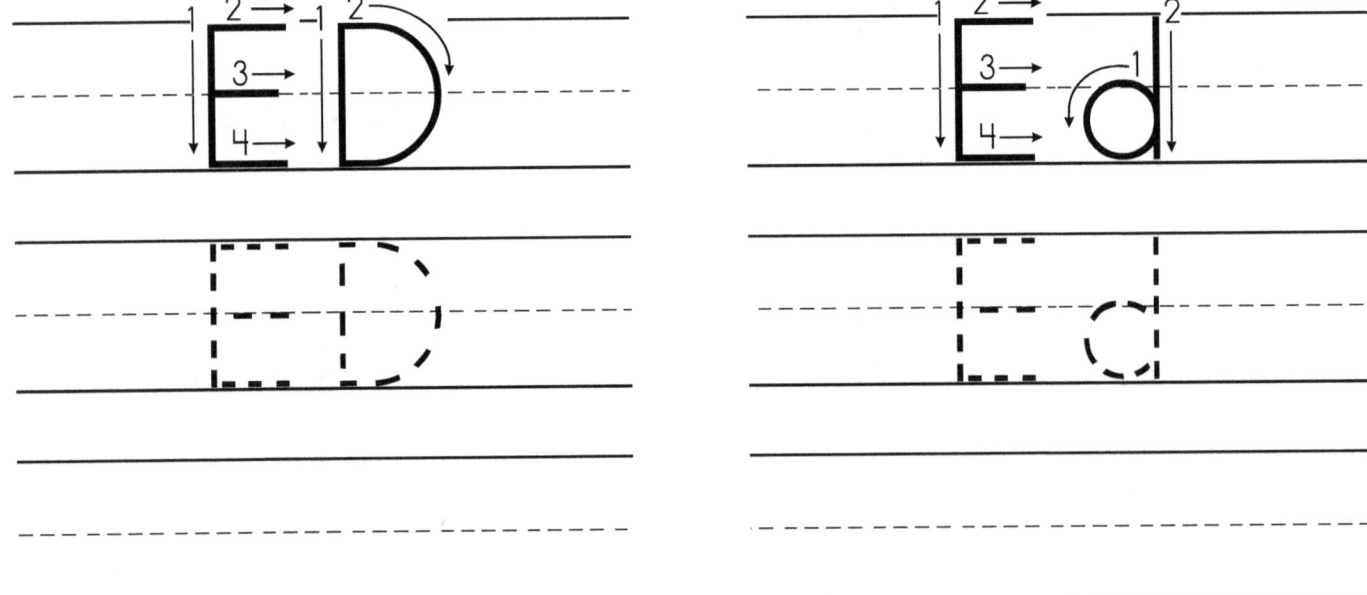

JED

# Jed

8

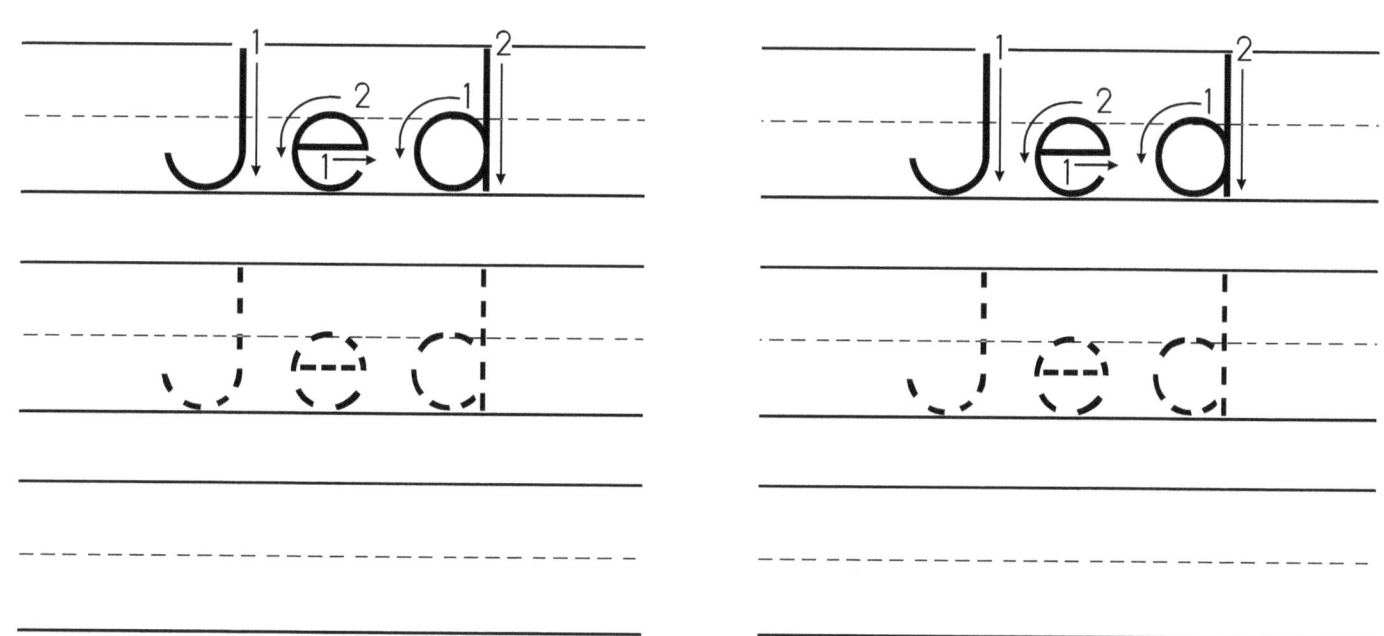

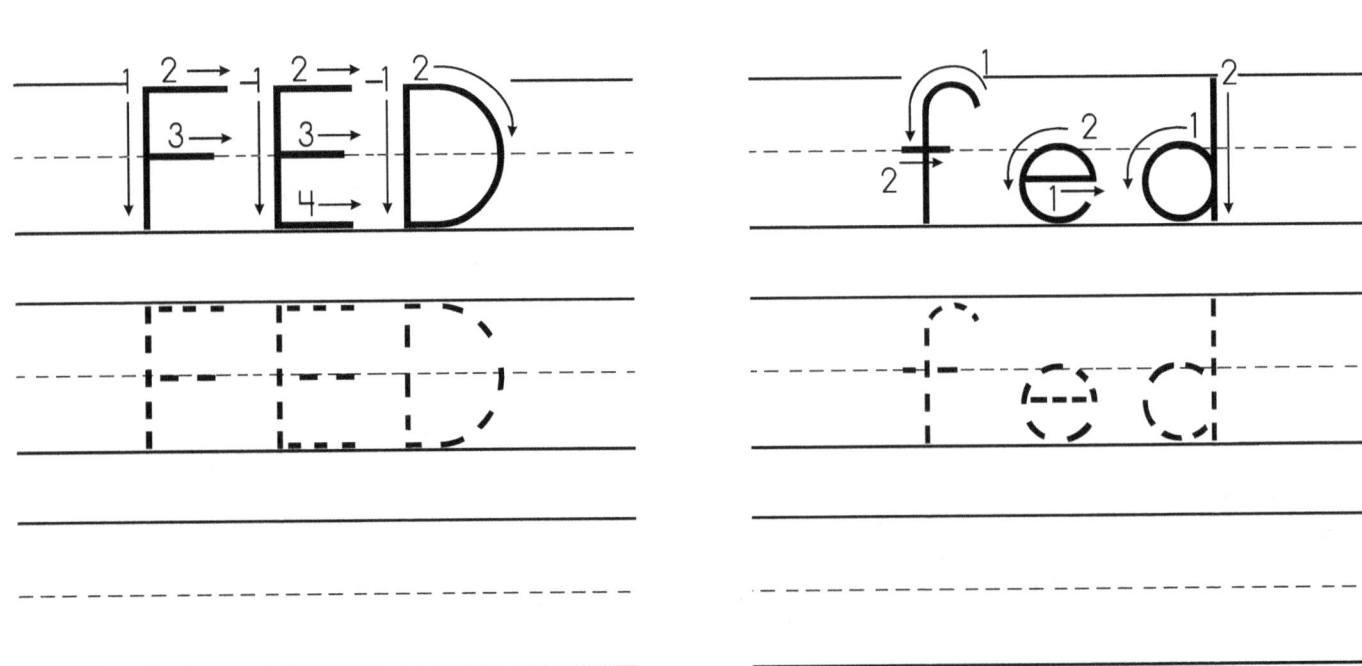

BED

bed

10

BED

bed

BED

bed

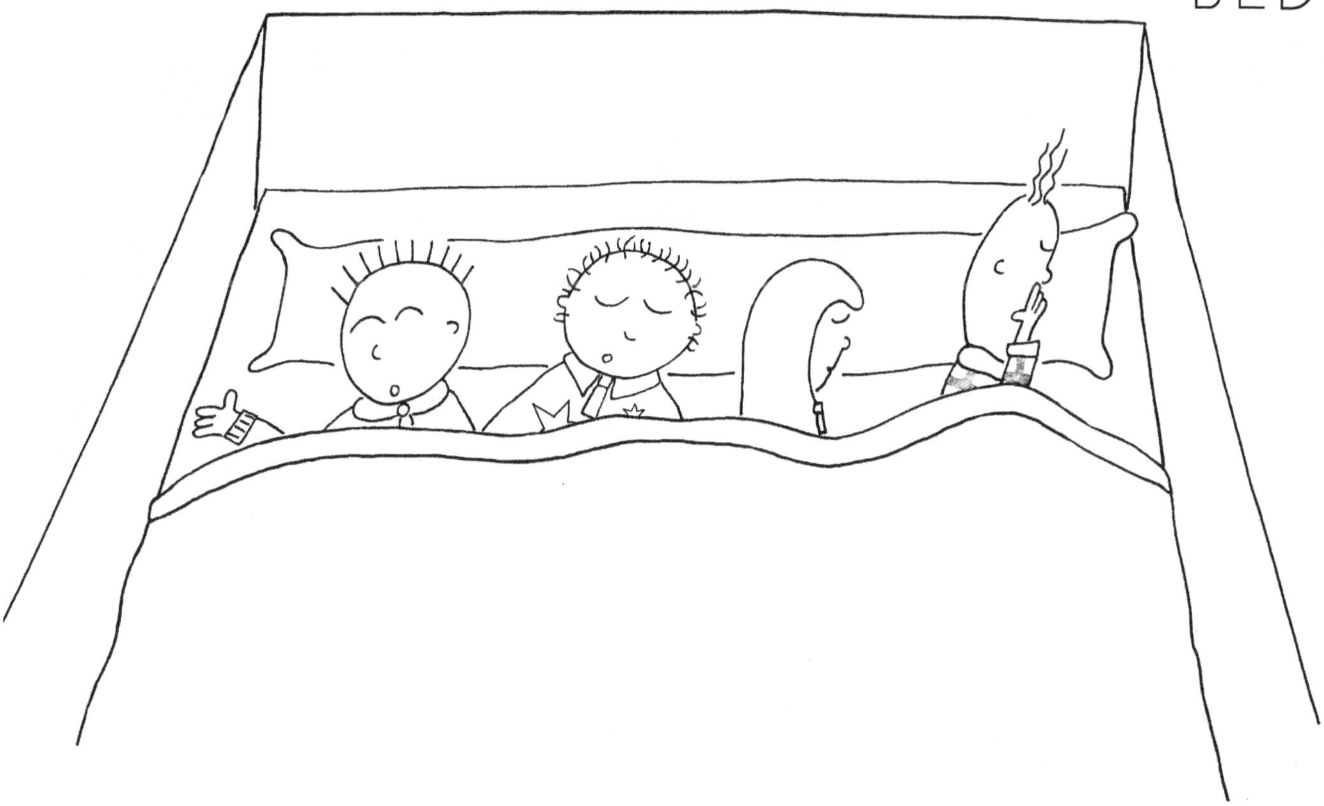

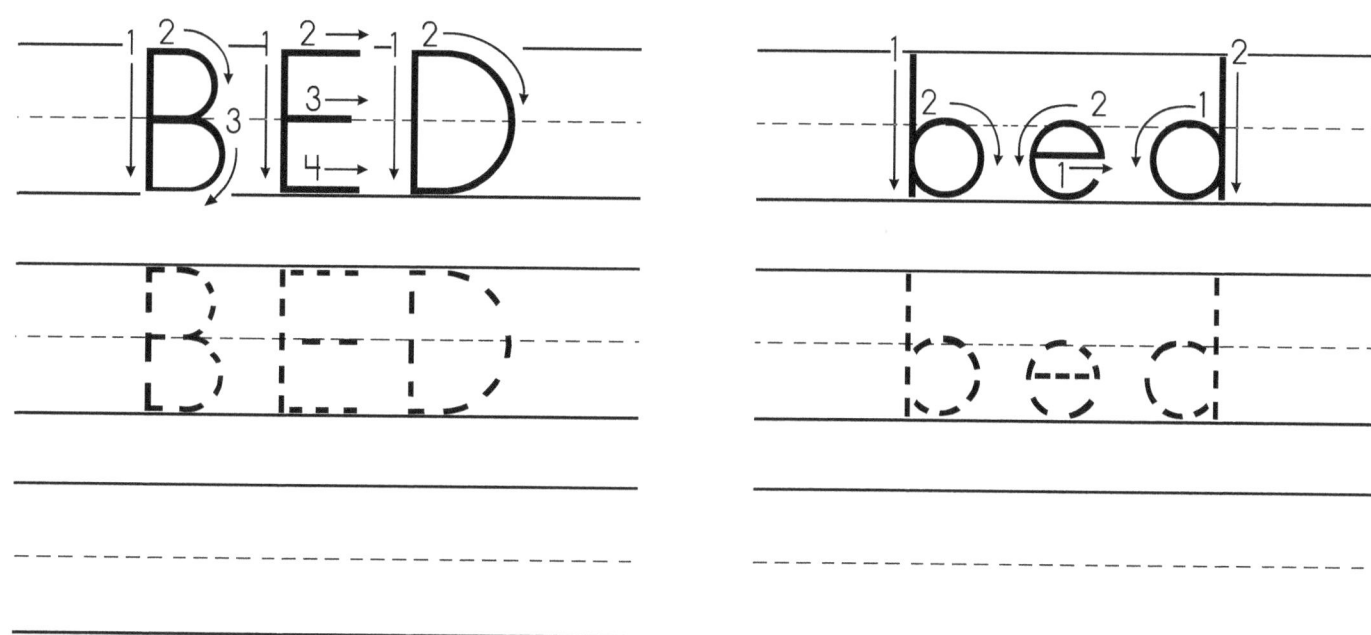

# FED

Ted   fed
Ned   bed
Ed
Jed

Got it!

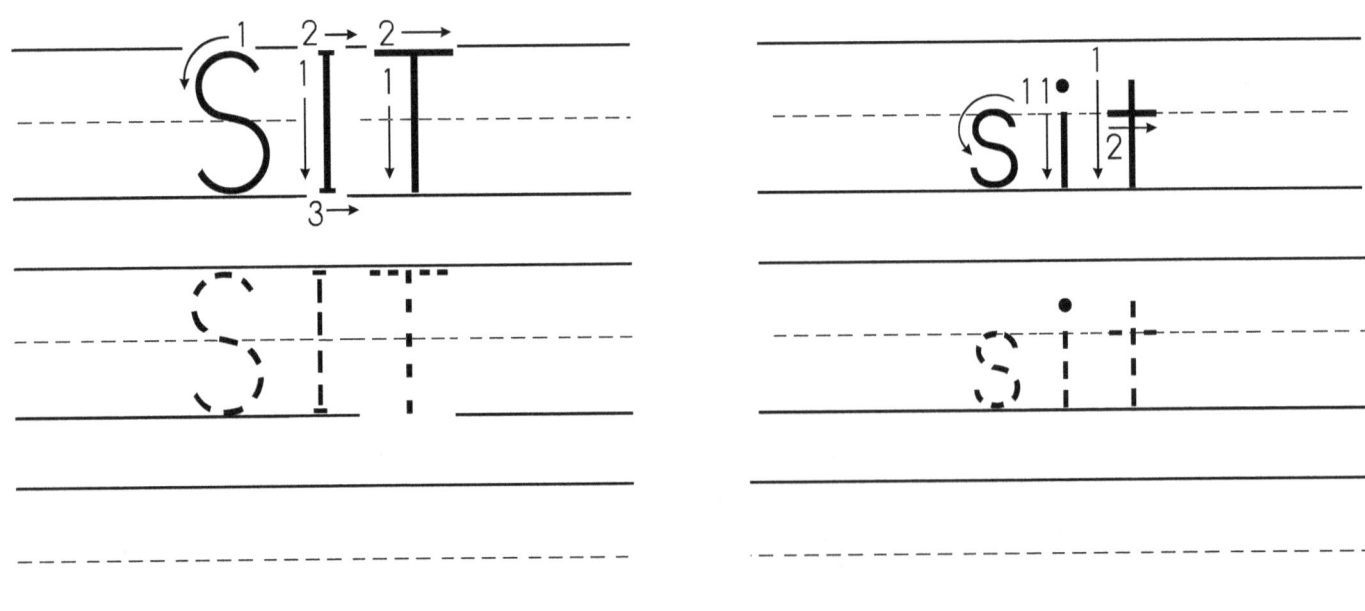

SIT

# sit

2

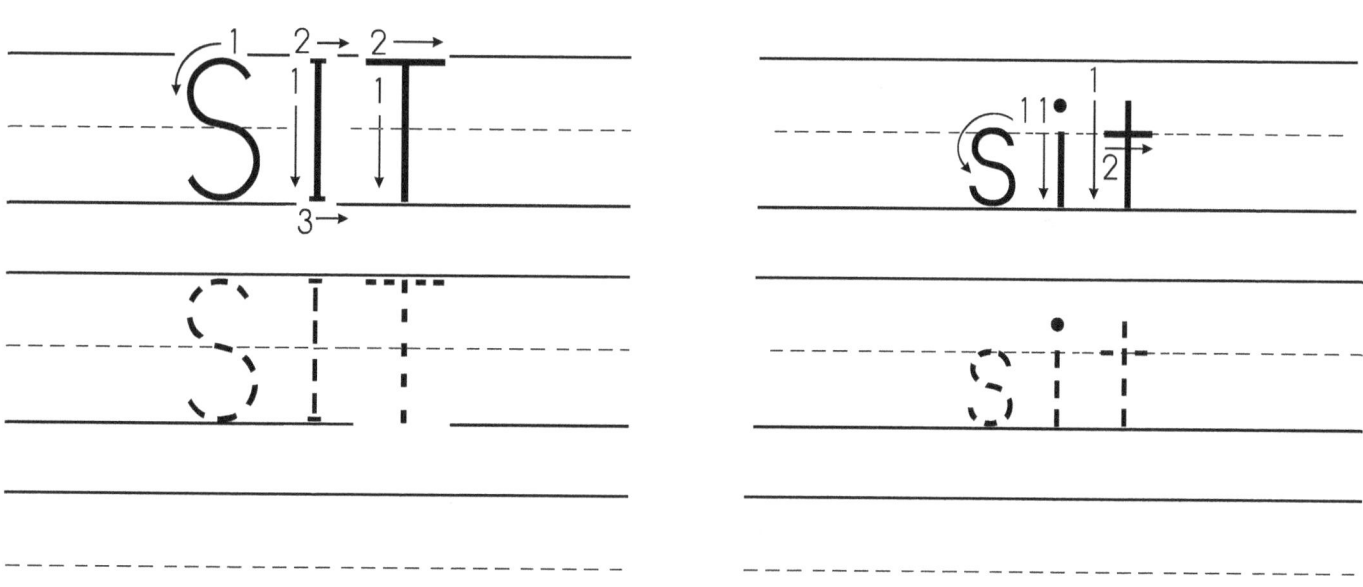

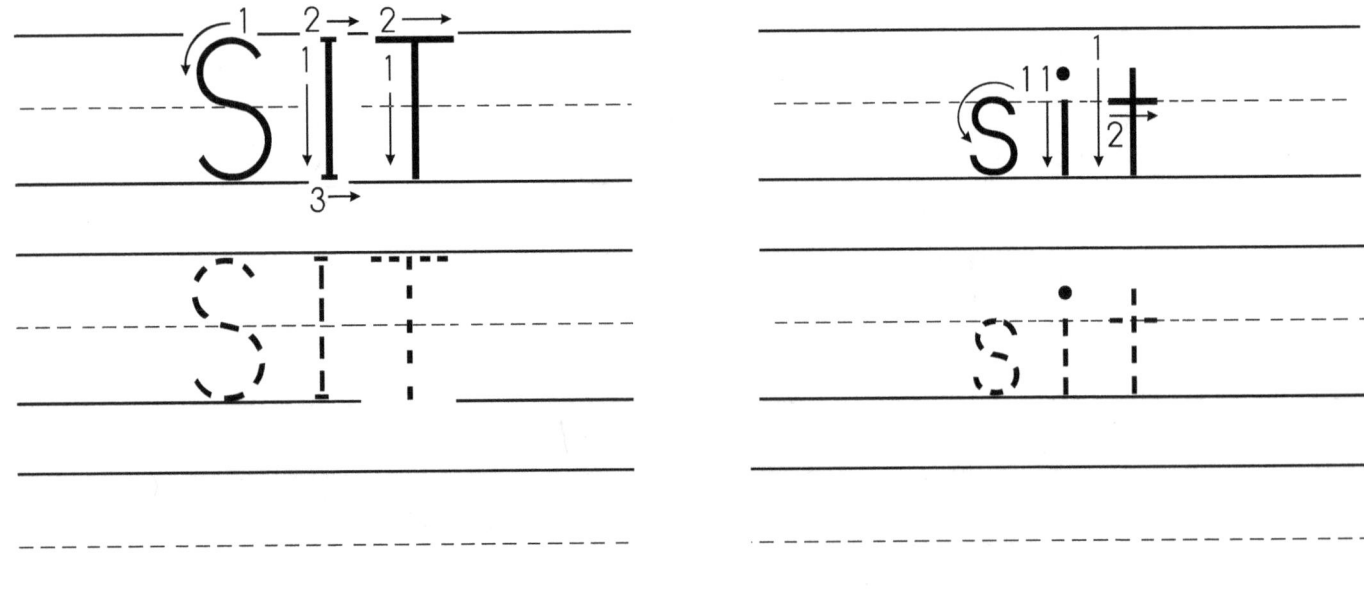

3     sit

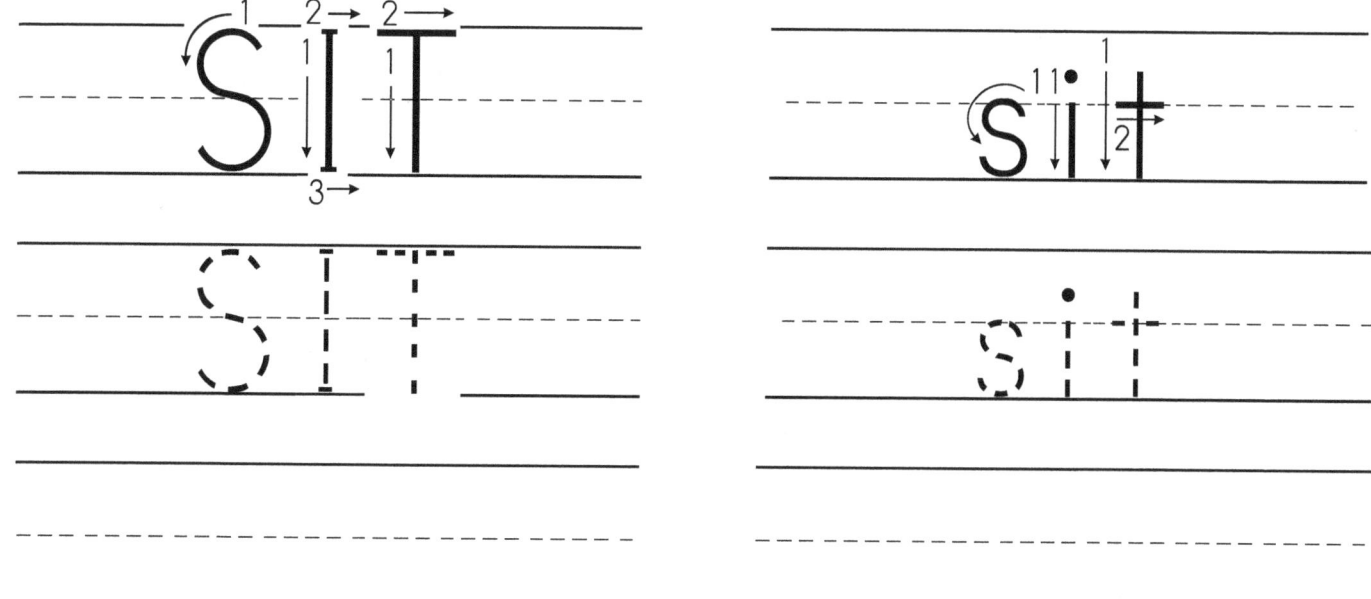

sit

4

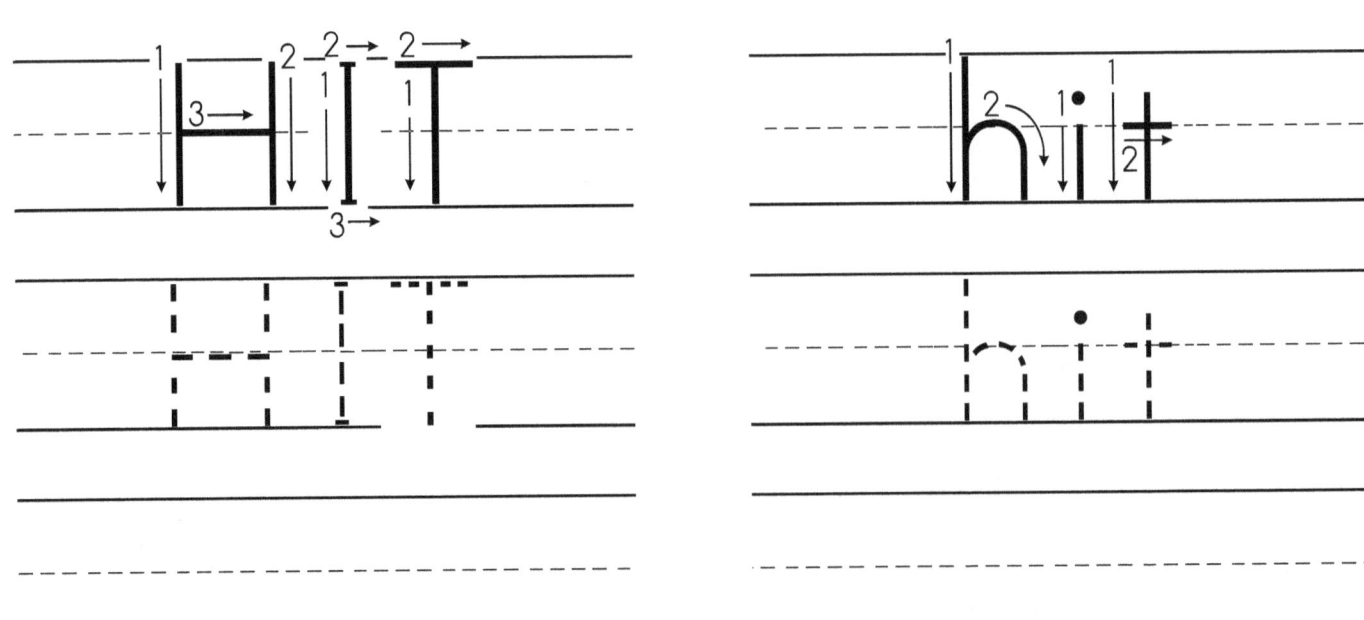

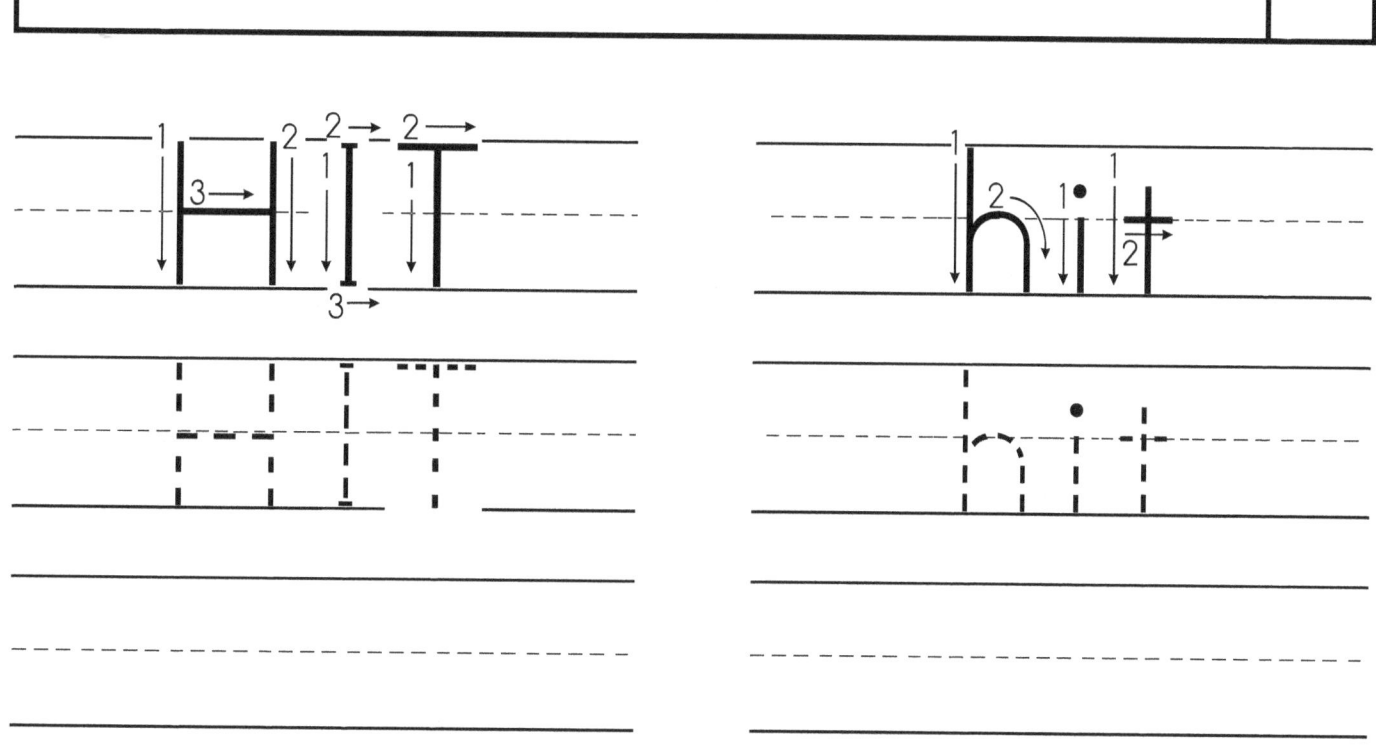

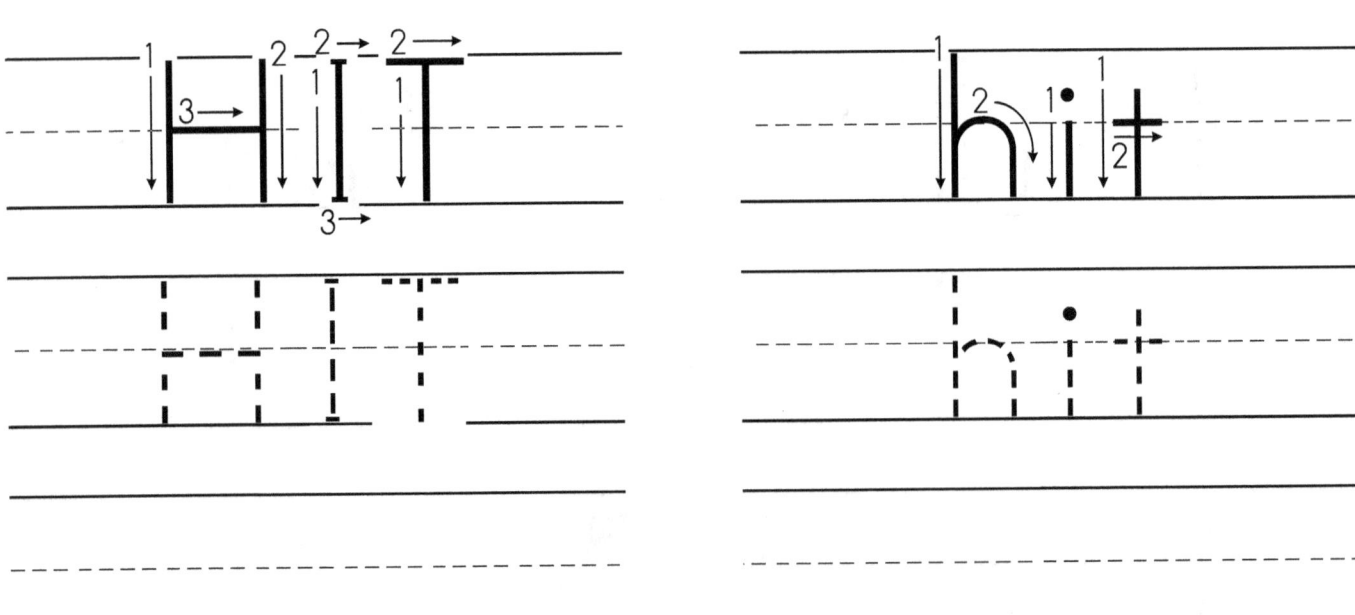

7 hit

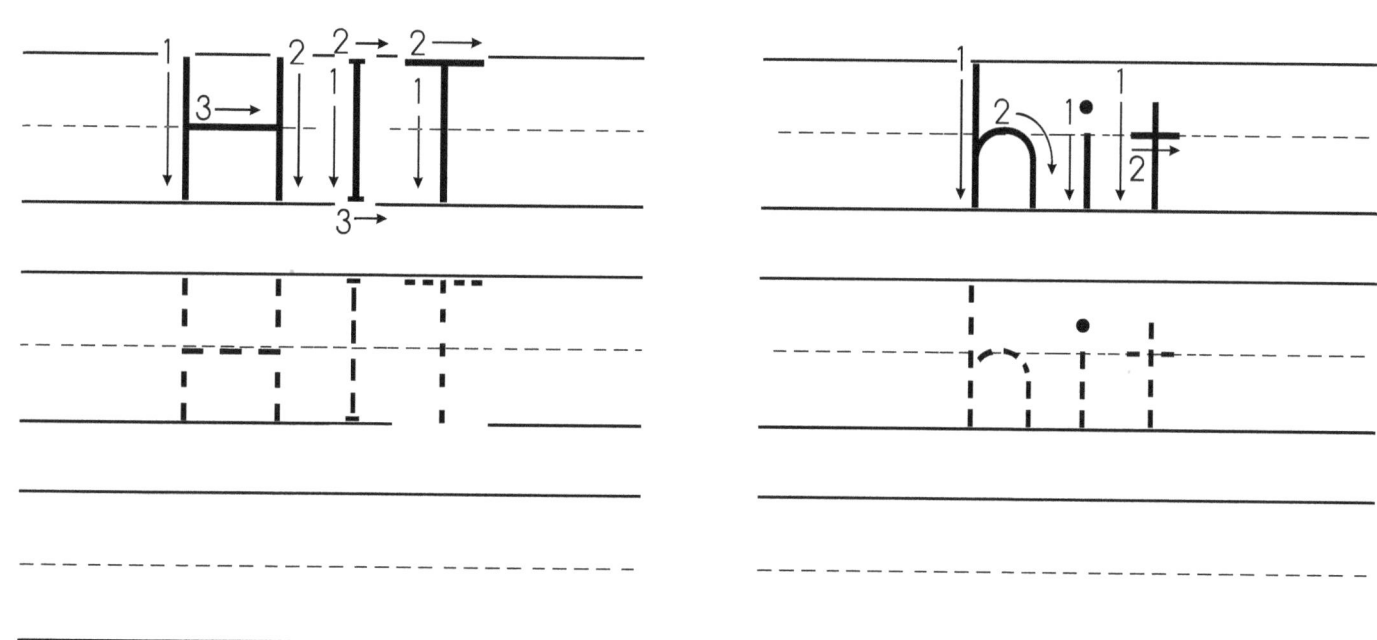

hit

8

| 9 | sit |

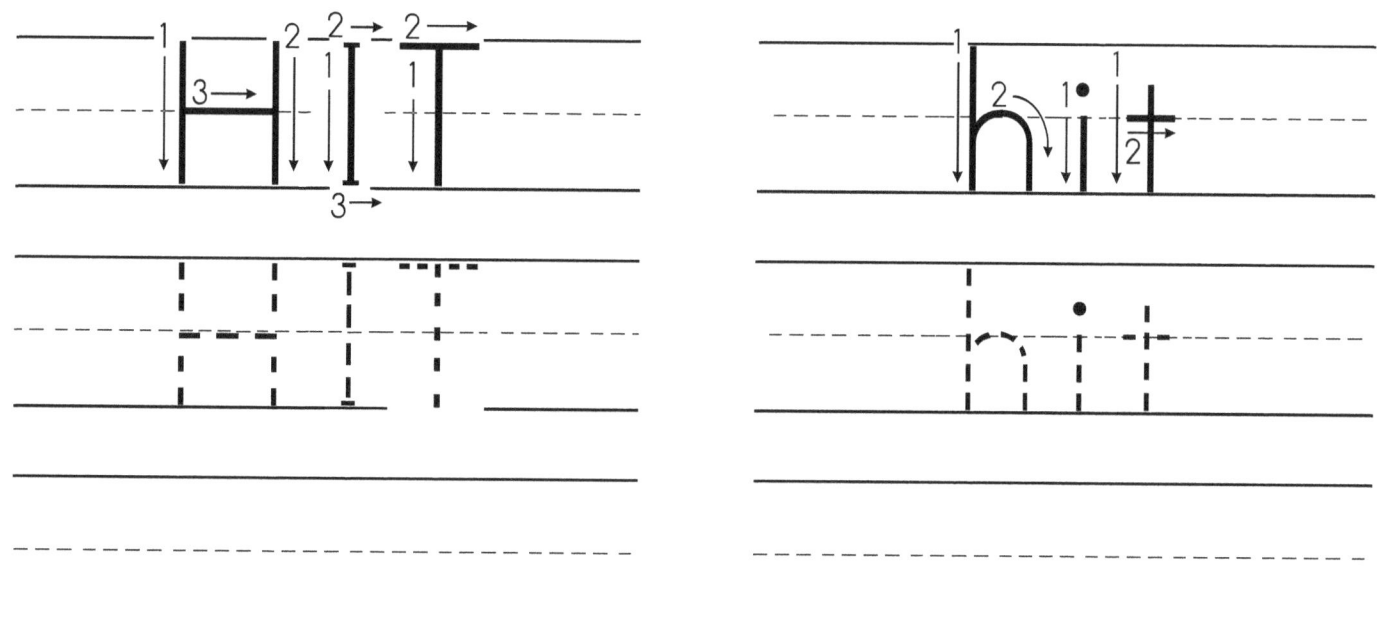

# HIT IT

sit    hit

Got it!

# MOM

MOM

1 | Mom

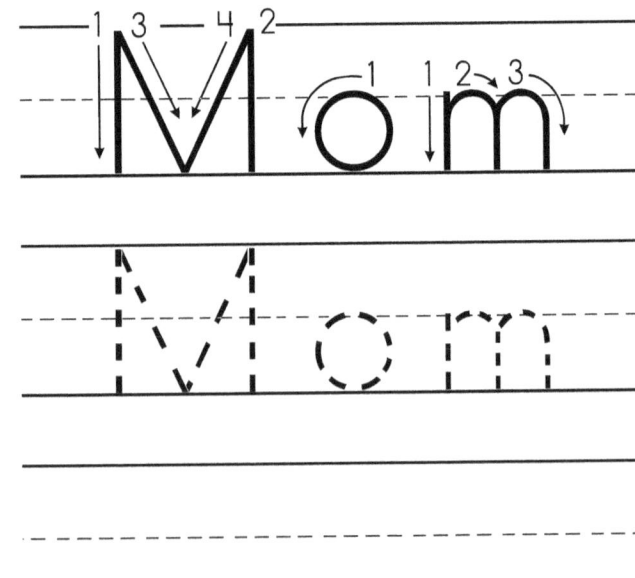

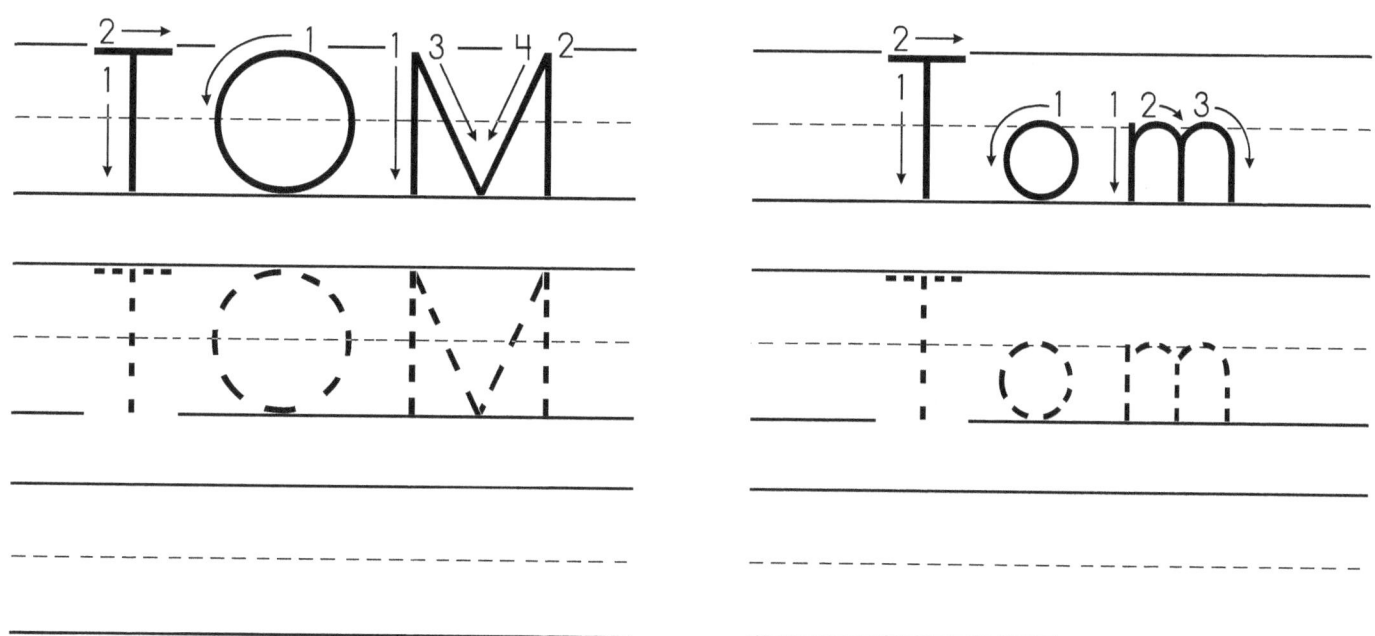

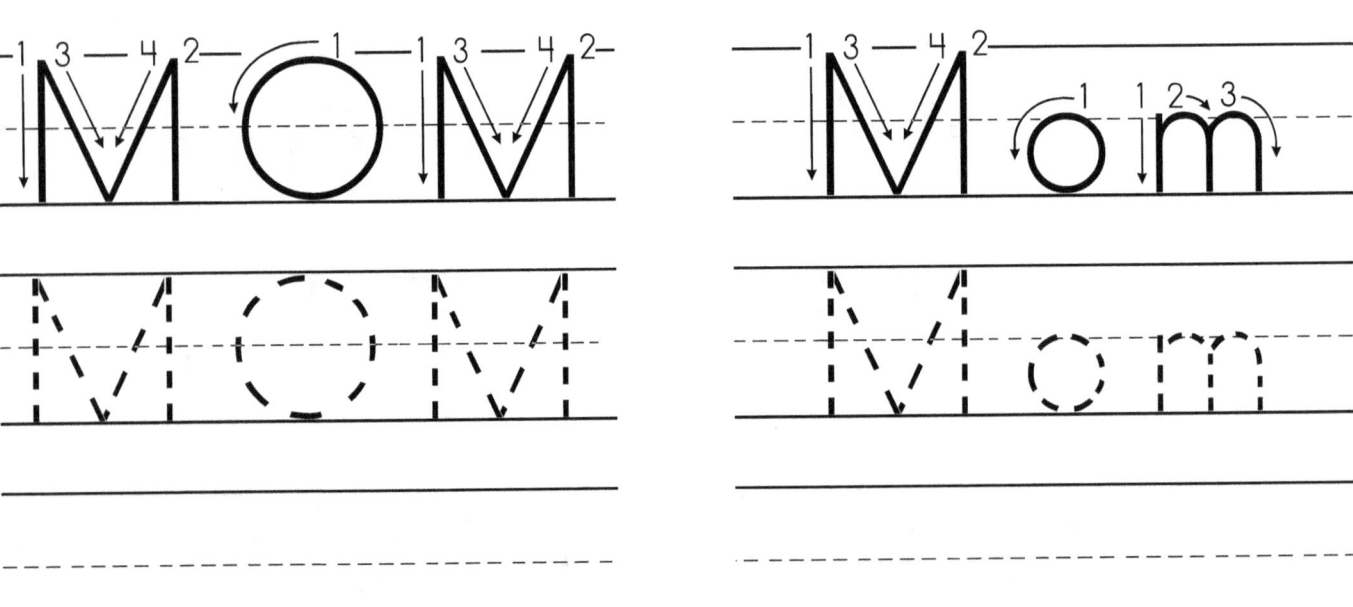

MOM

Mom

4

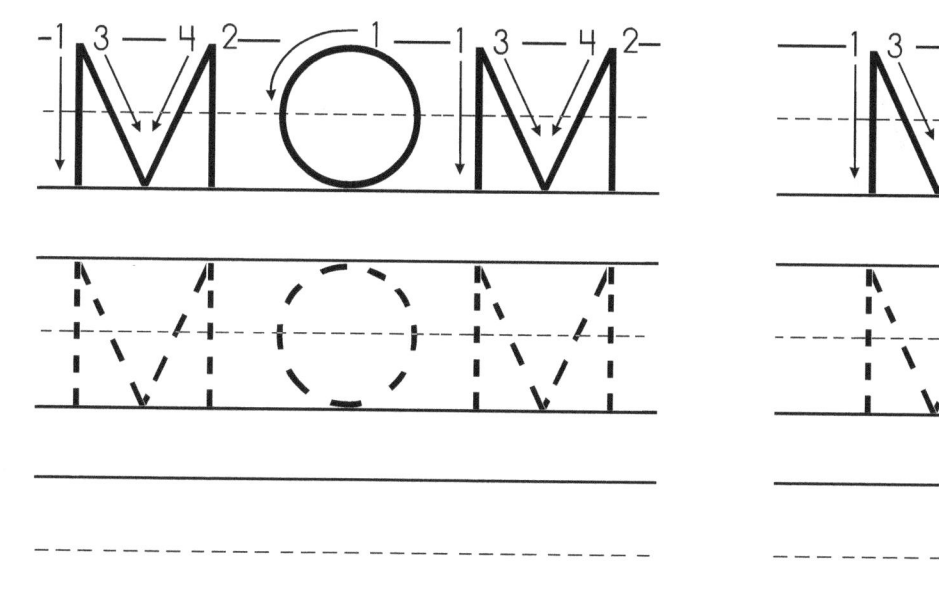

TOM

5 | Tom

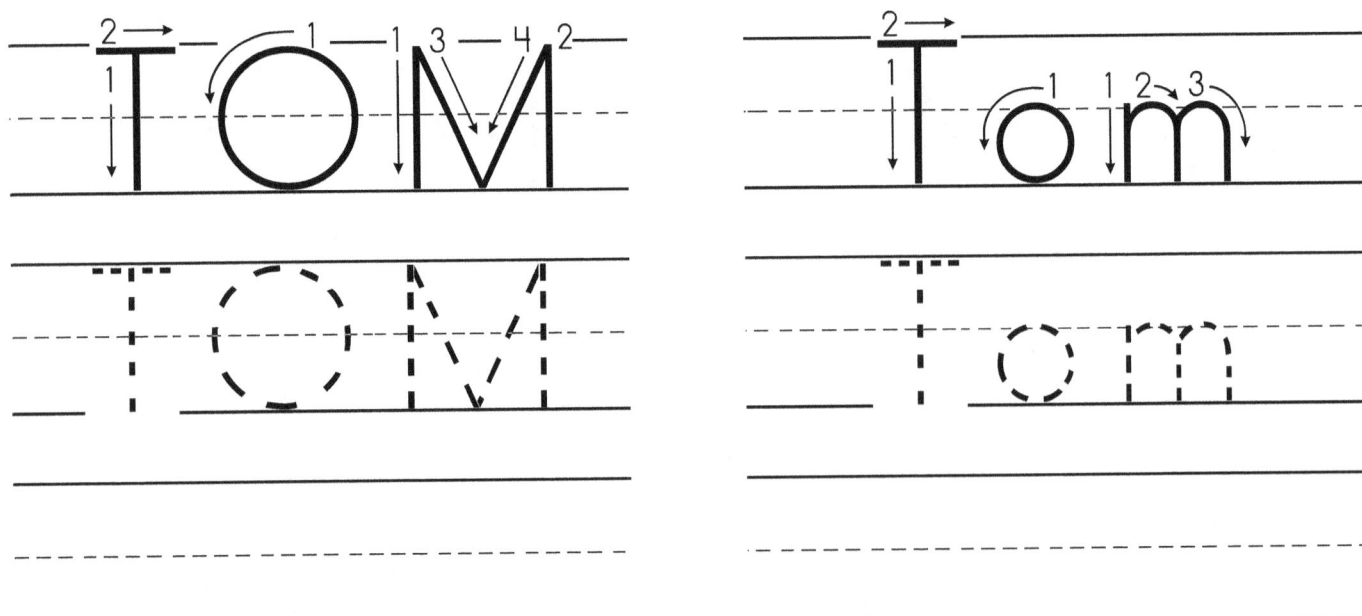

# TOM

## Tom 6

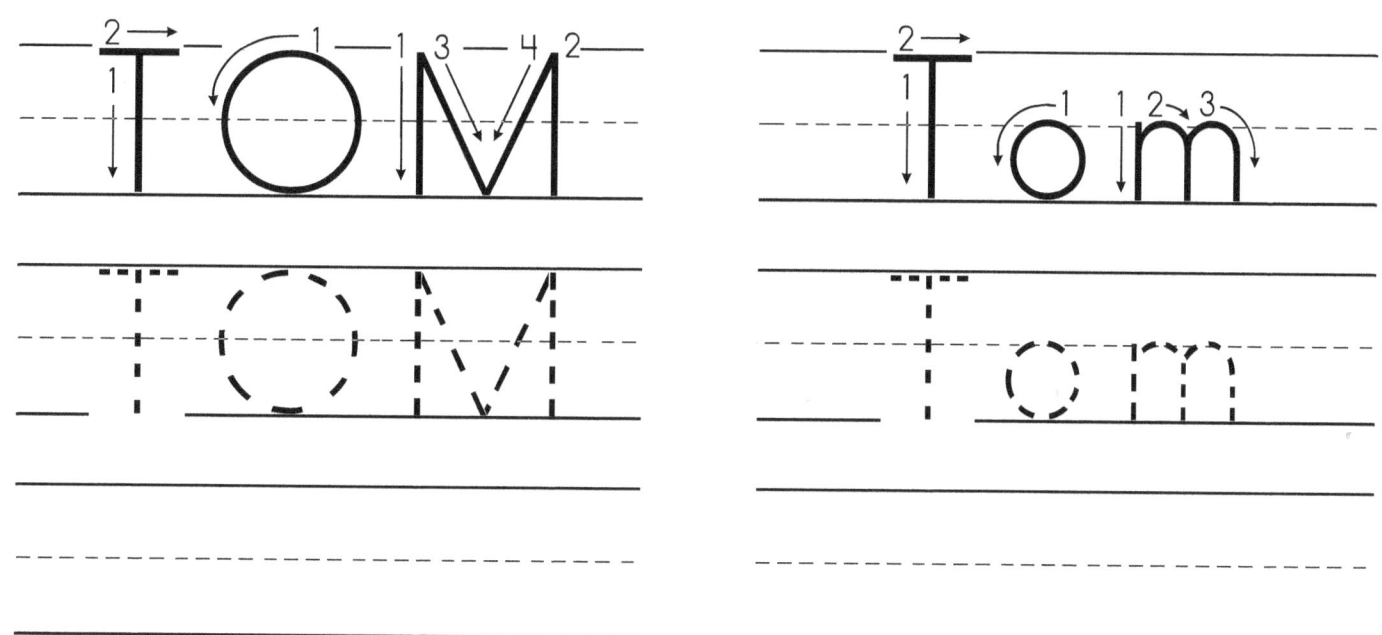

MOM

**7** Mom

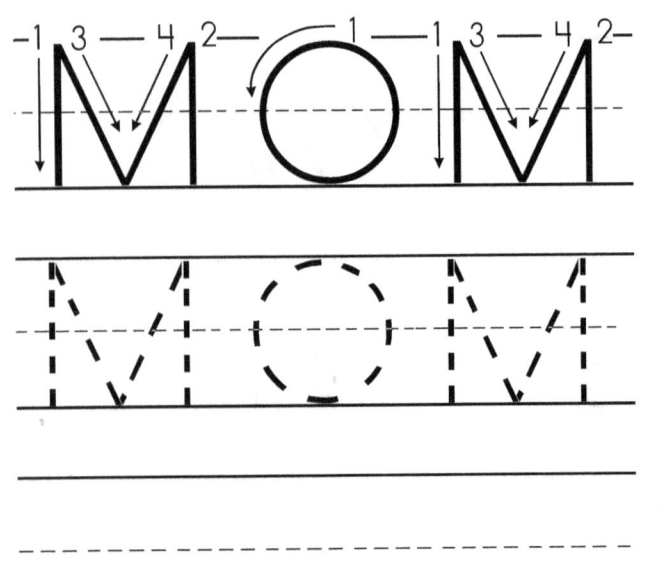
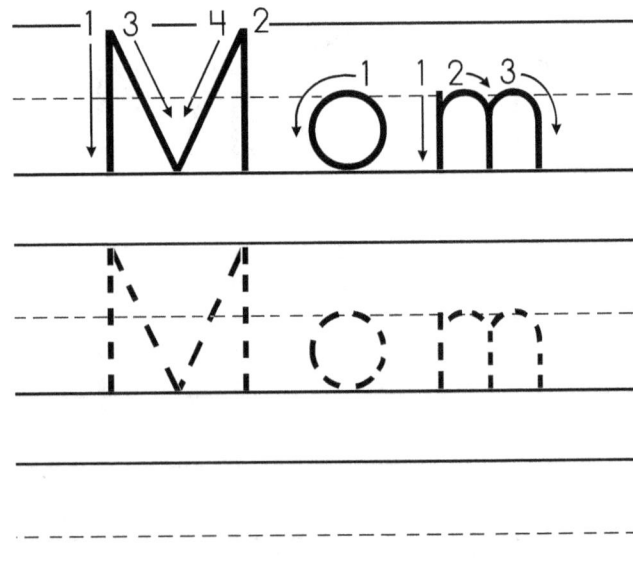

MOM

Mom | 8

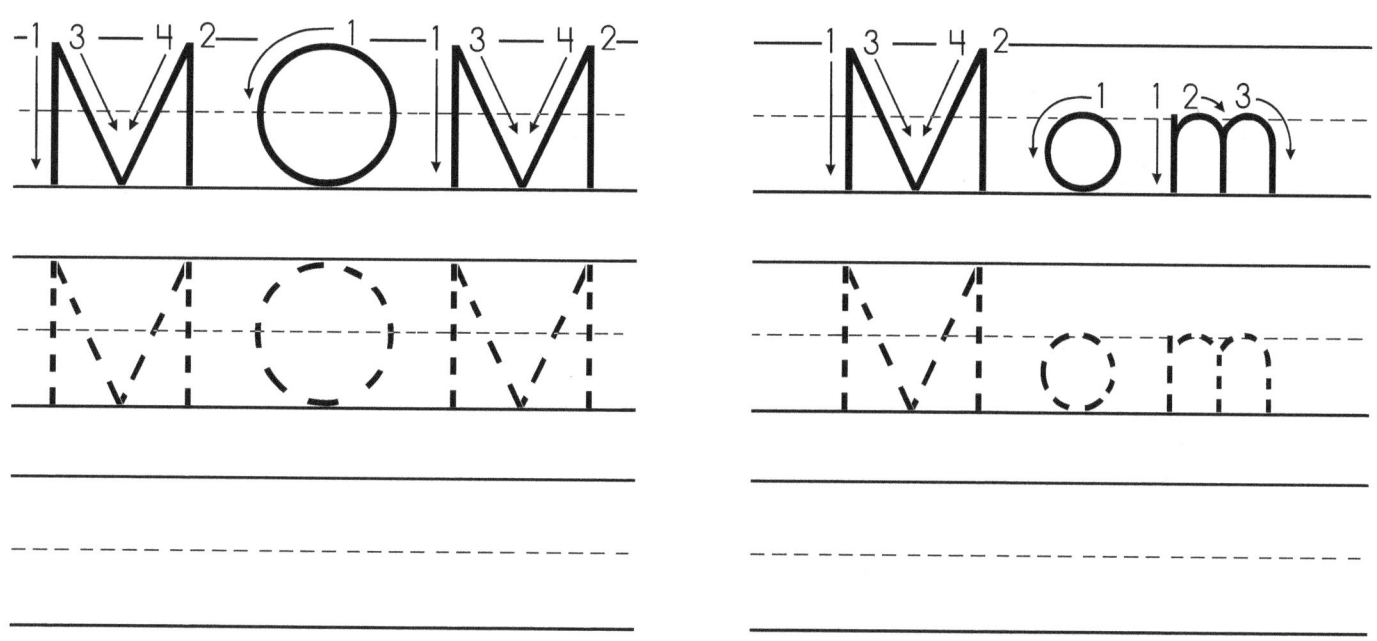

TOM

9 Tom

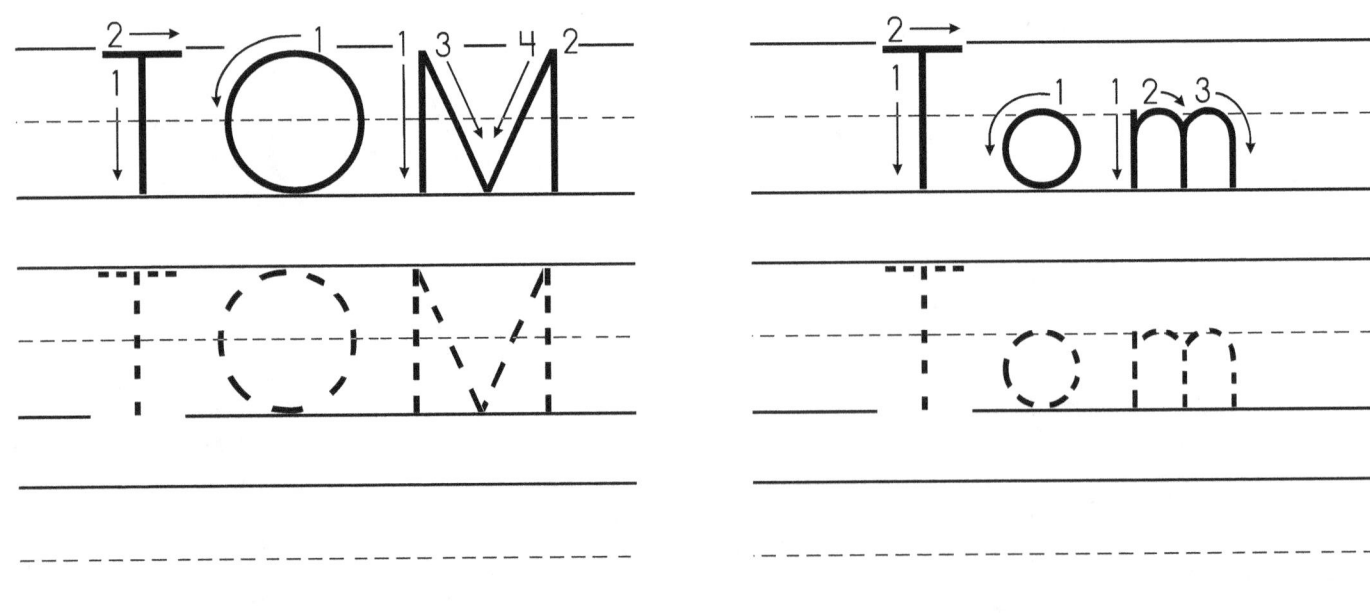

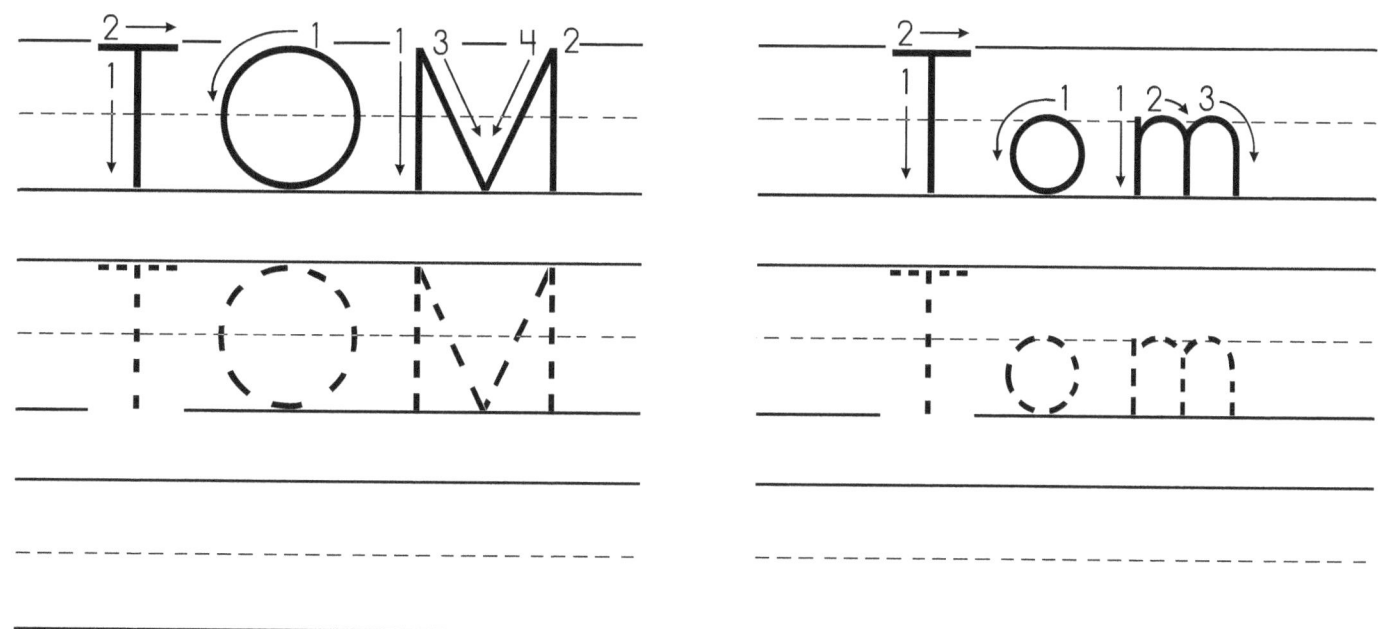

# MOM

Mom    Tom

Got it!

# SUN

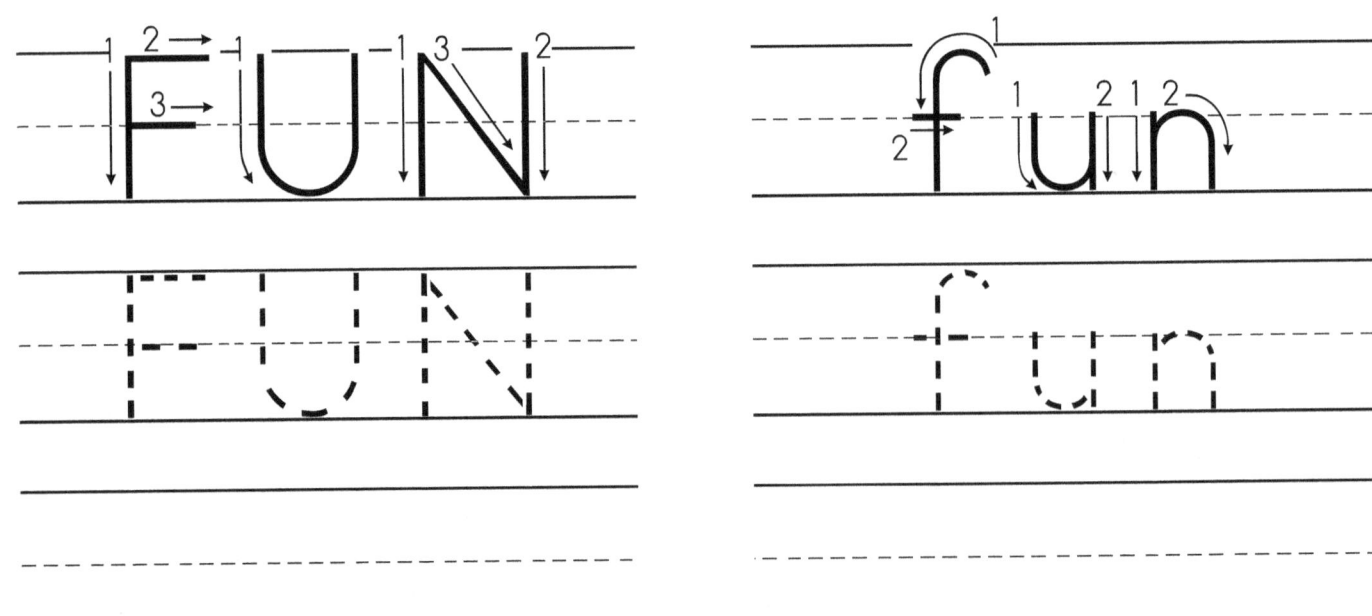

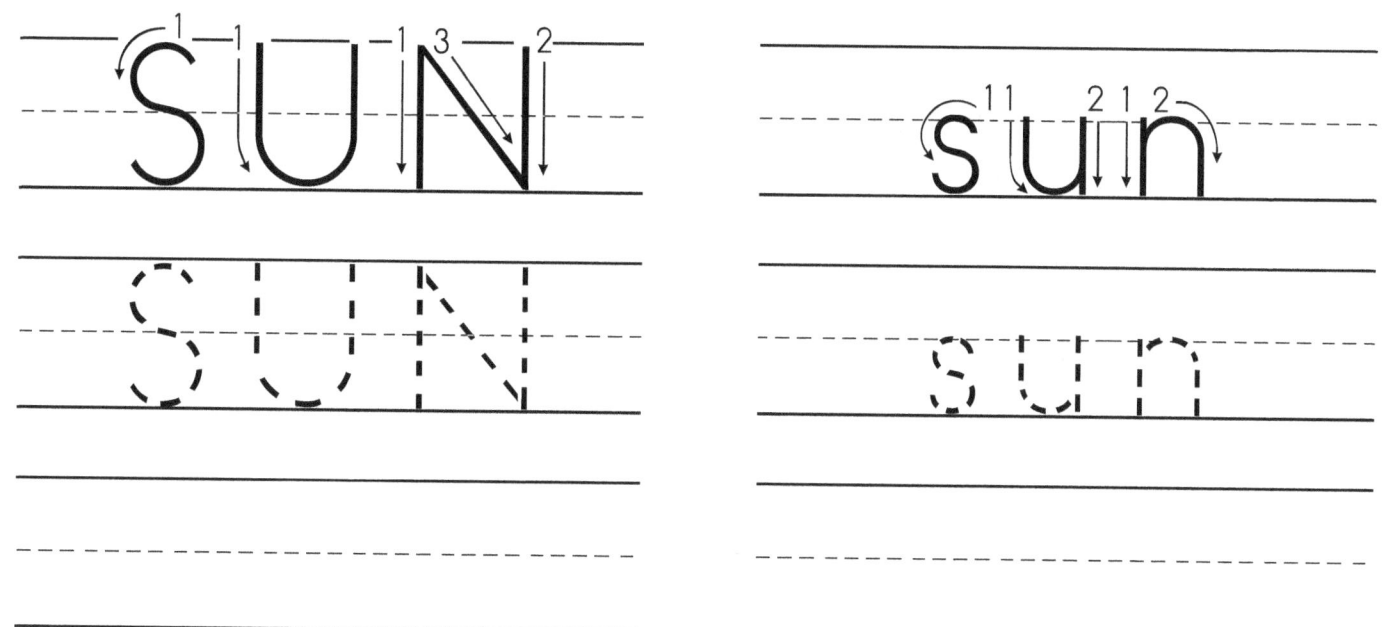

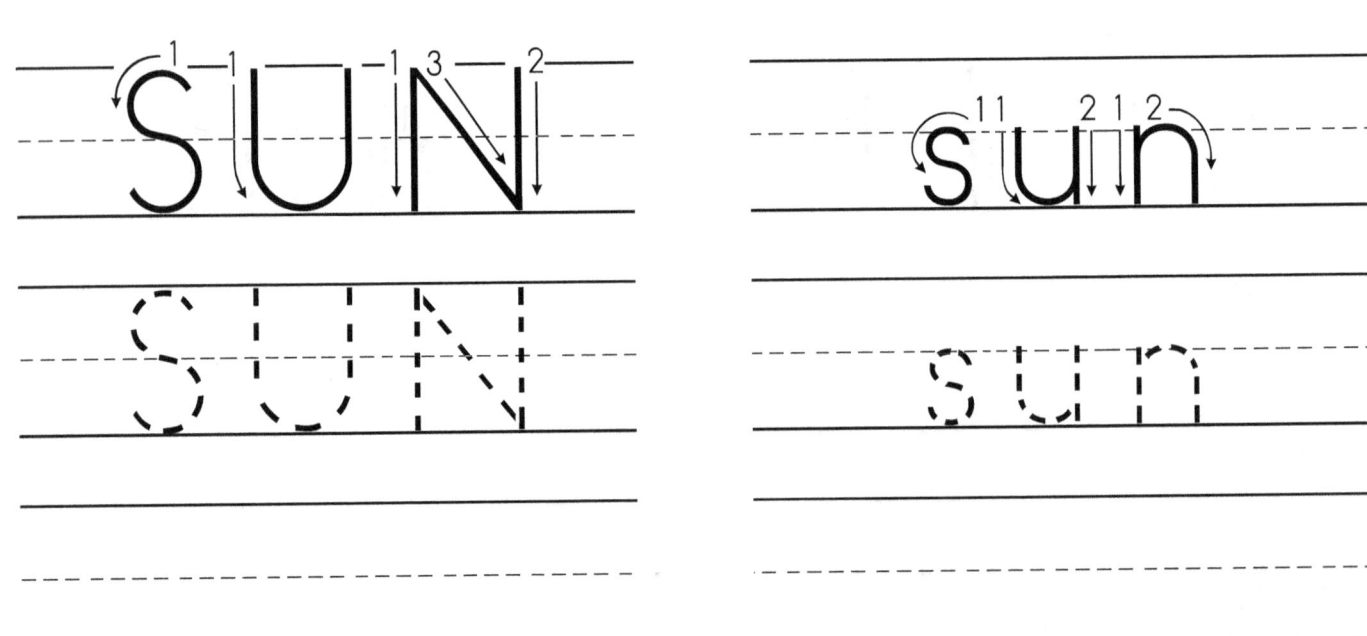

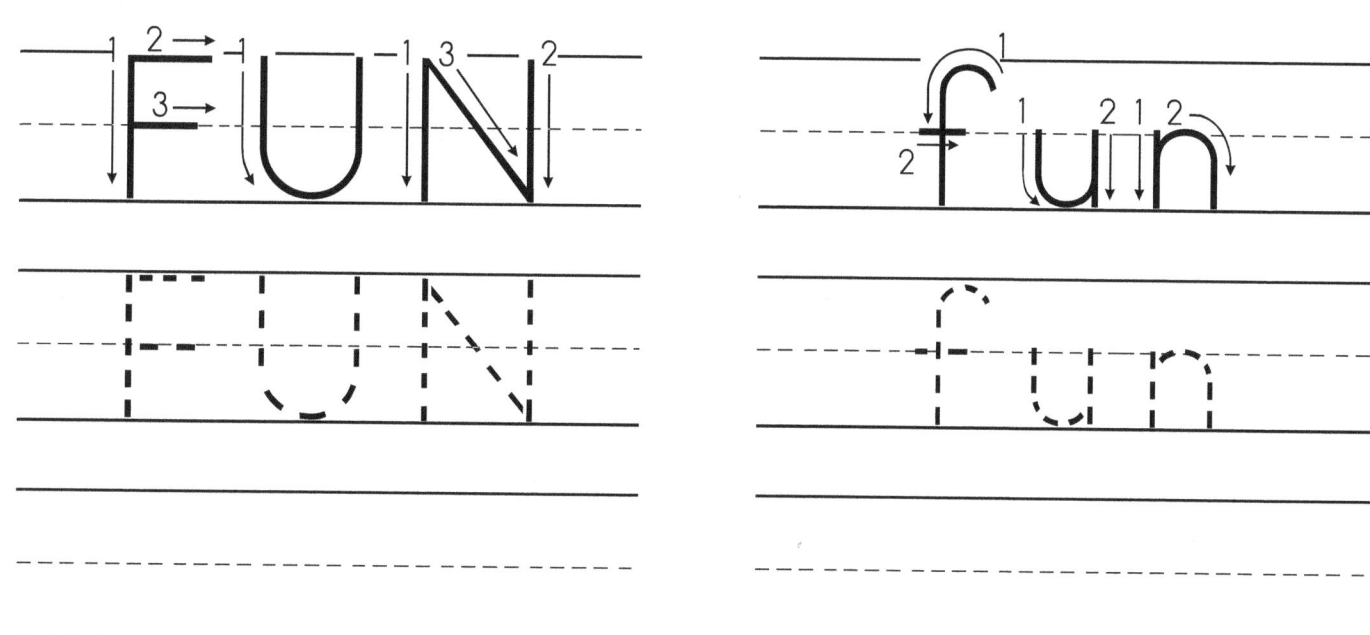

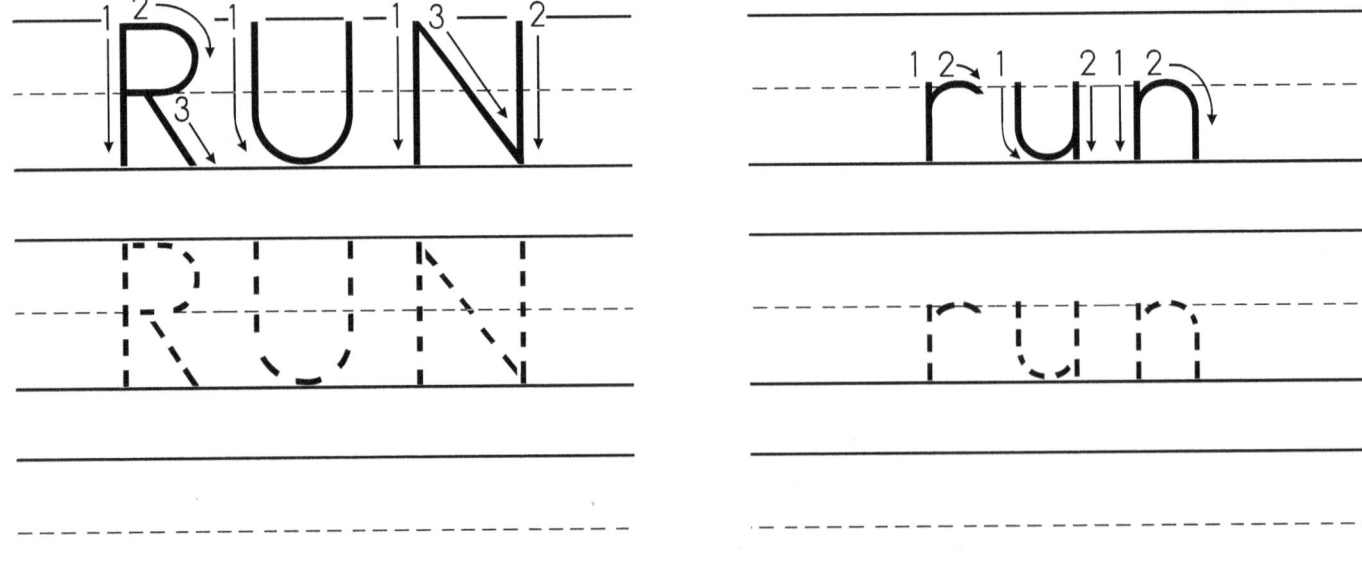

RUN

run

6

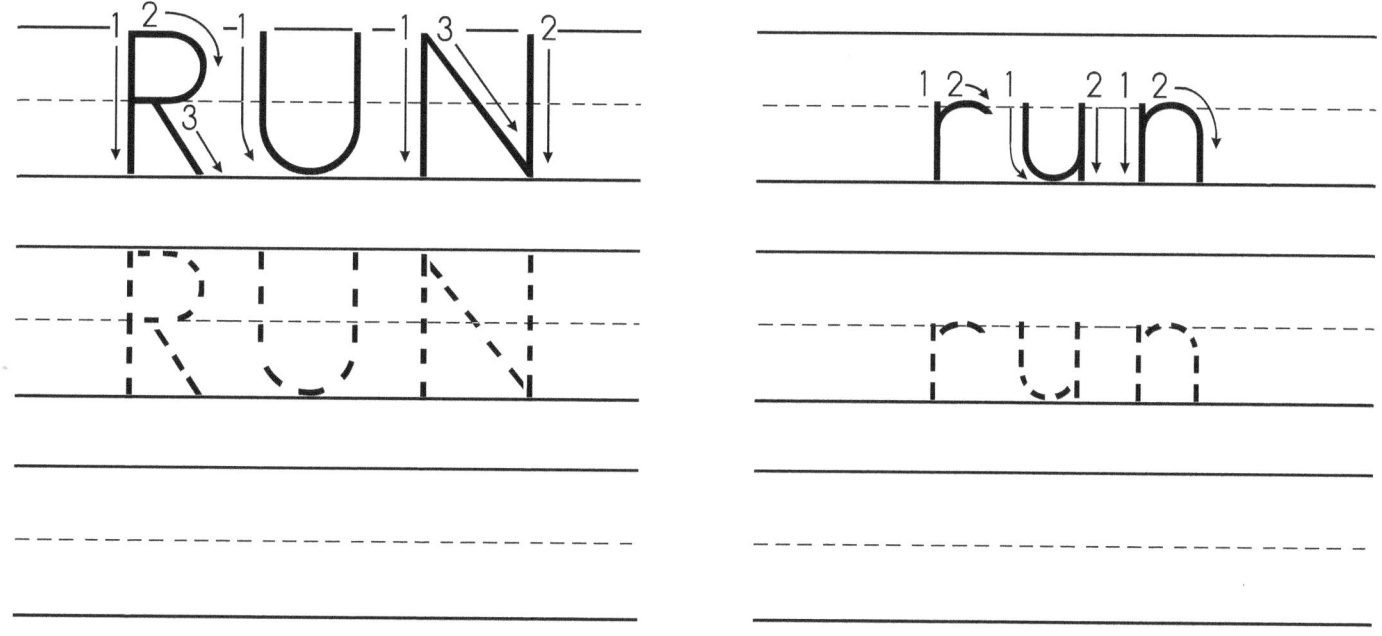

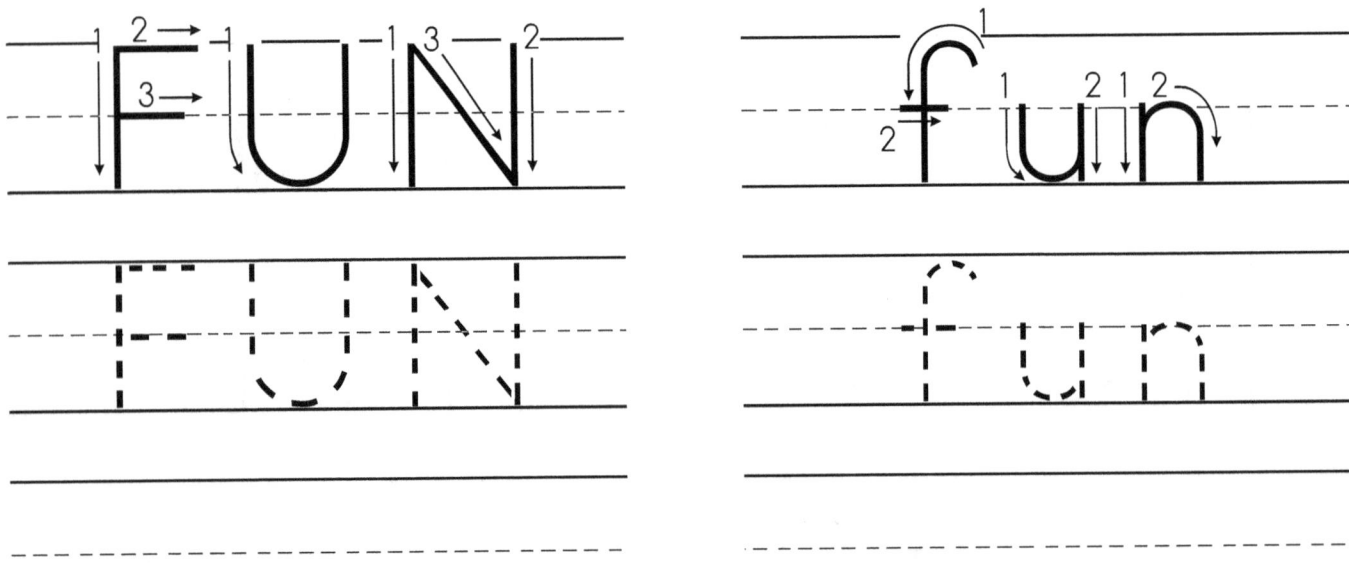

FUN

**7** fun

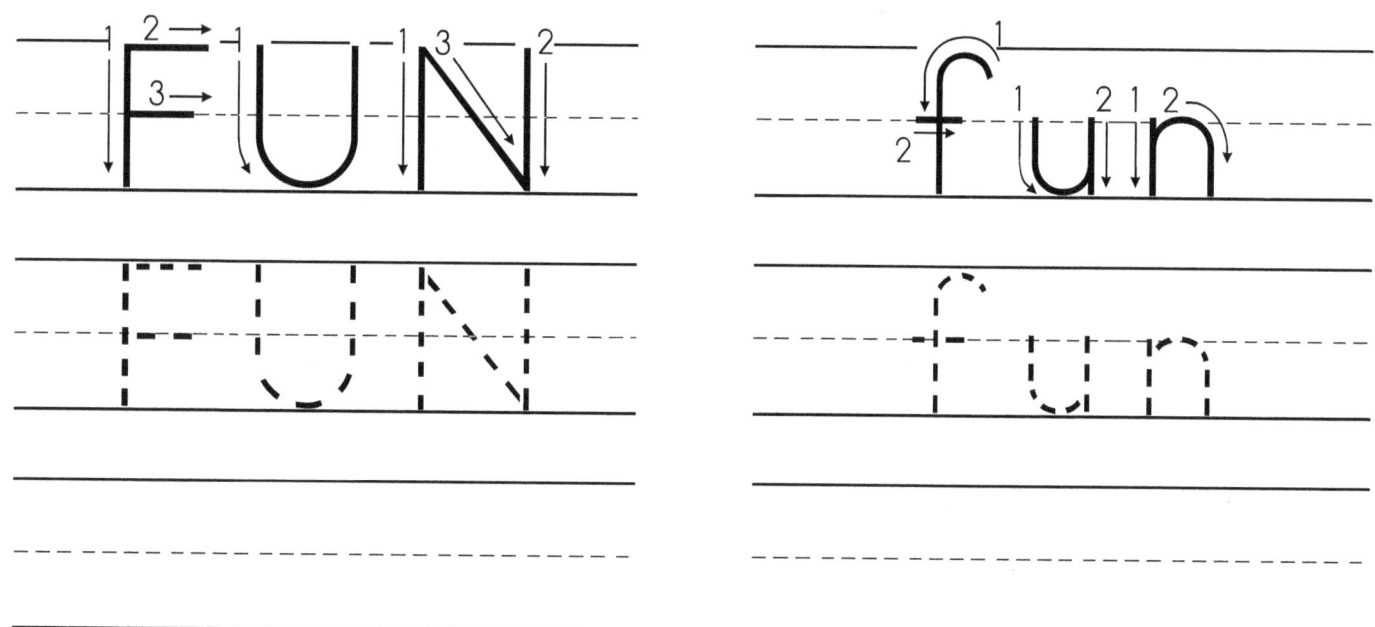

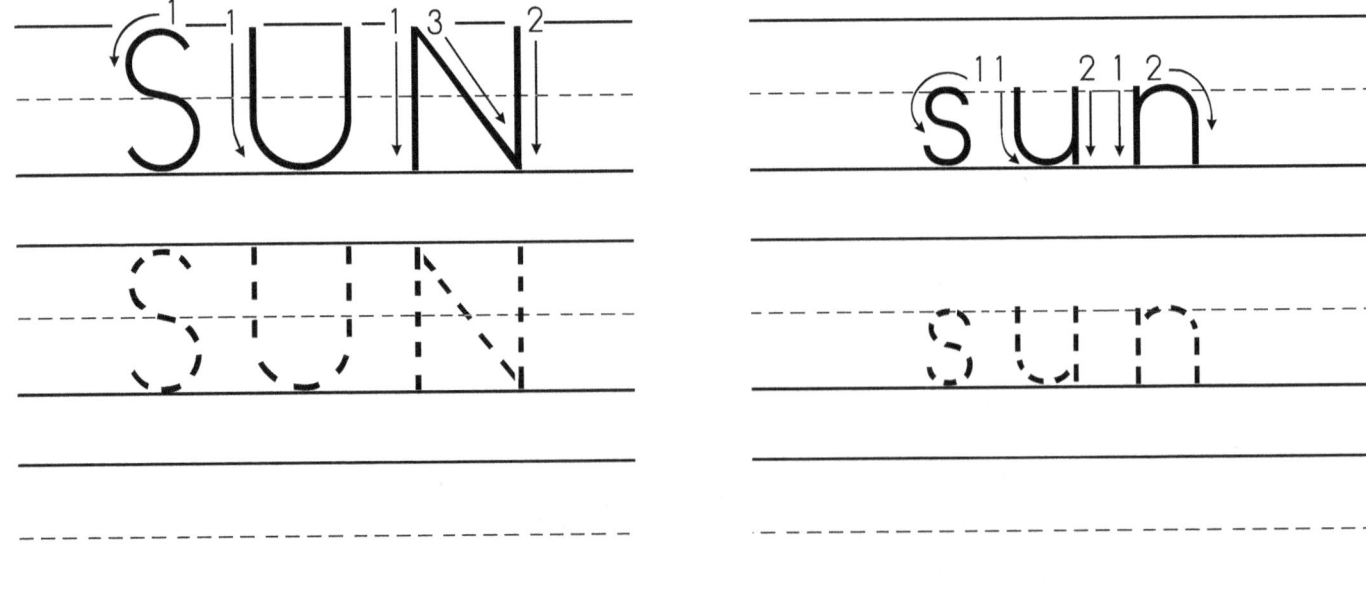

9 sun

FUN

fun

10

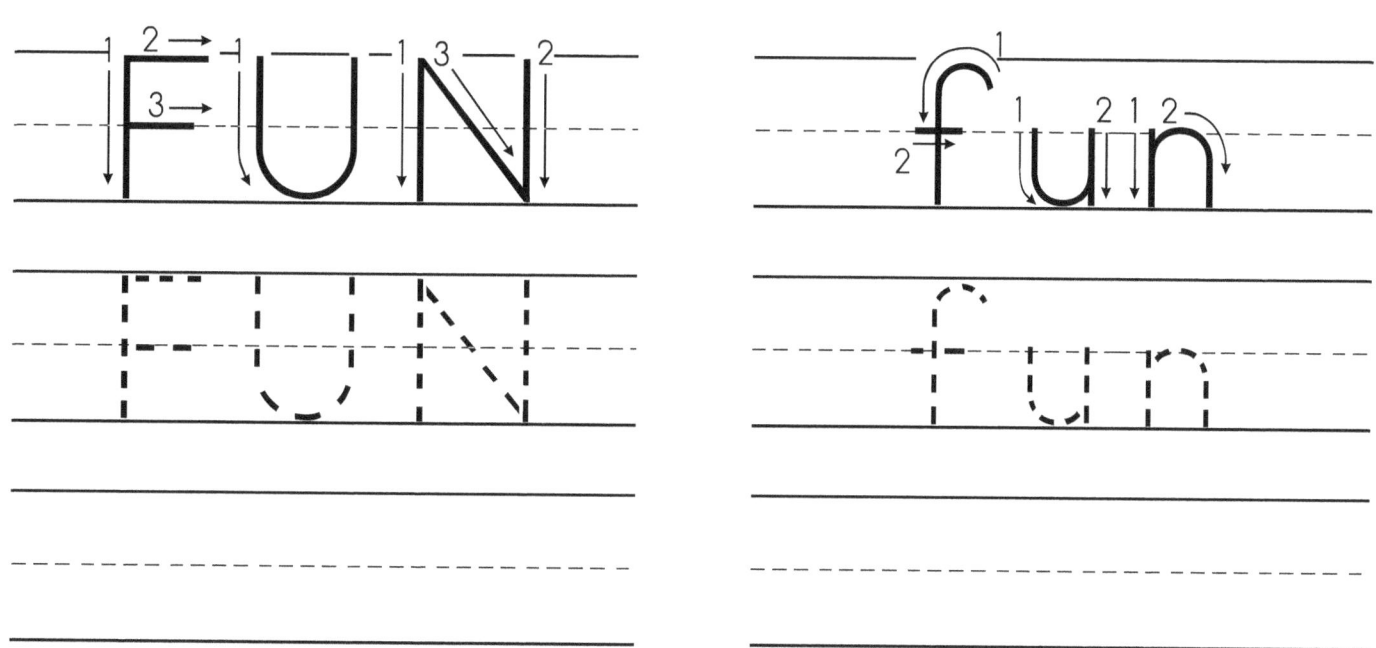

# SUN

fun   run

sun

Got it!

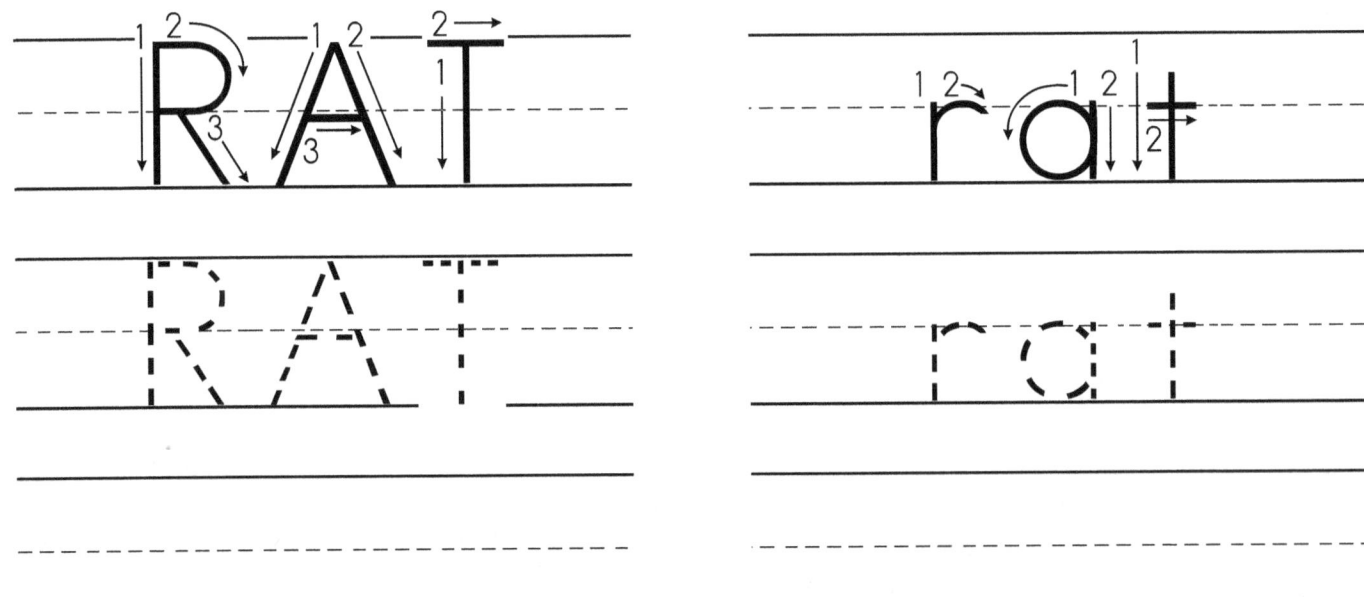

| 1 | rat |

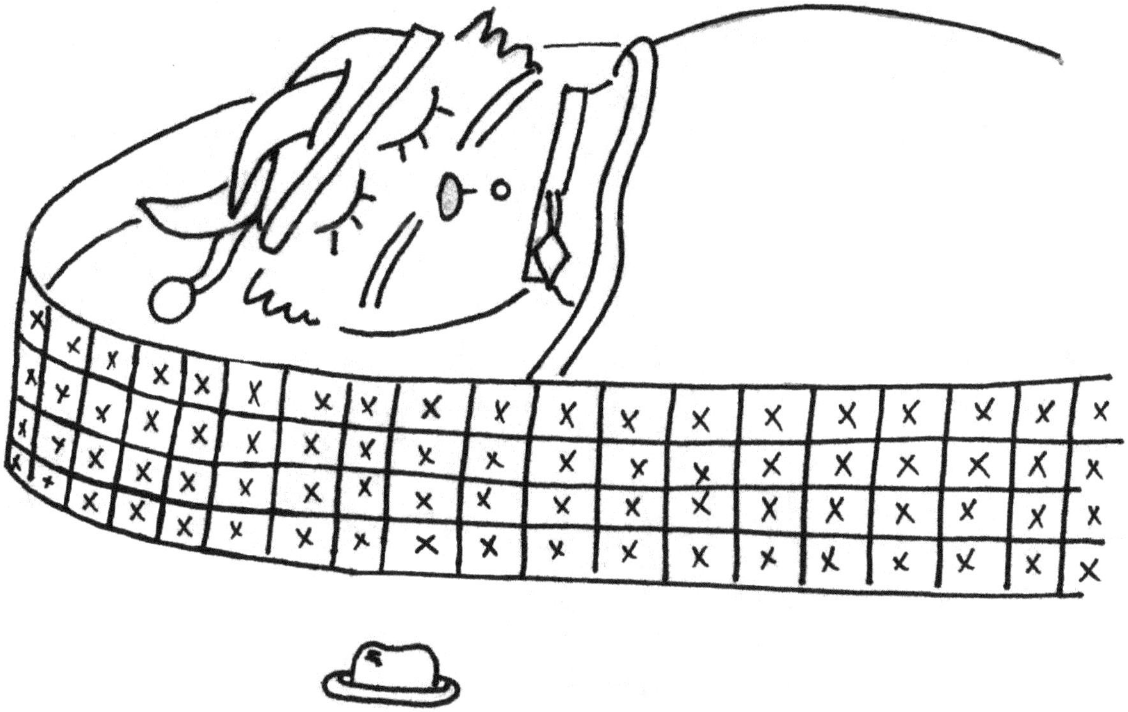

CAT

cat

2

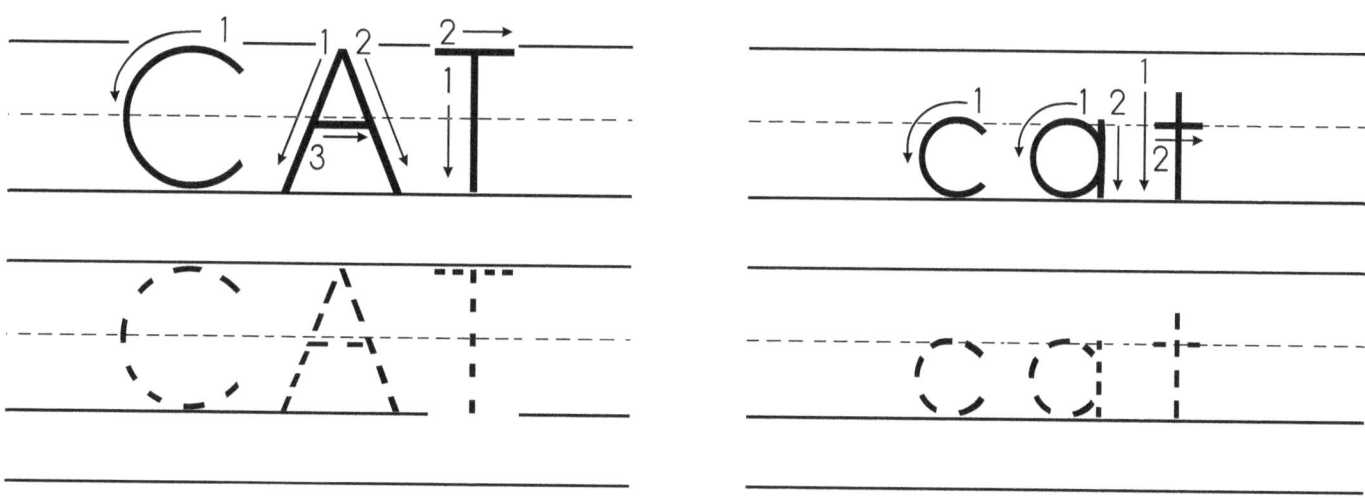

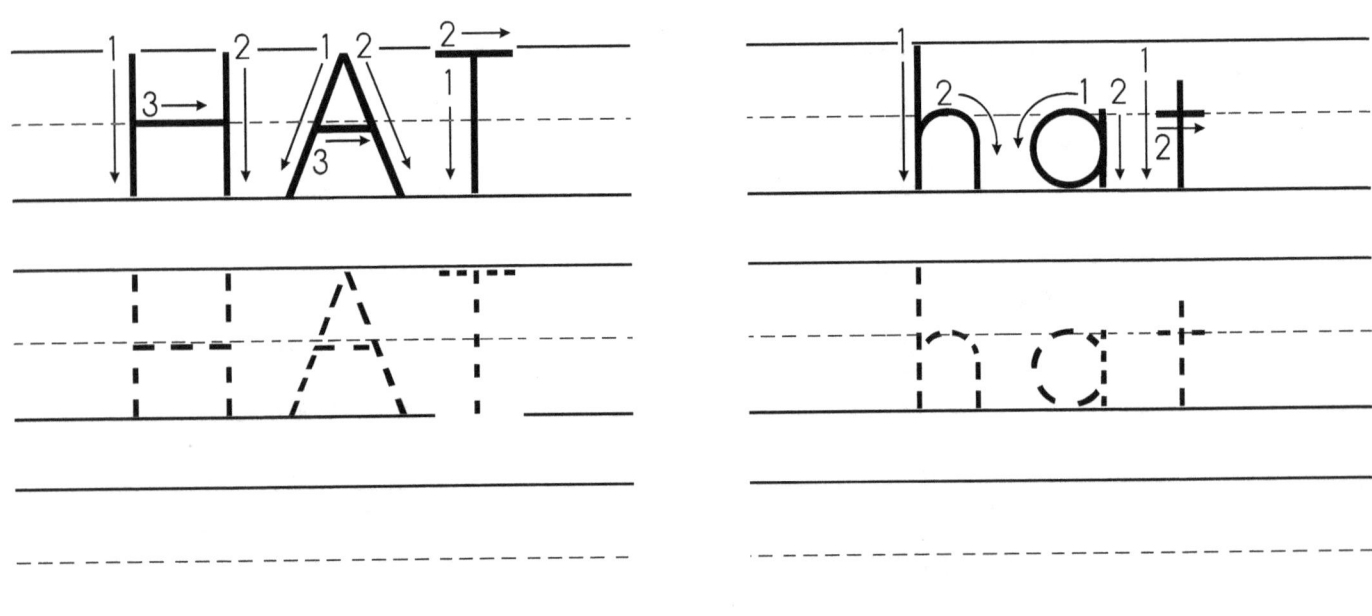

3 hat

HAT

HAT

hat

4

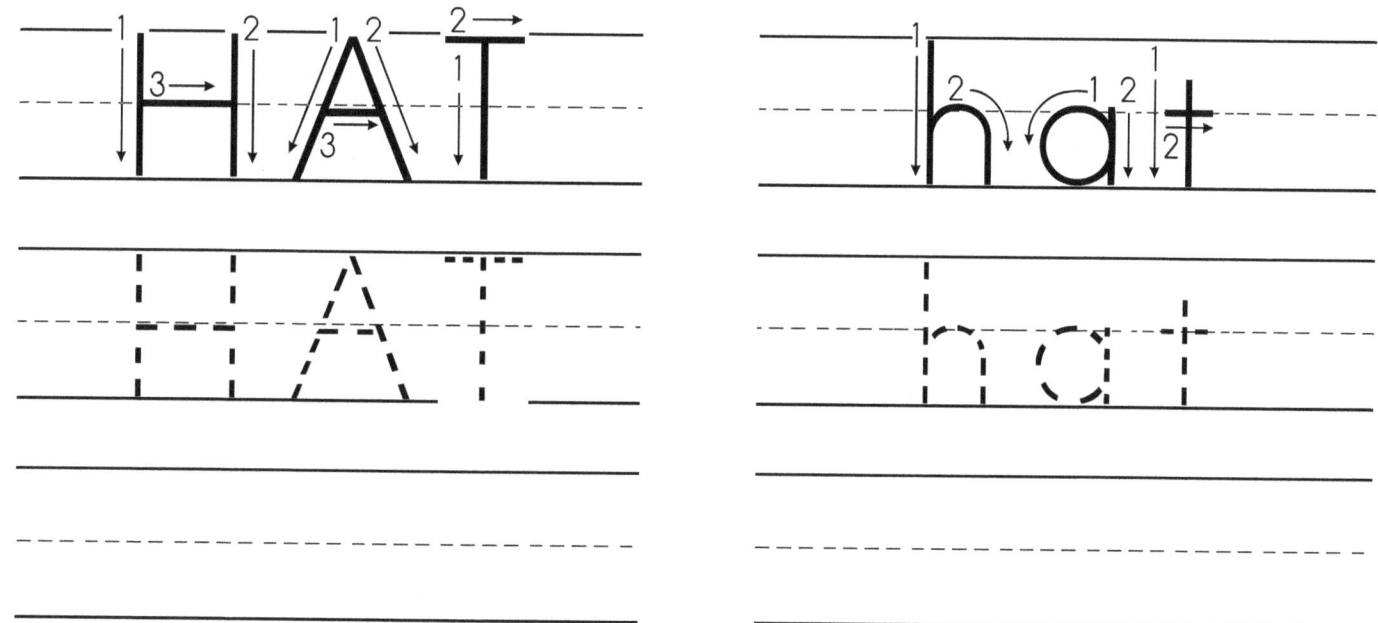

CAT

5 cat

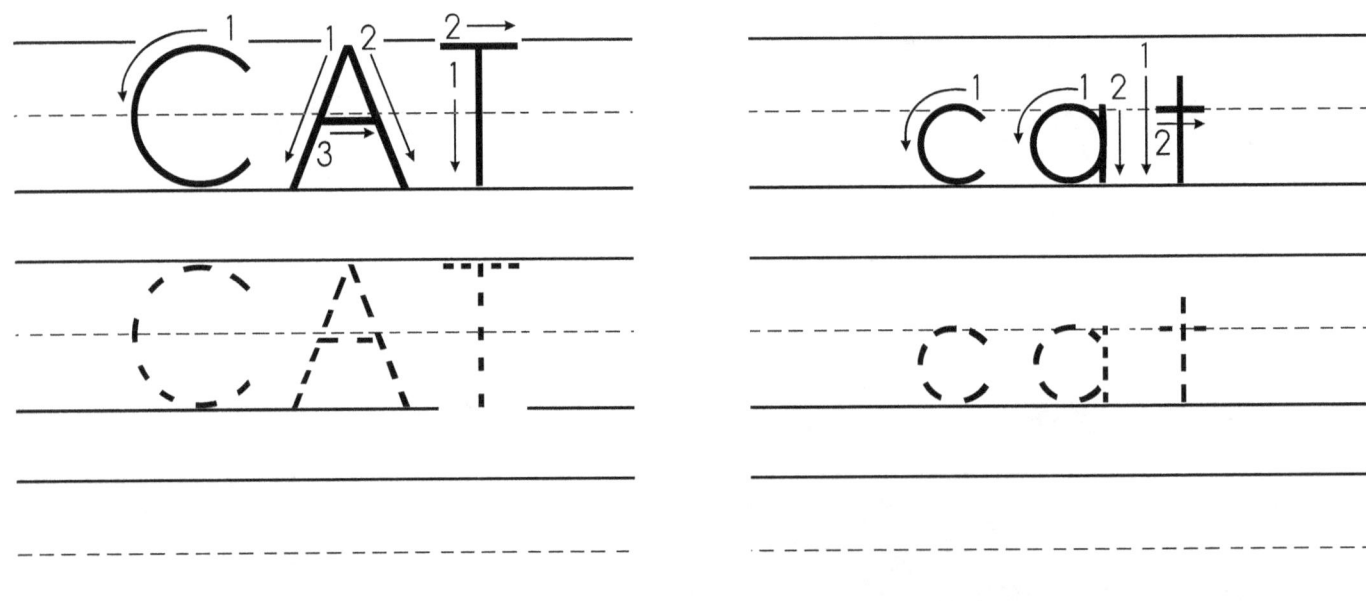

HAT

hat

6

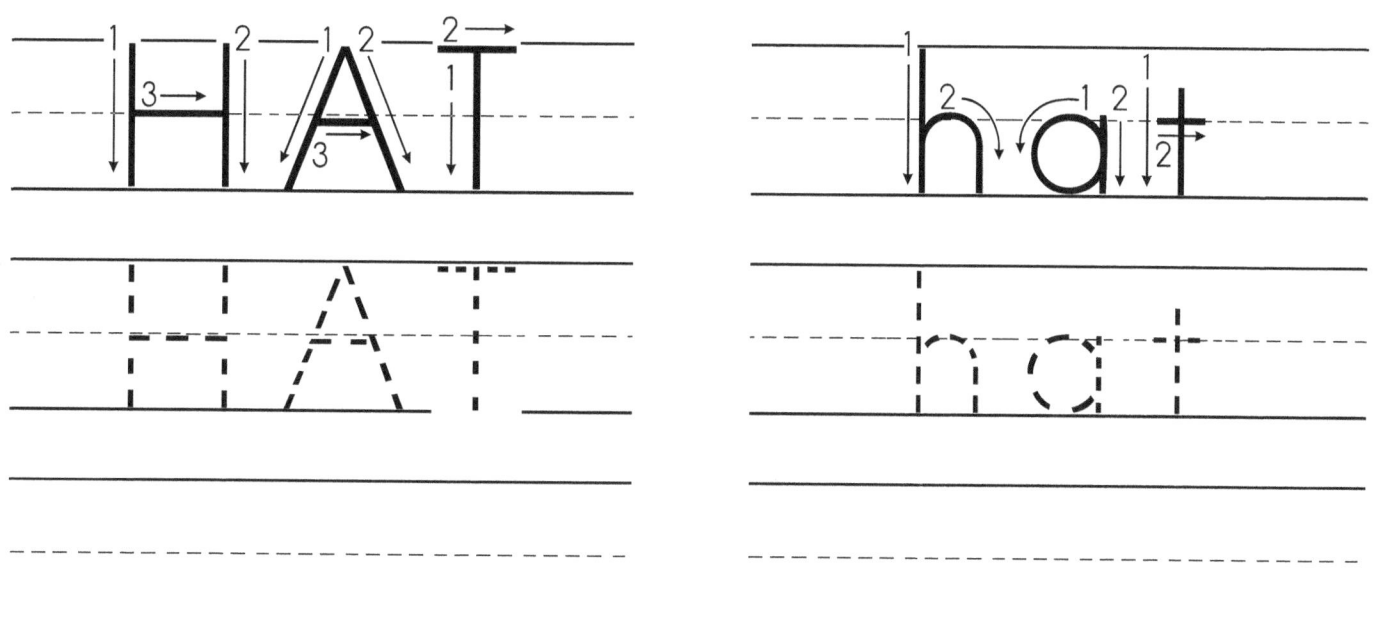

CAT

cat

7

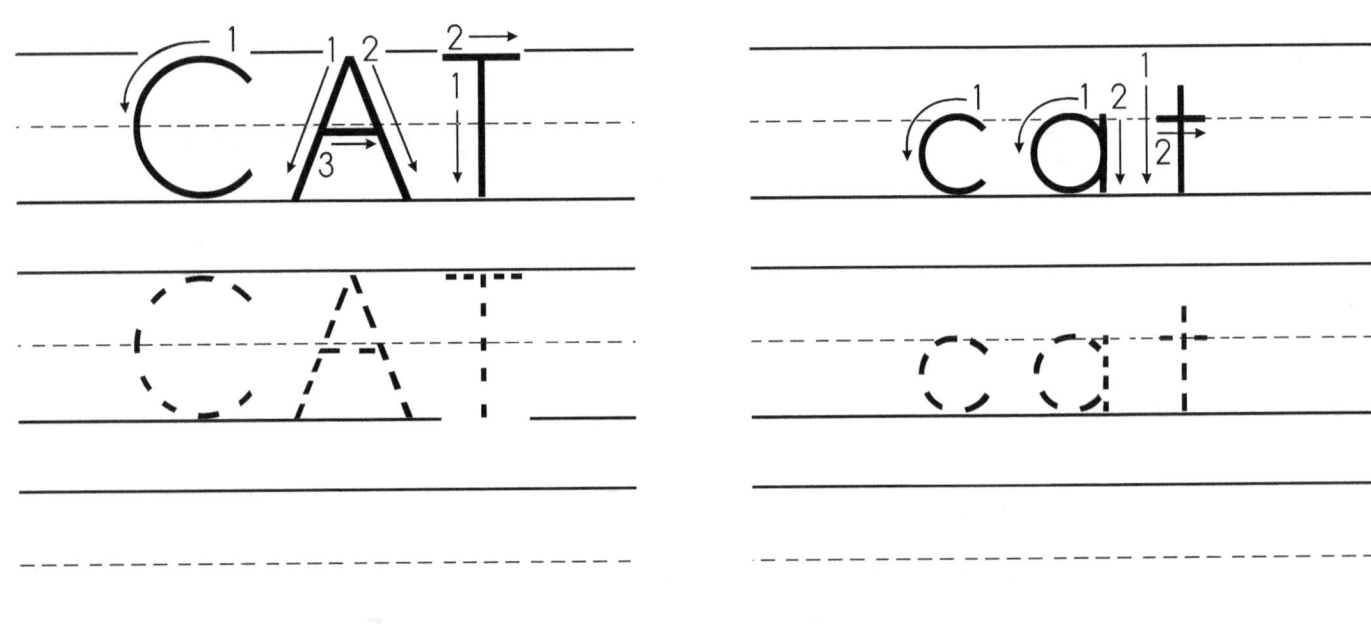

CAT

cat  8

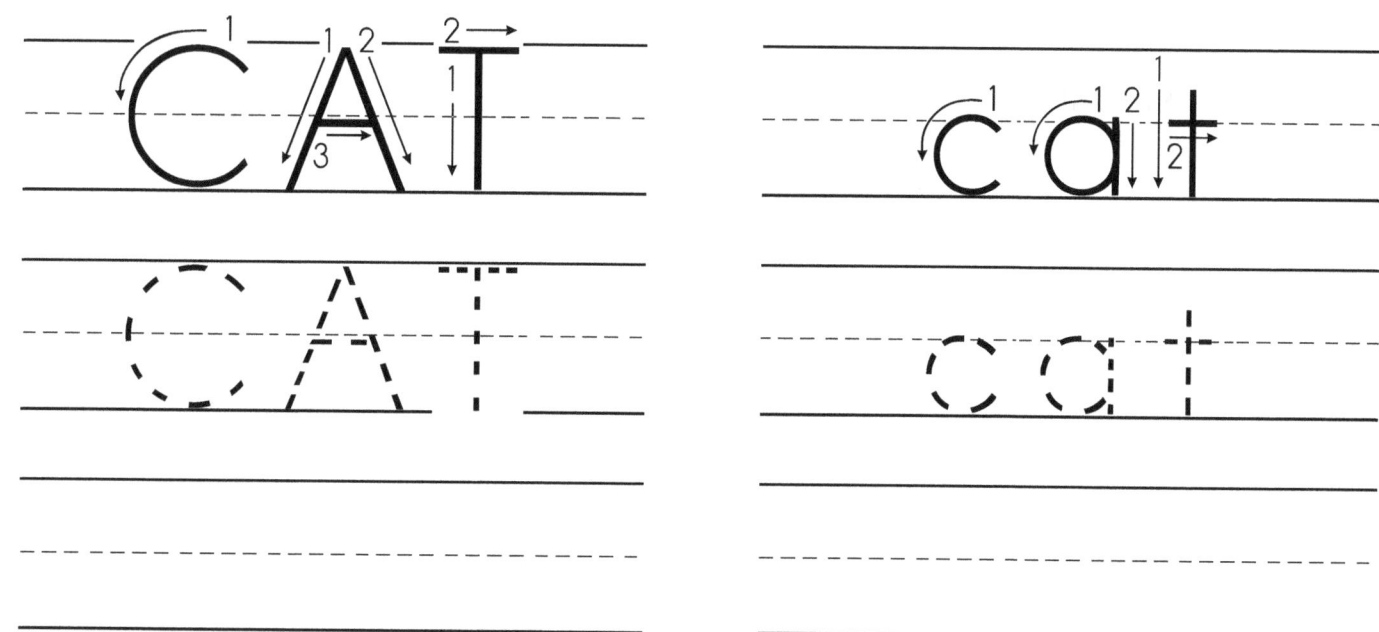

HAT

hat

9

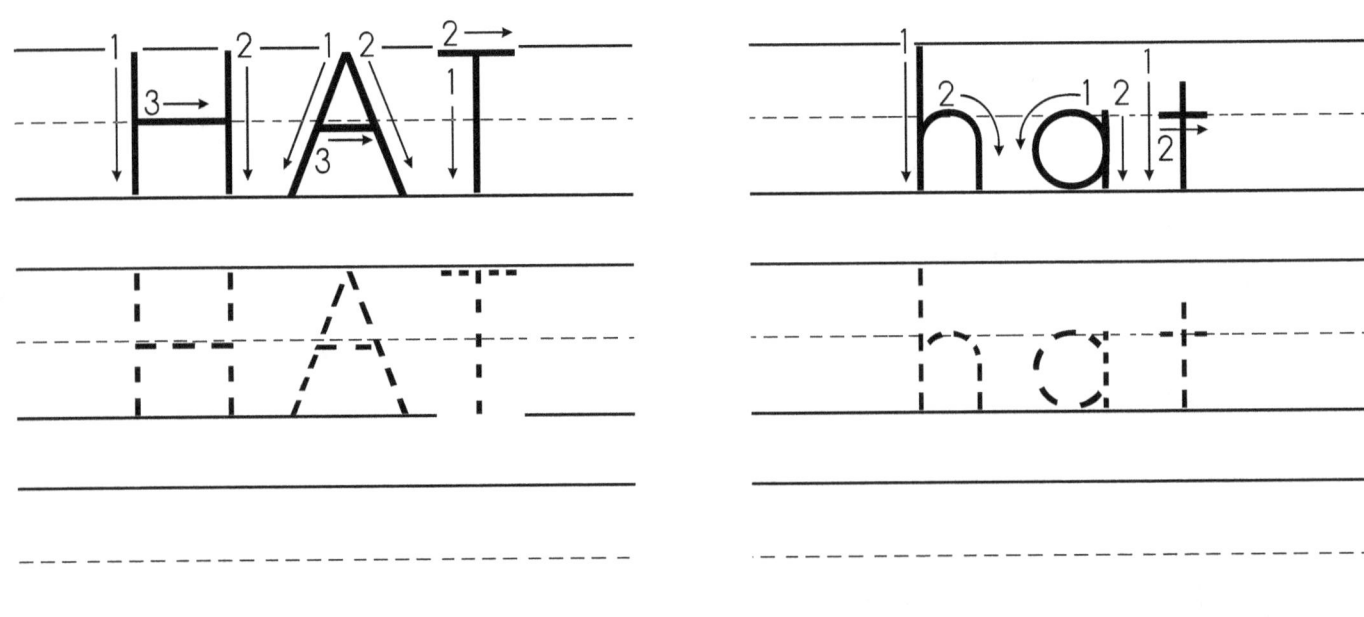

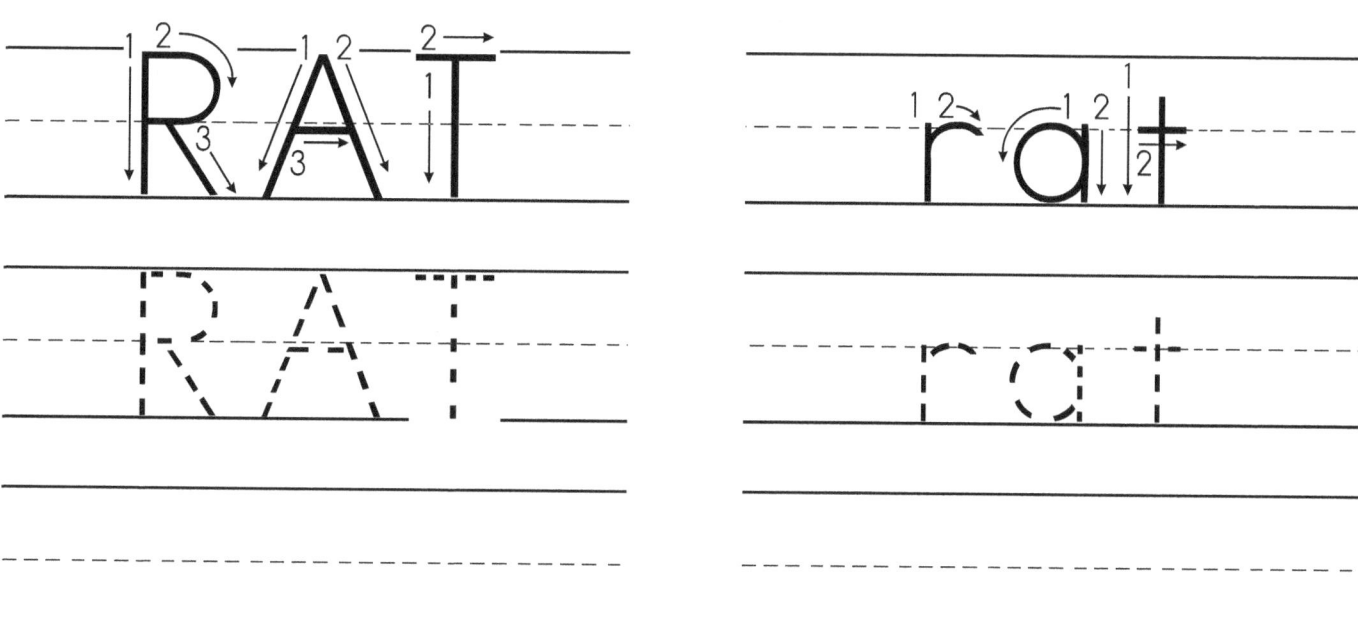

rat 10

# HAT

rat   hat

cat   mat

Got it!

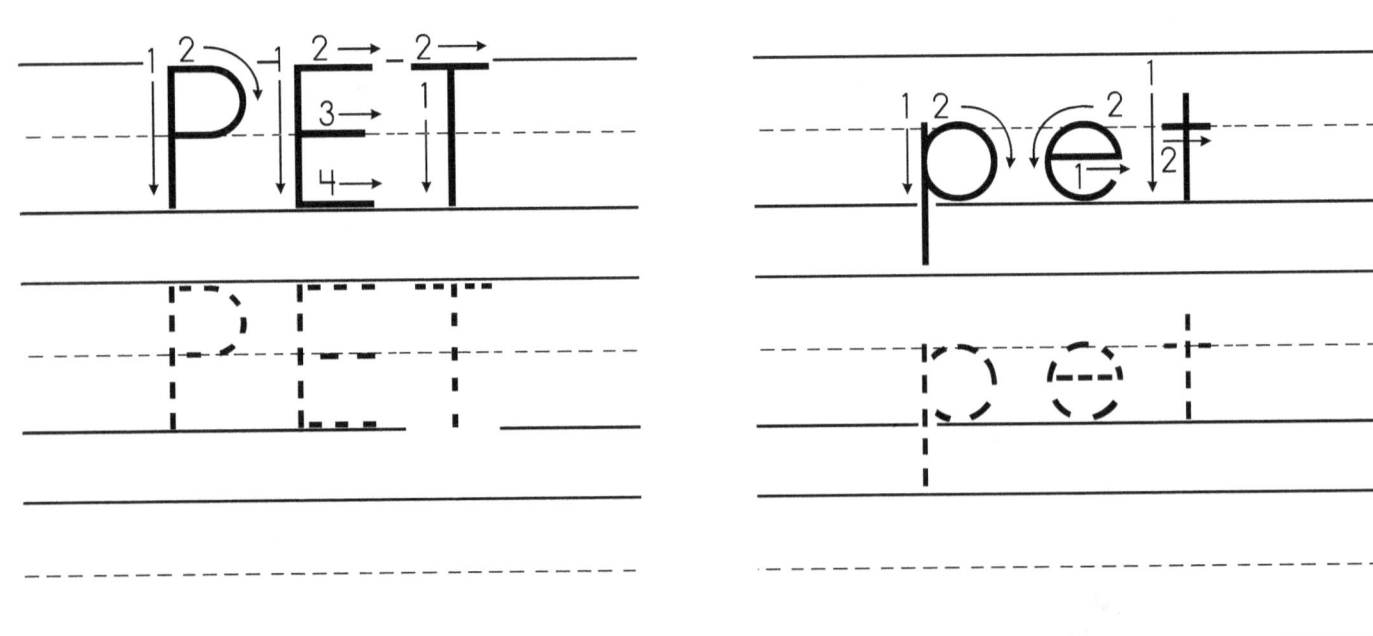

1   pet

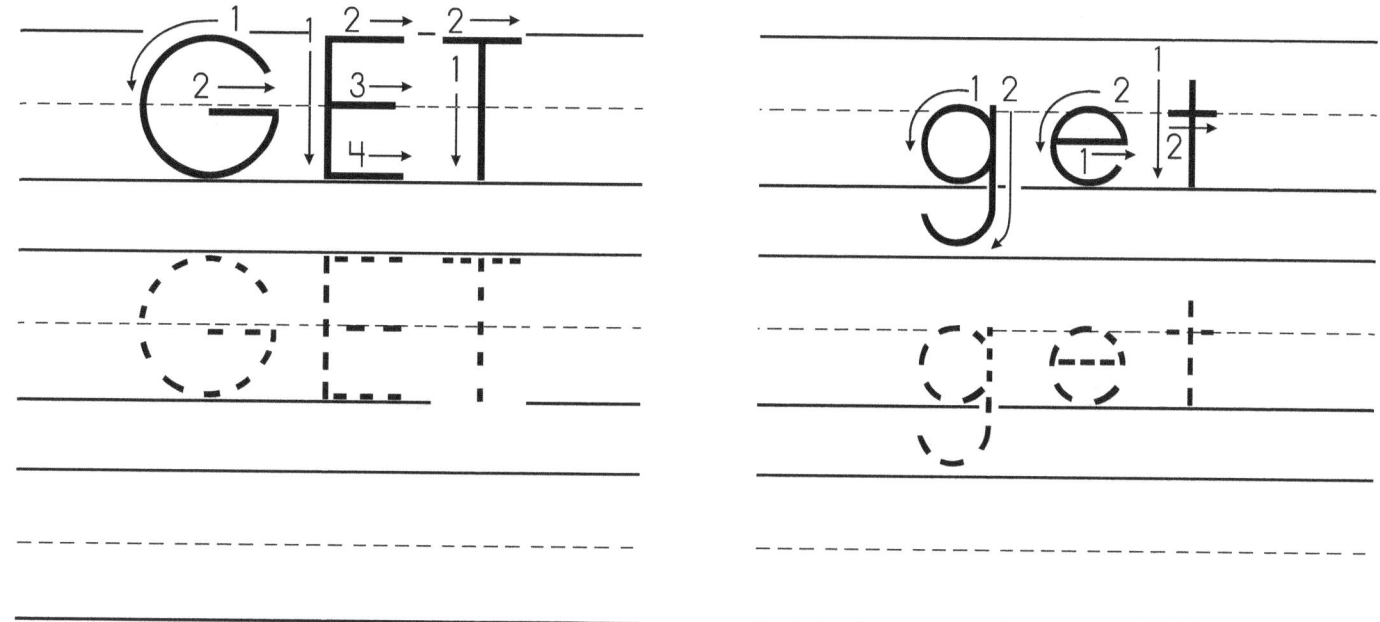

GET

get

2

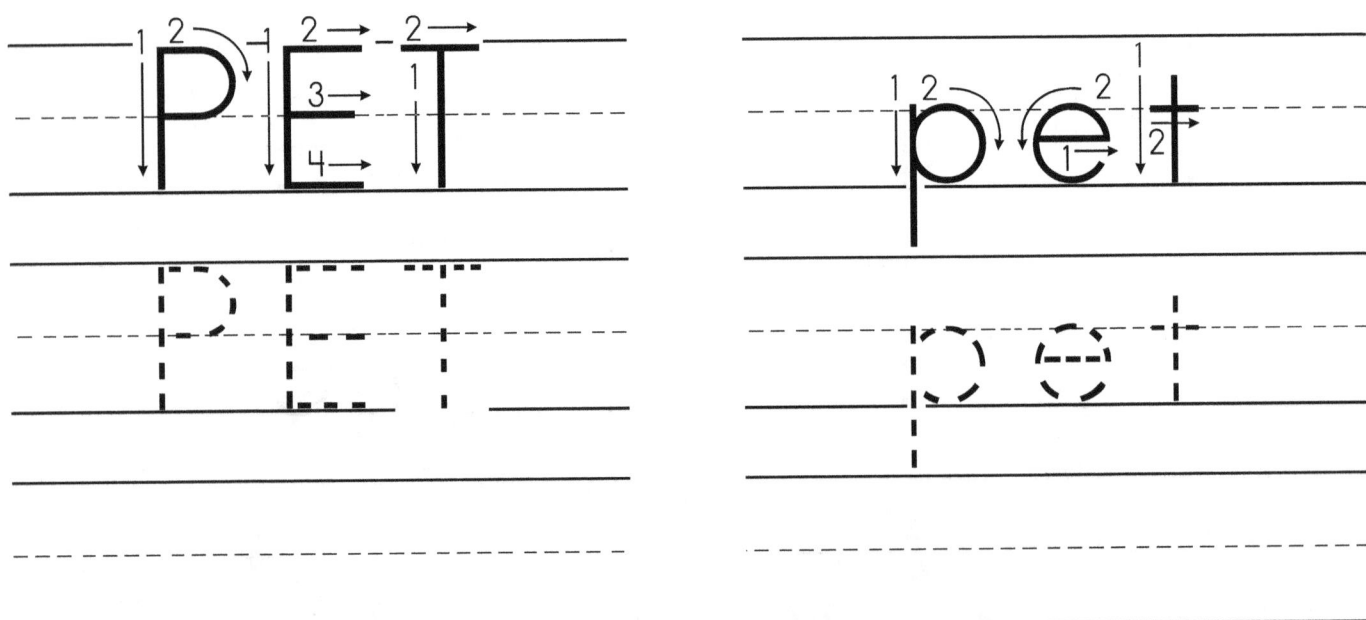

3 pet

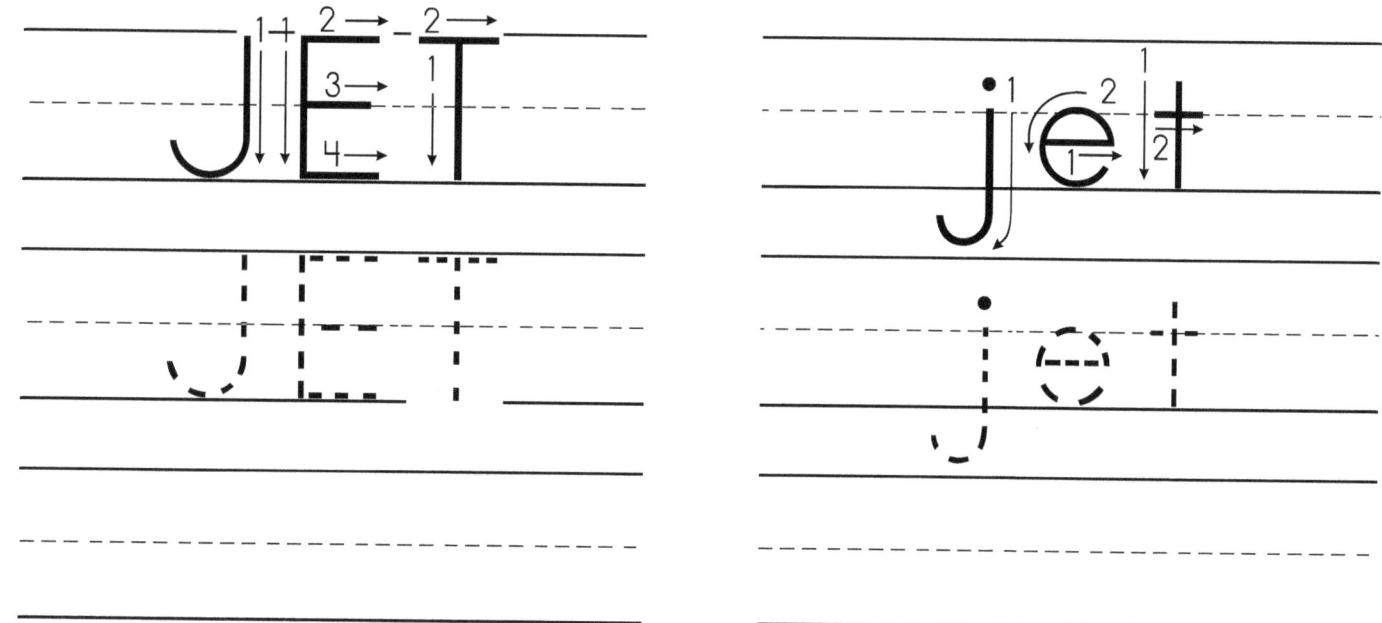

MET

5 met

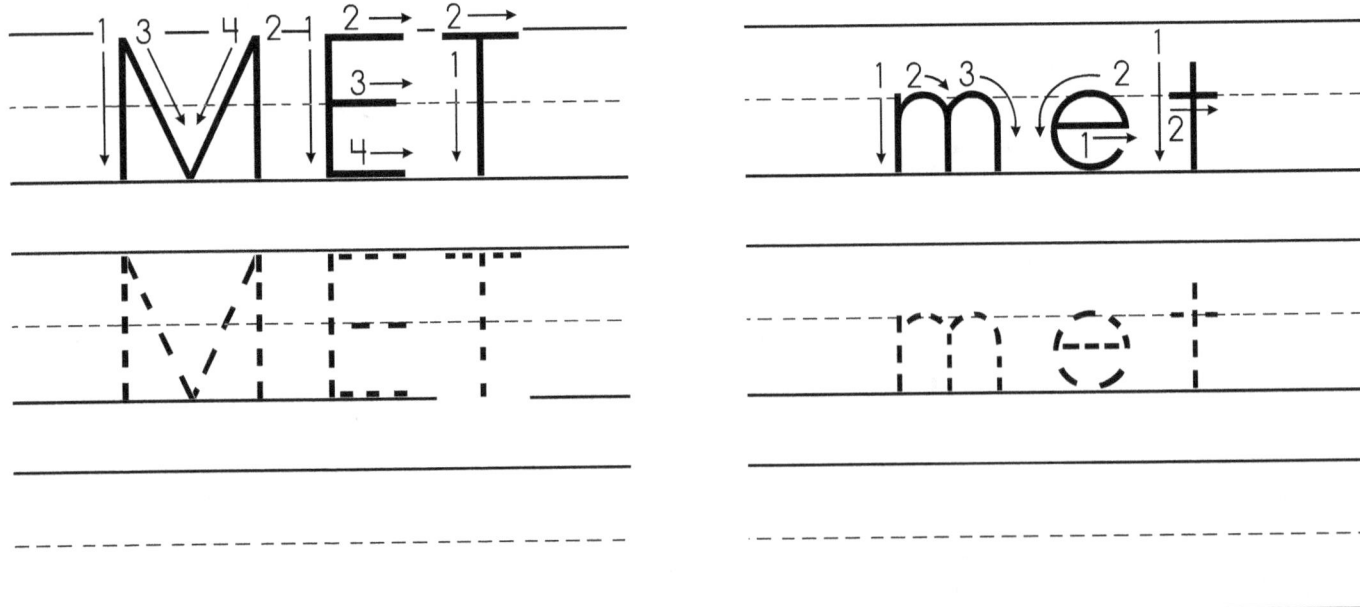

WET

wet

6

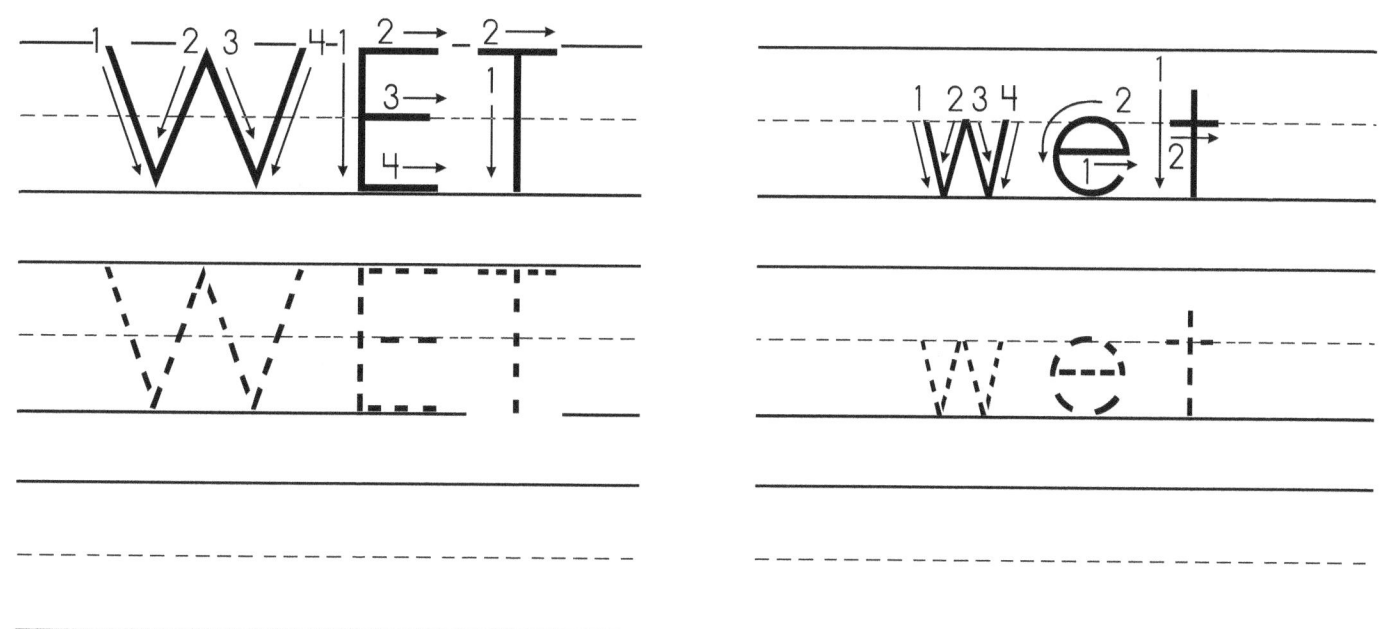

# 7 wet

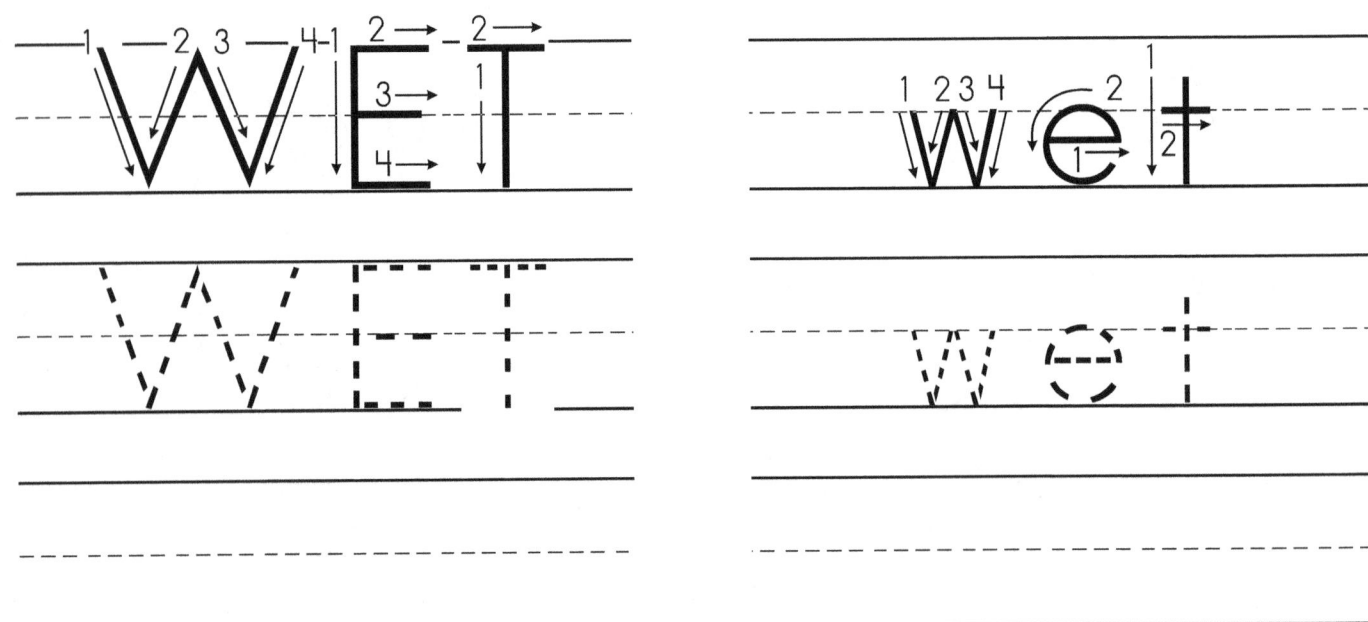

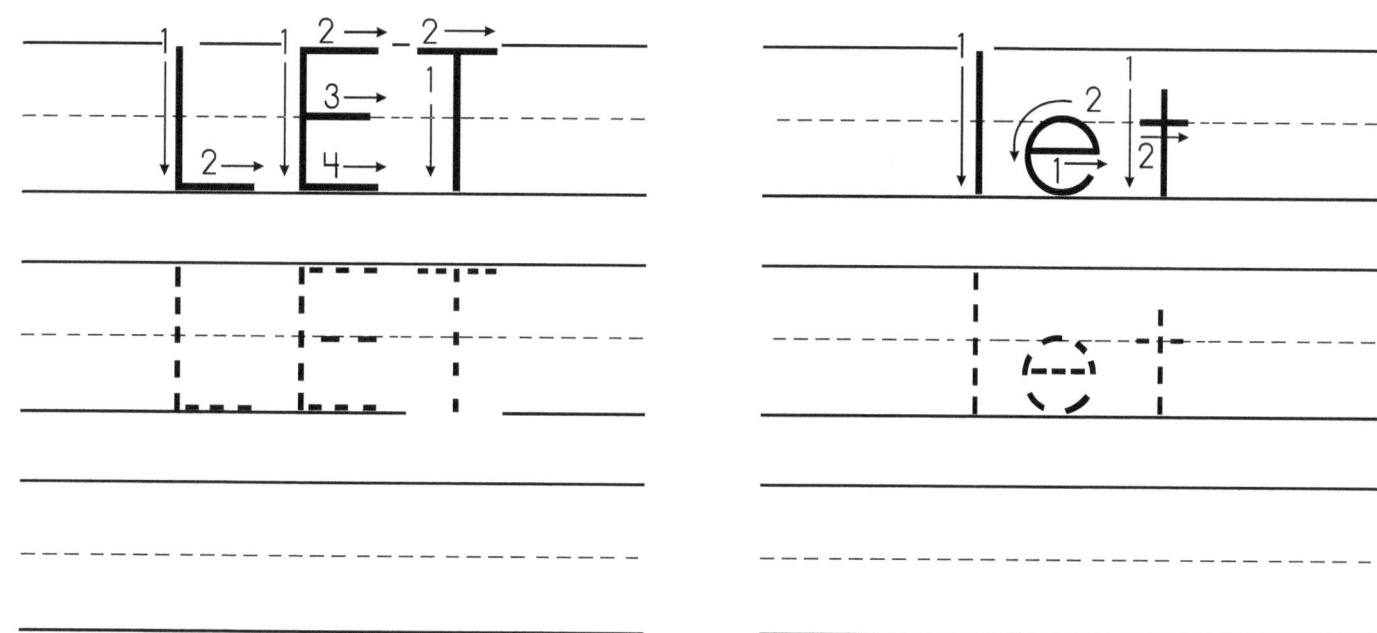

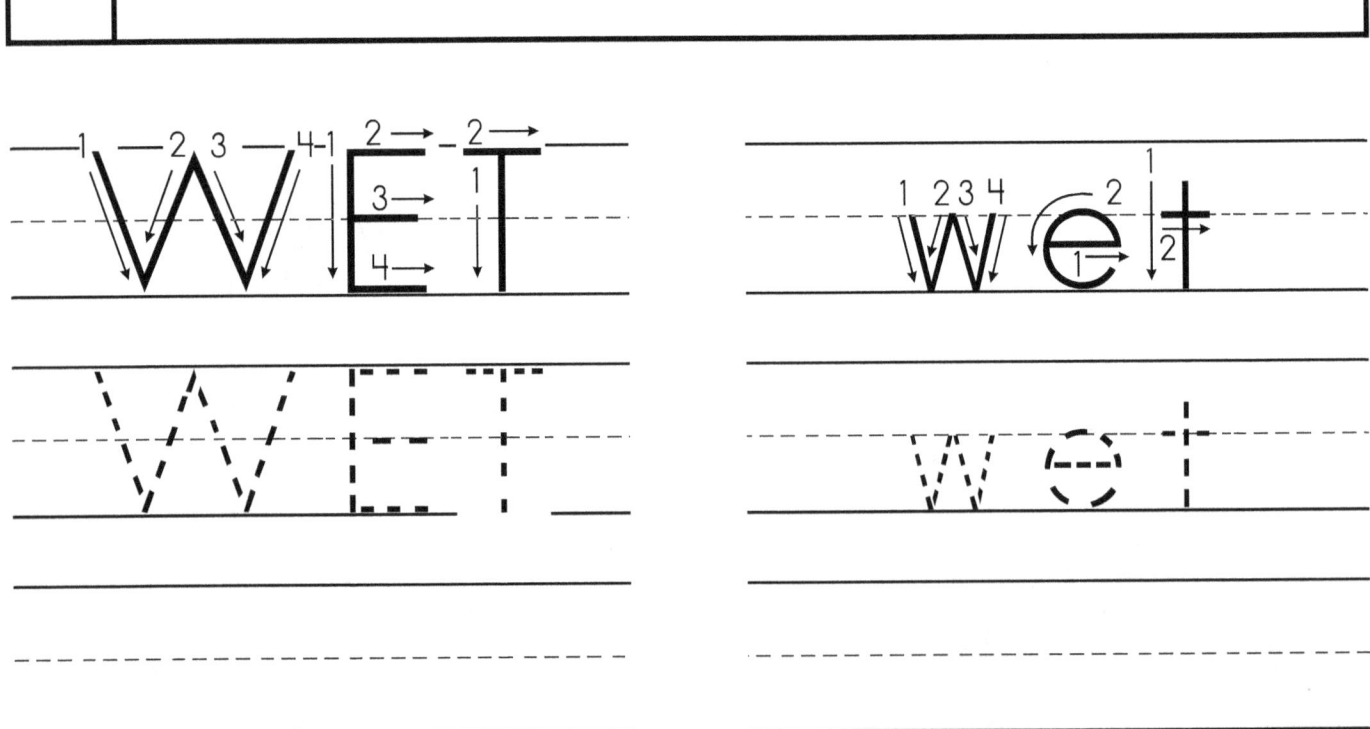

9 wet

SET

set

10

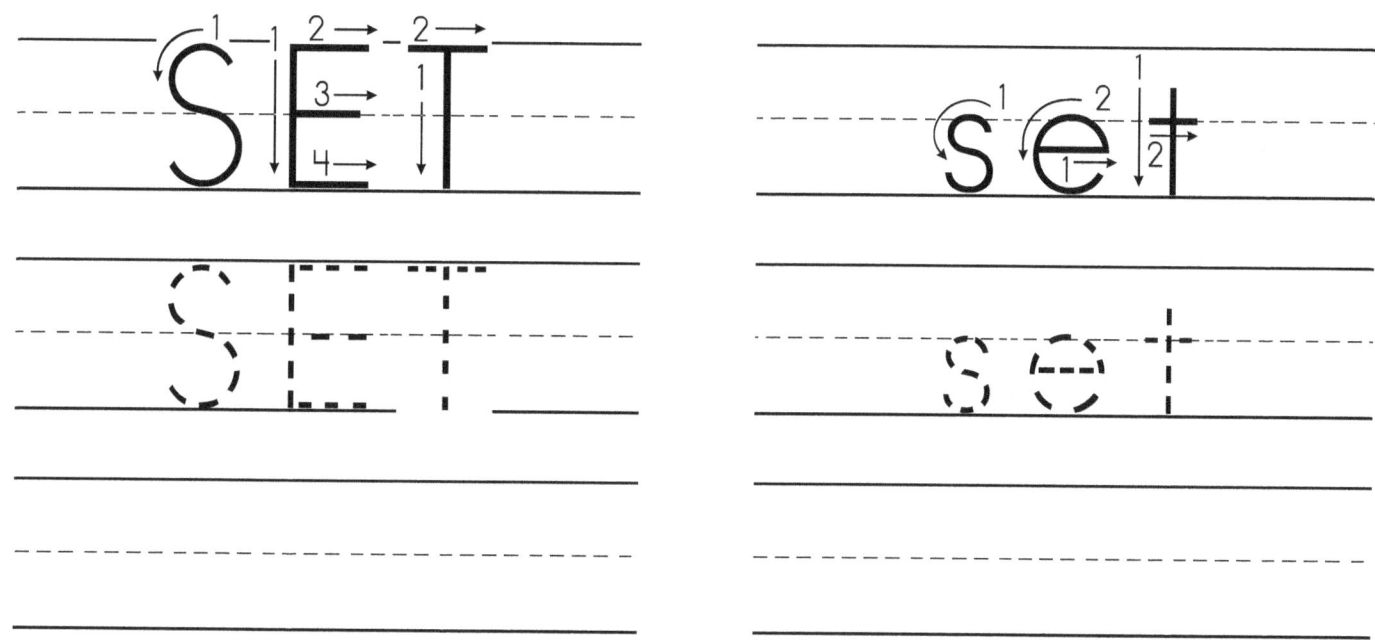

# WET

pet     wet

get     let

jet     set

met

Got it!

# PIG DIGS

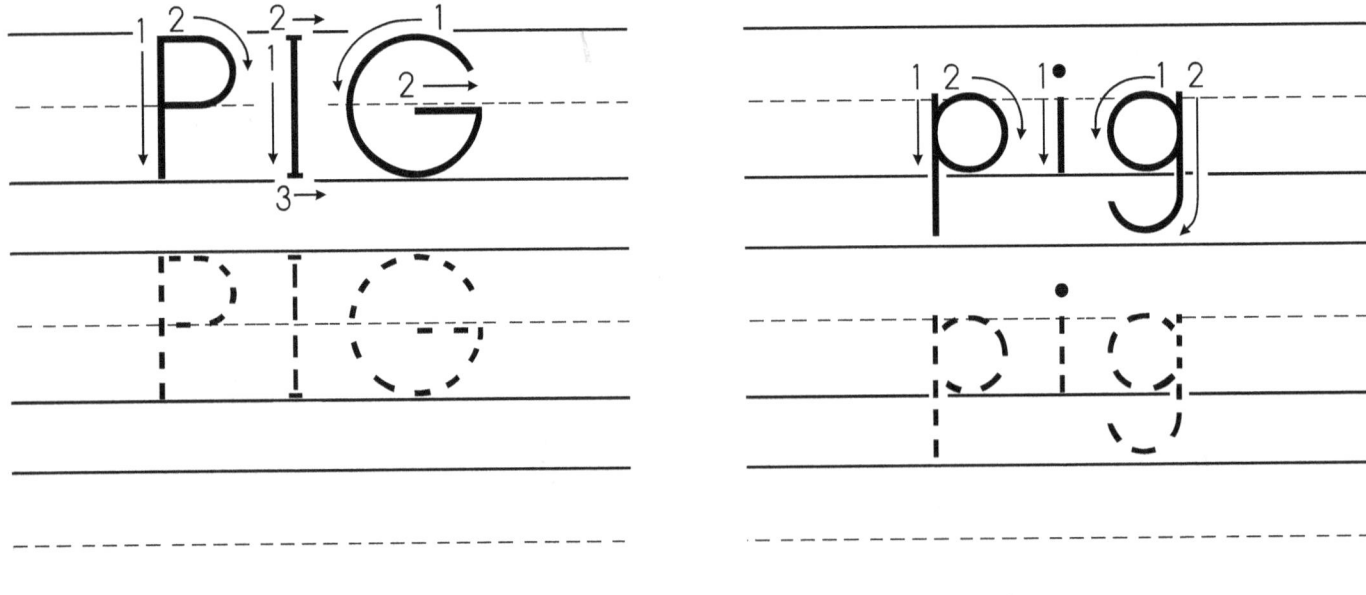

DIG

dig

2

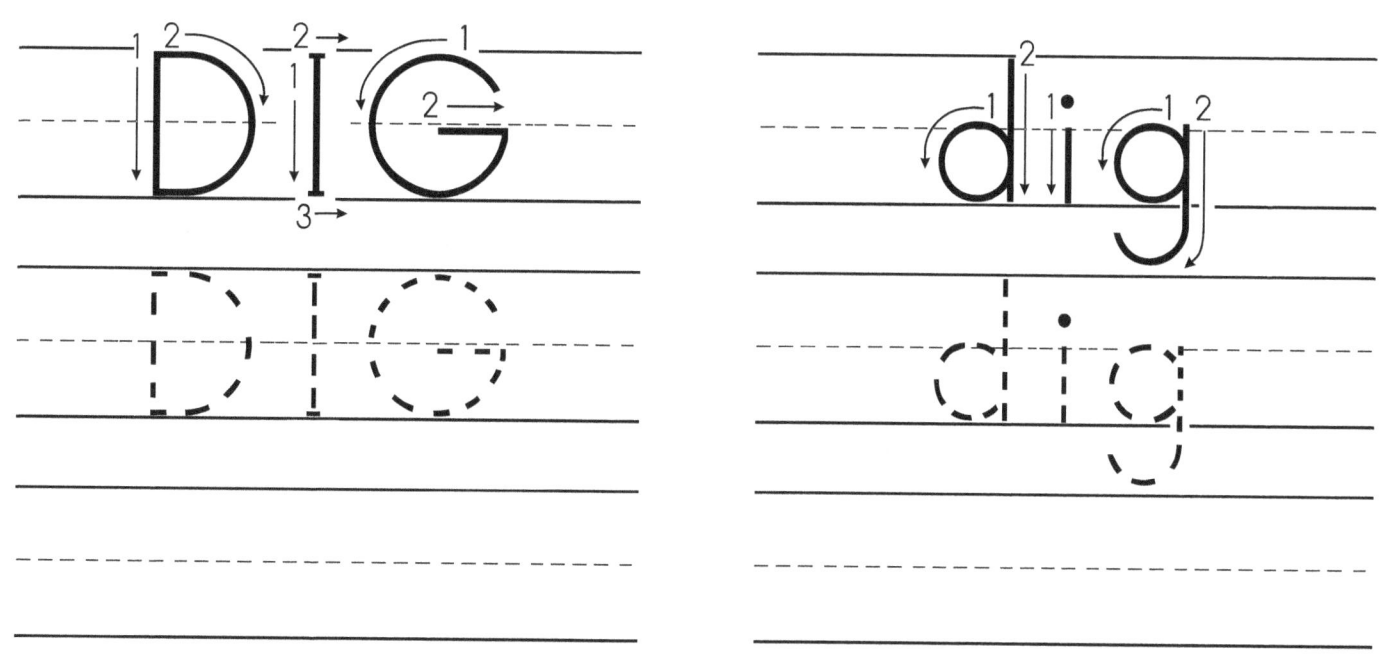

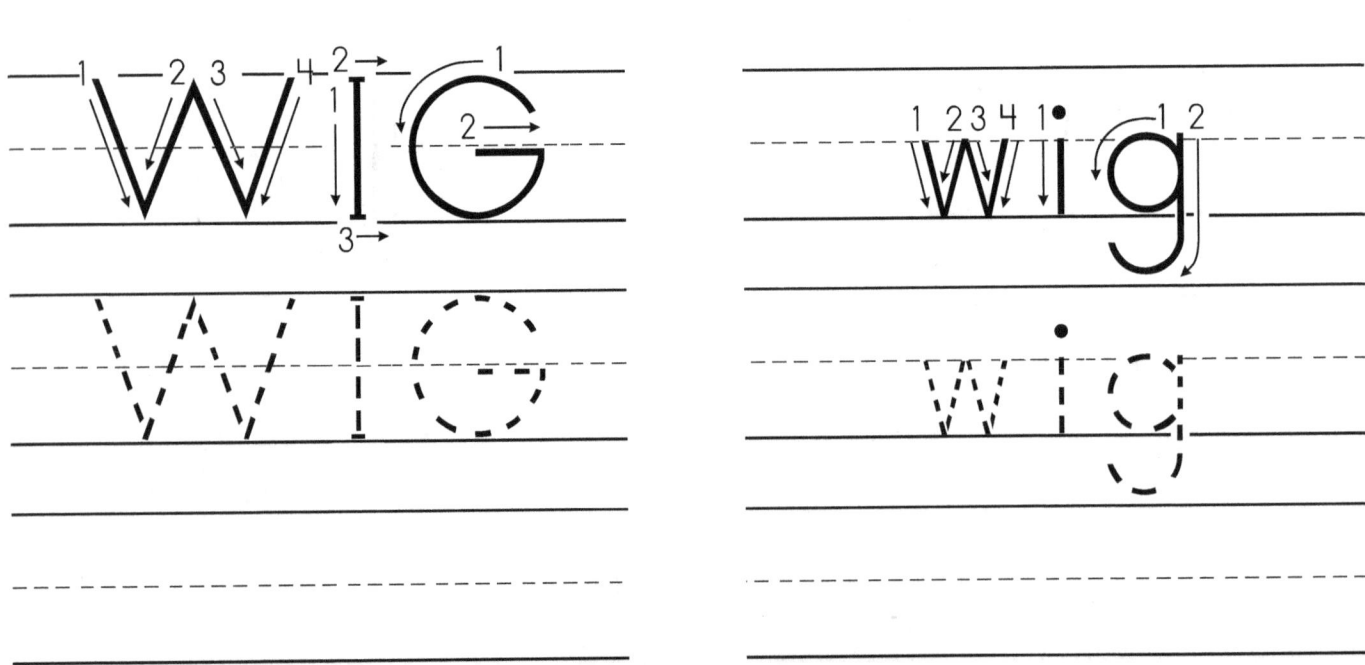

WIG

3 wig

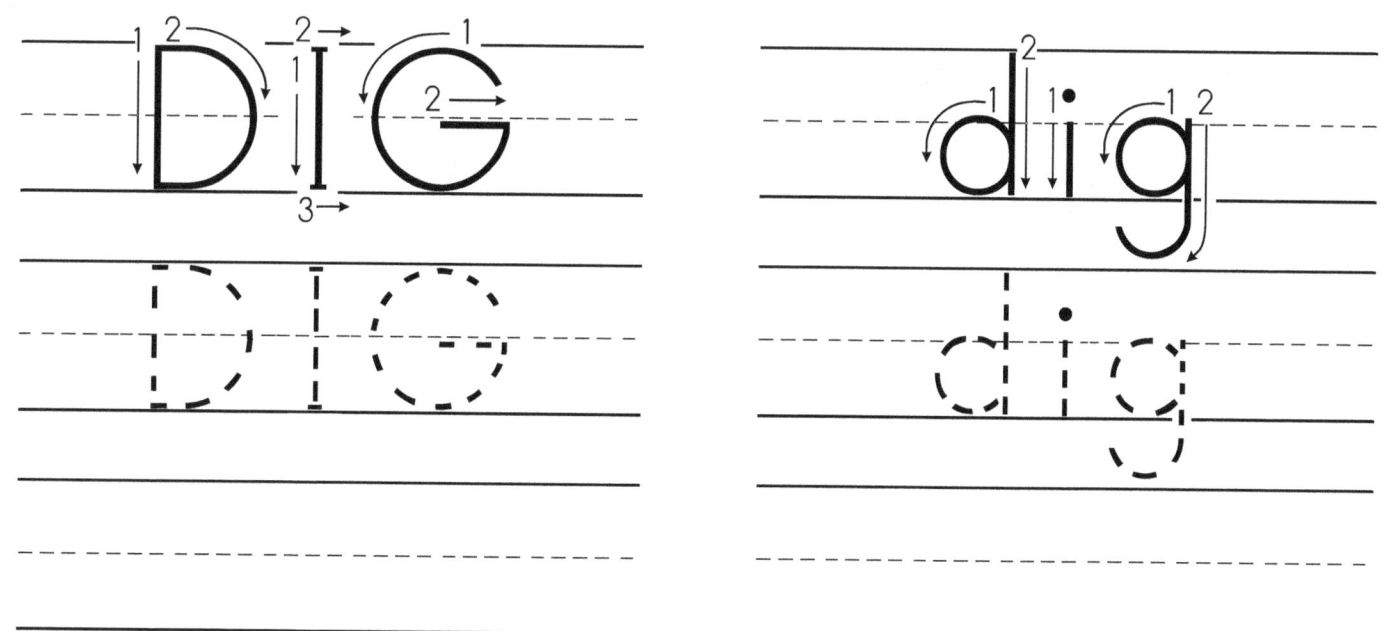

PIG

pig

5

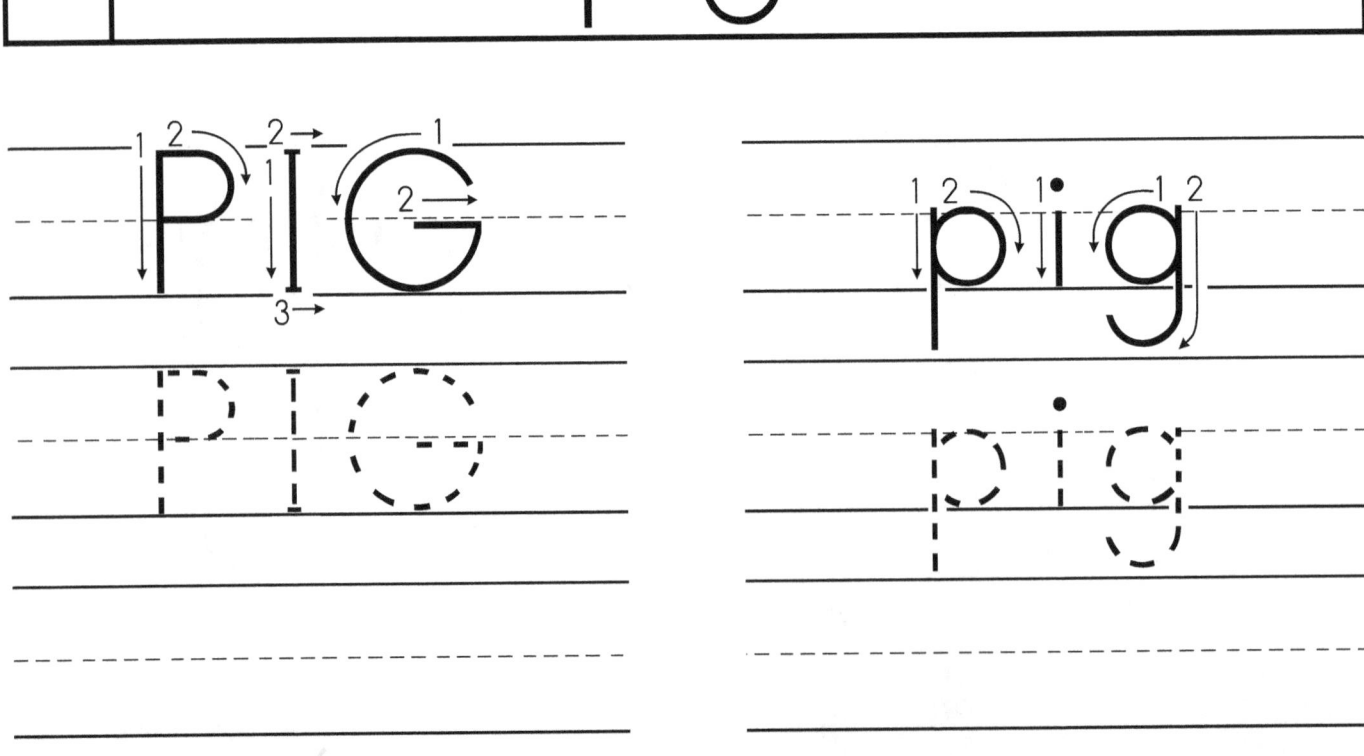

DIG

dig | 6

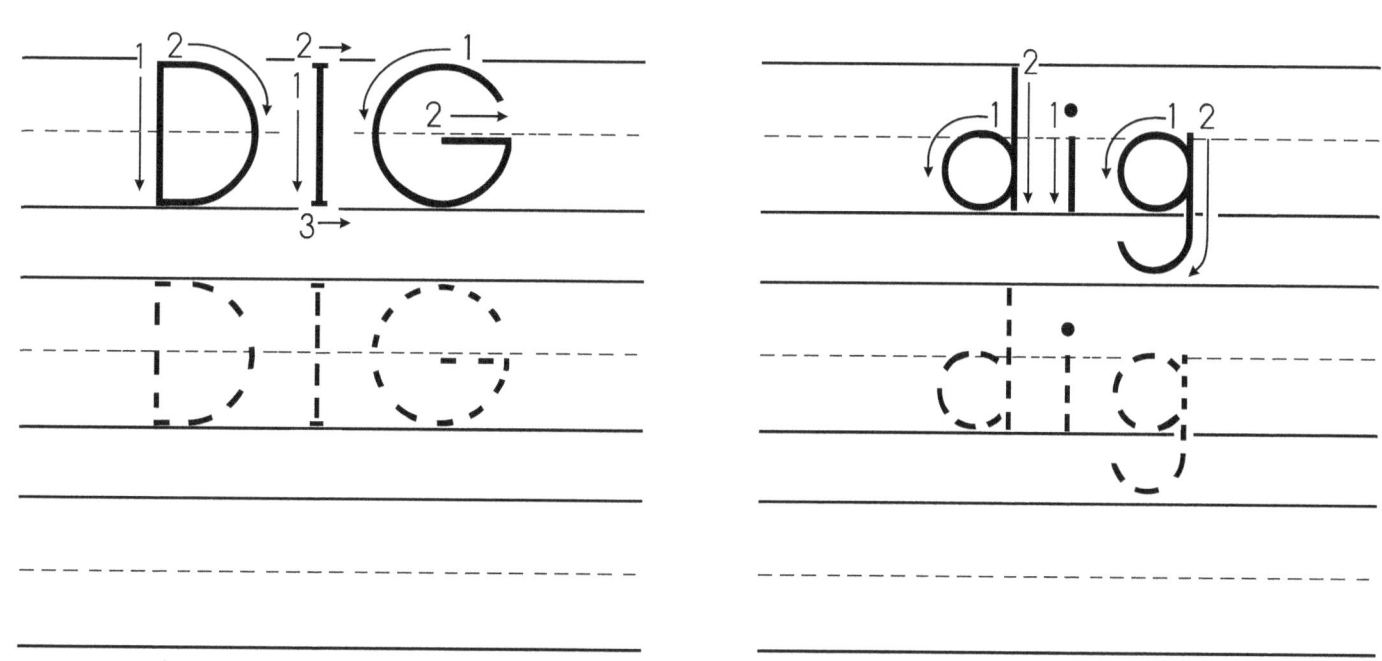

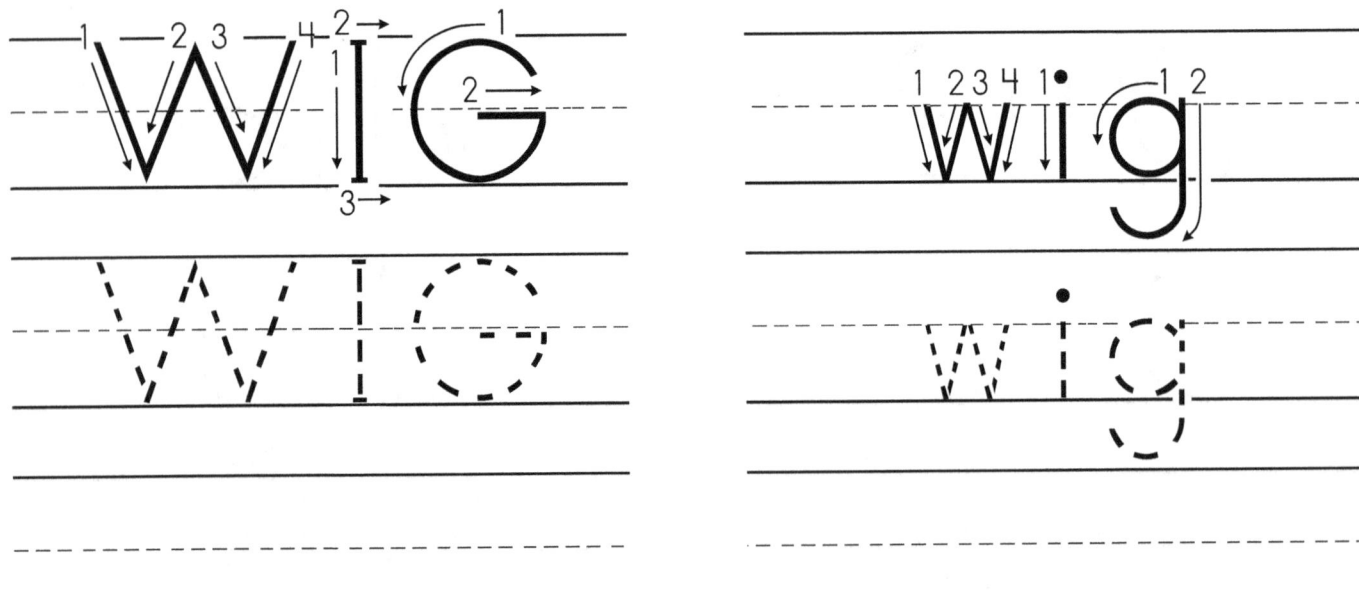

7 wig

DIG

dig

8

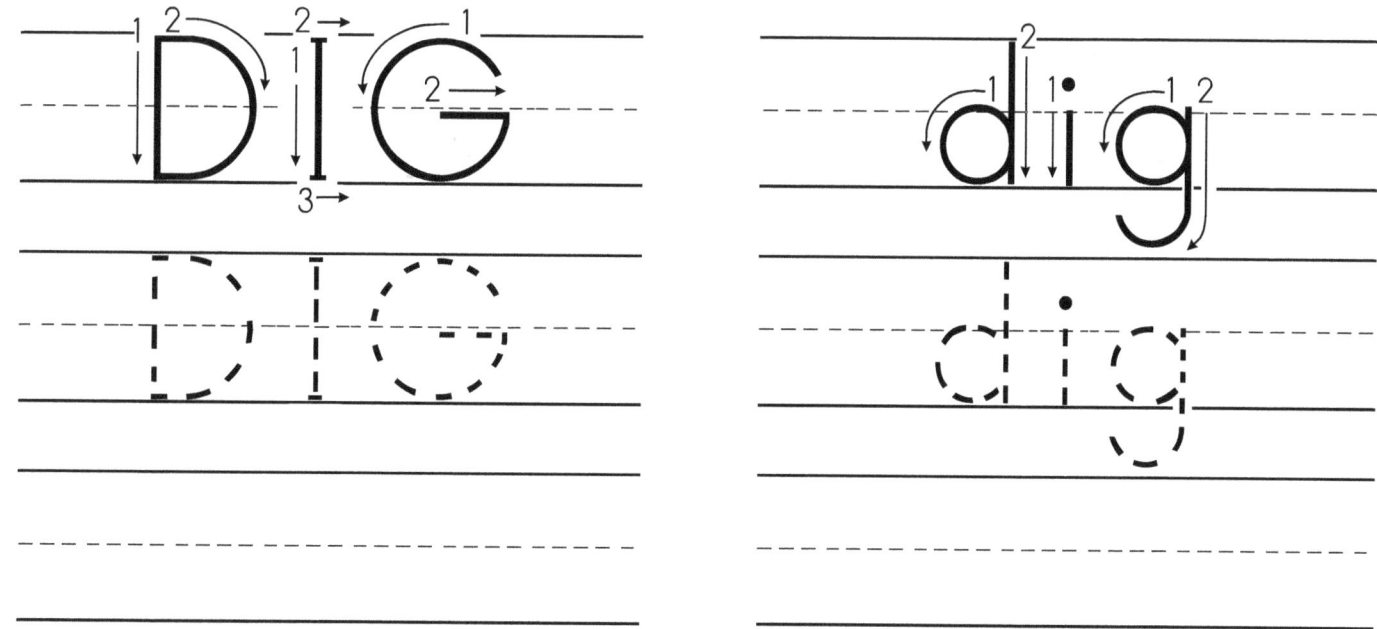

BIG

9 | big

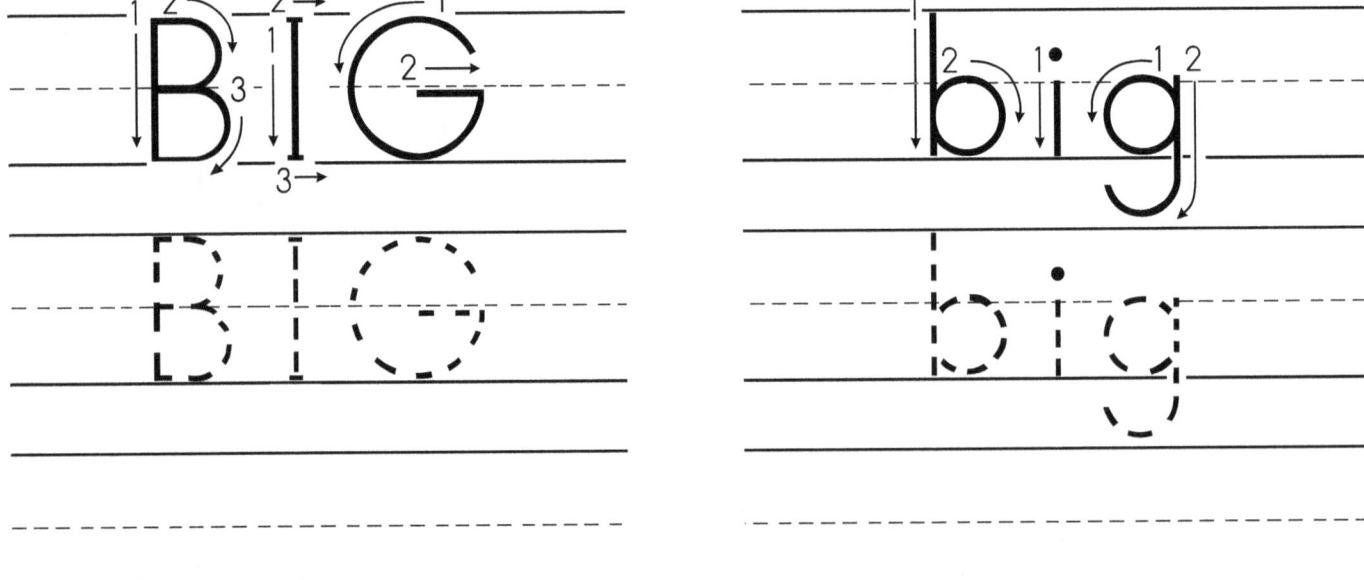

# PIG DIGS

pig     big
dig     jig
wig

Got it!

# DOG JOGS

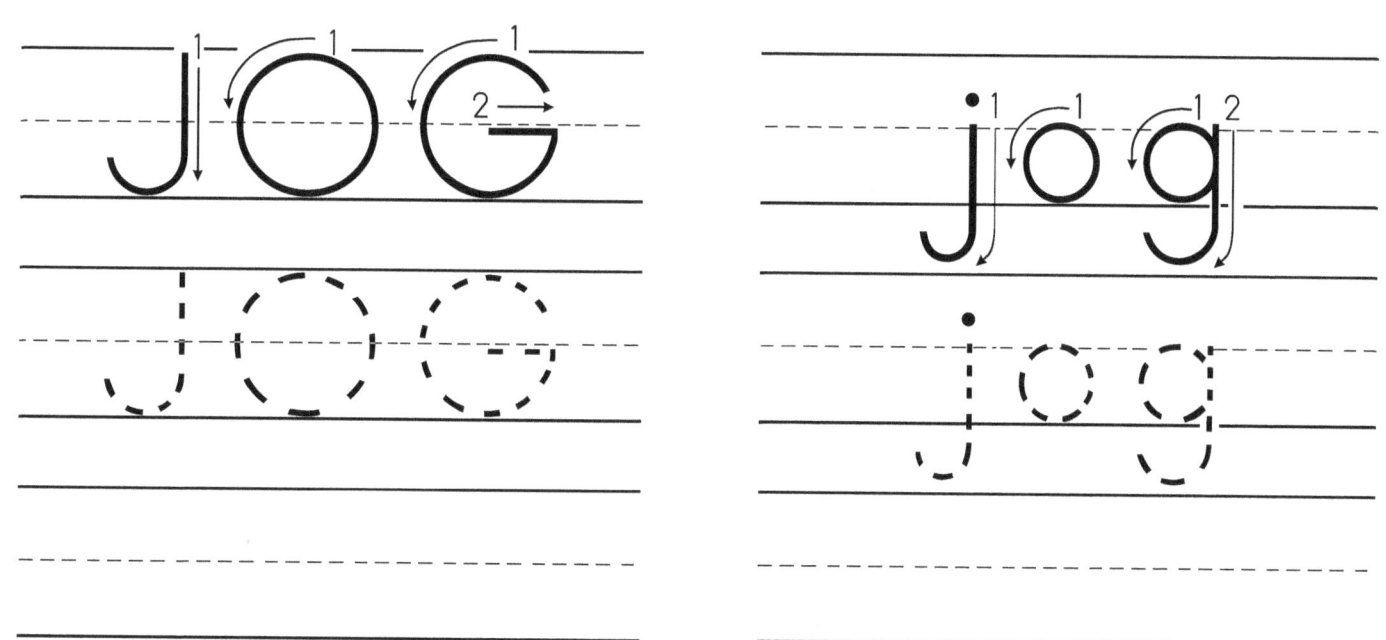

JOG

3   jog

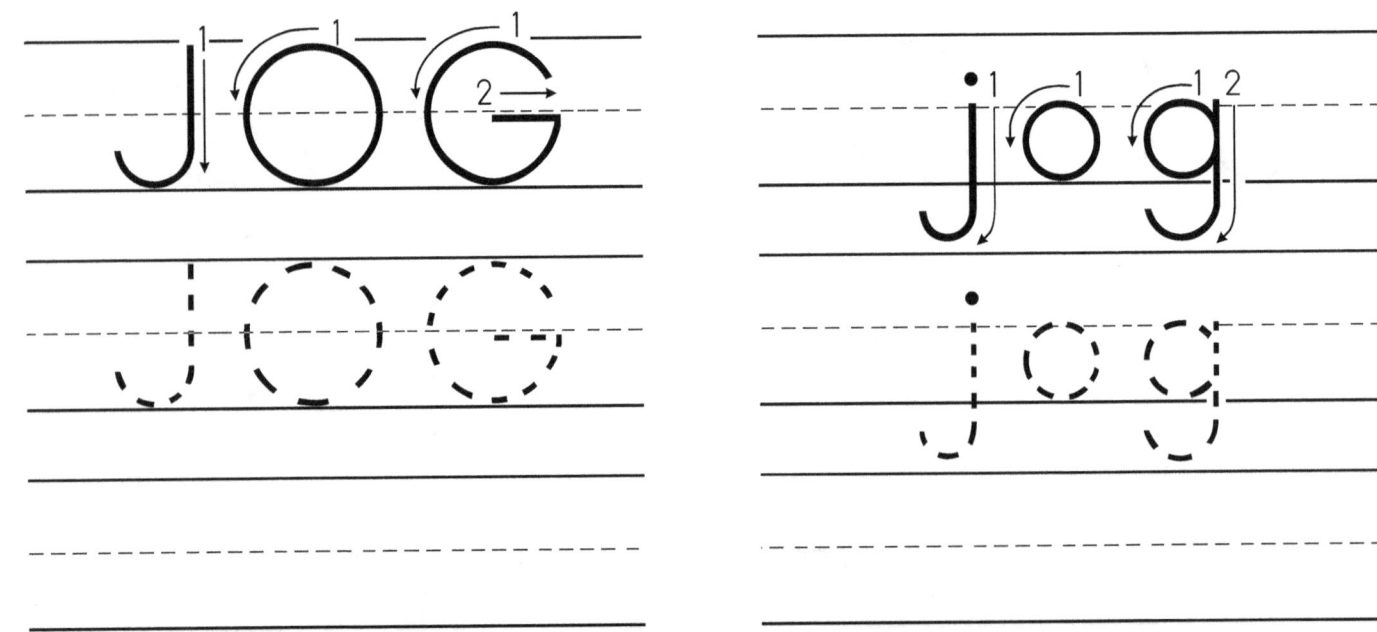

FOG

fog

4

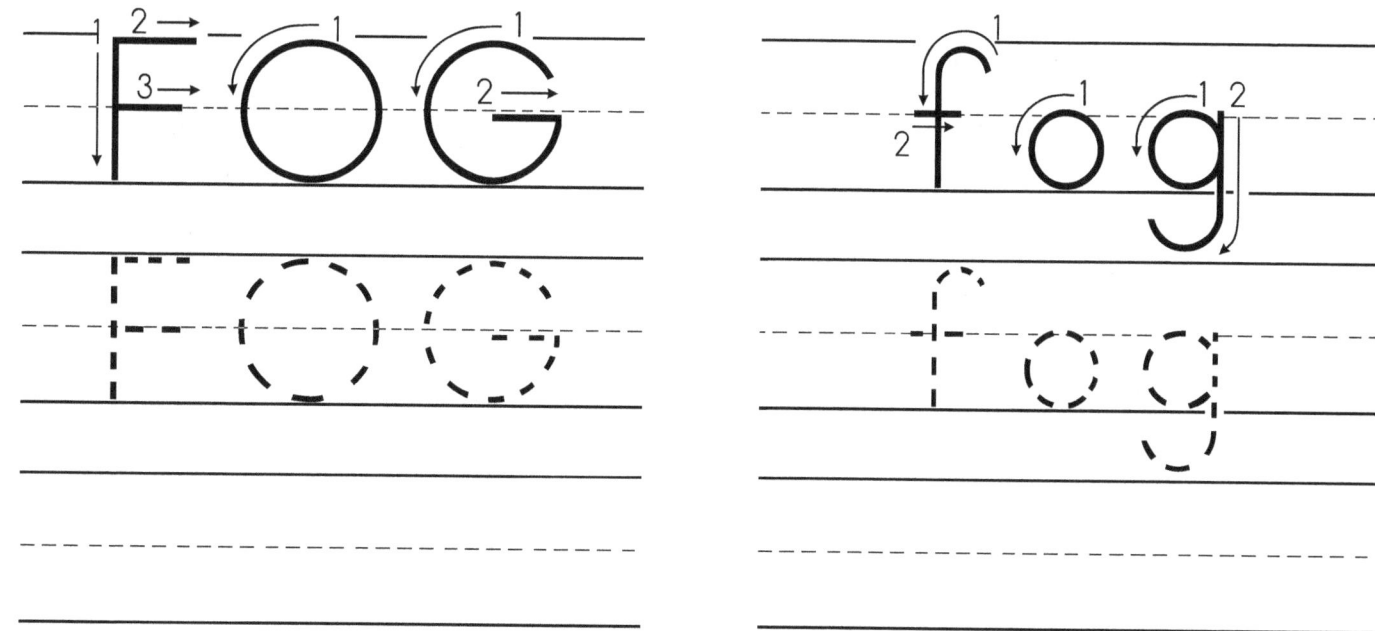

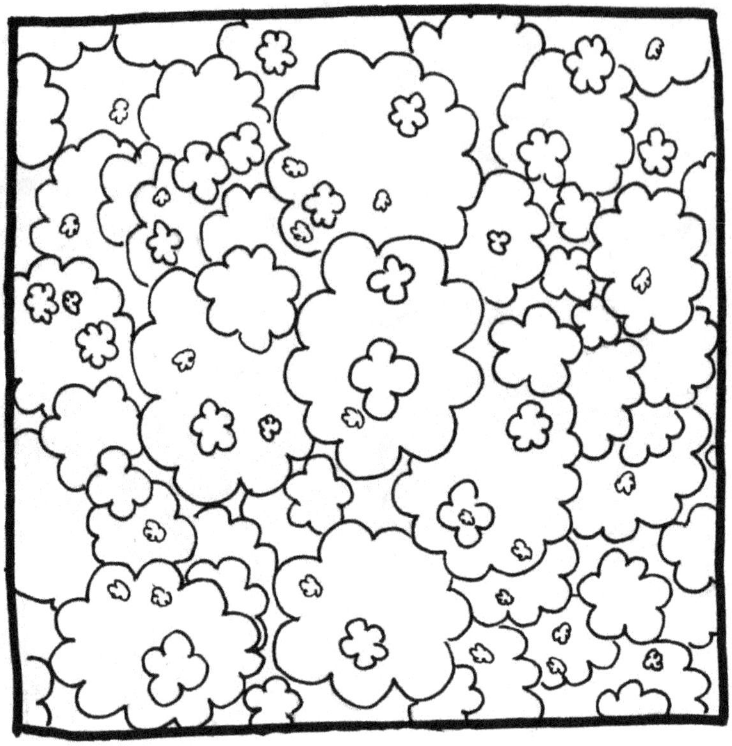

FOG

5 | fog

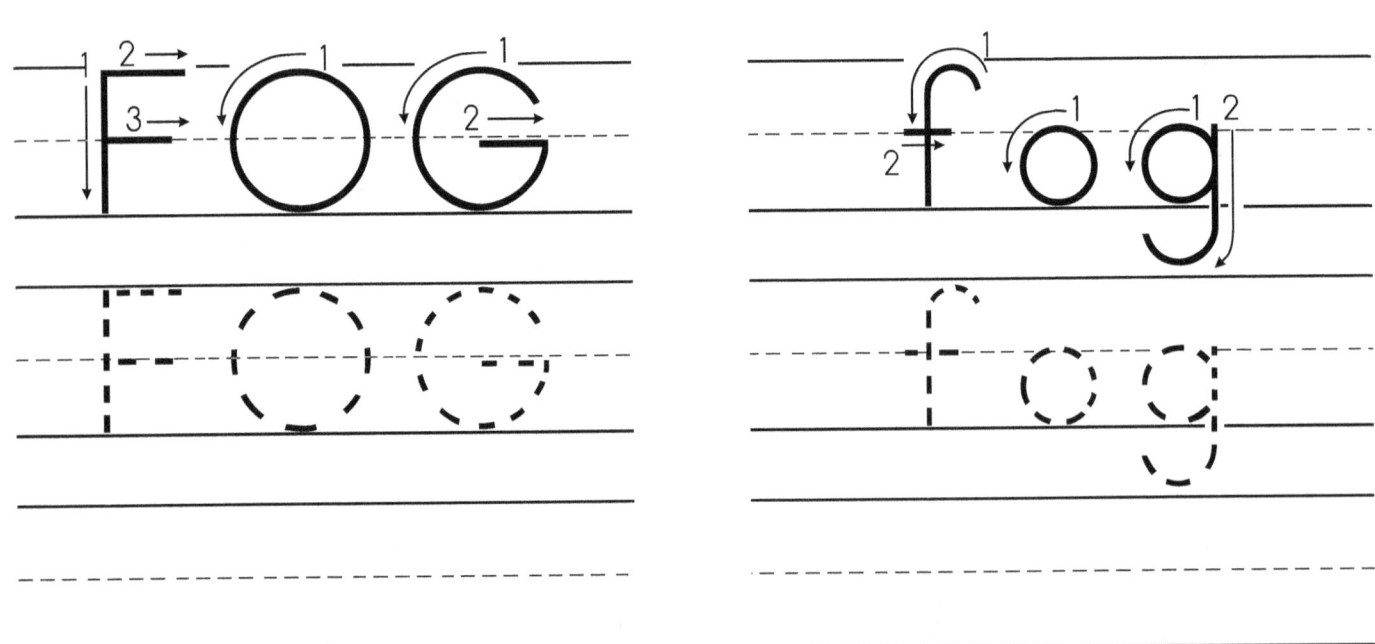

log

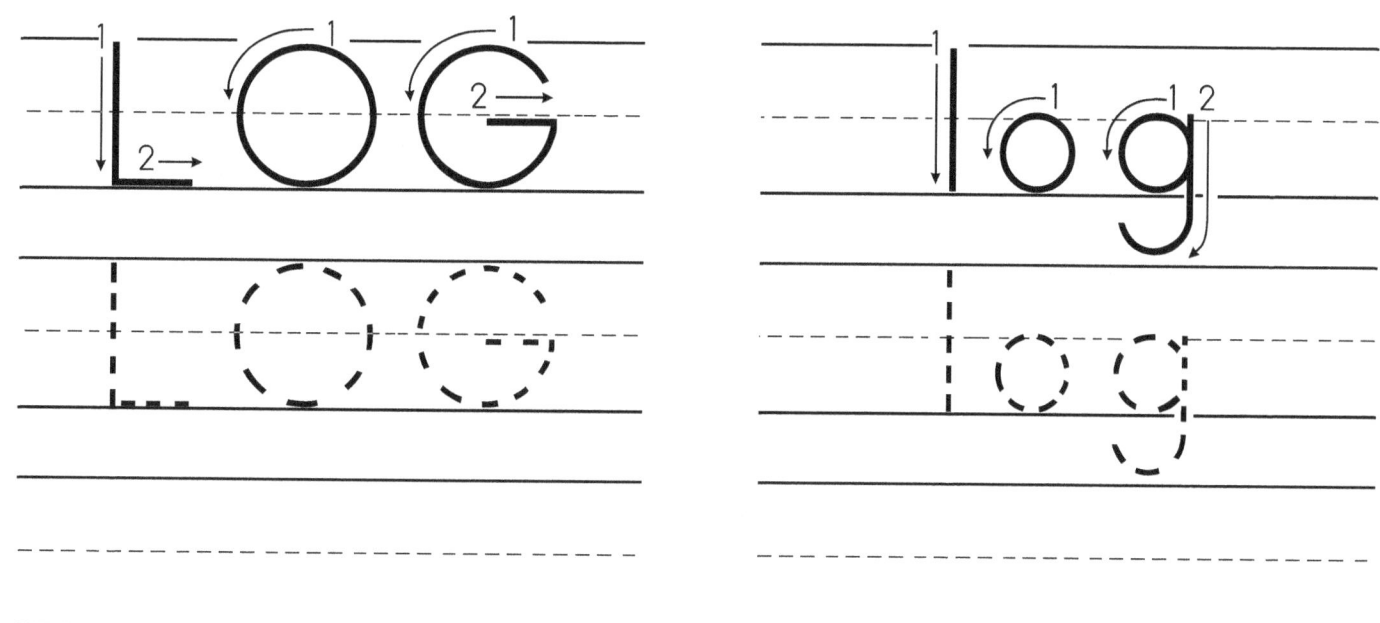

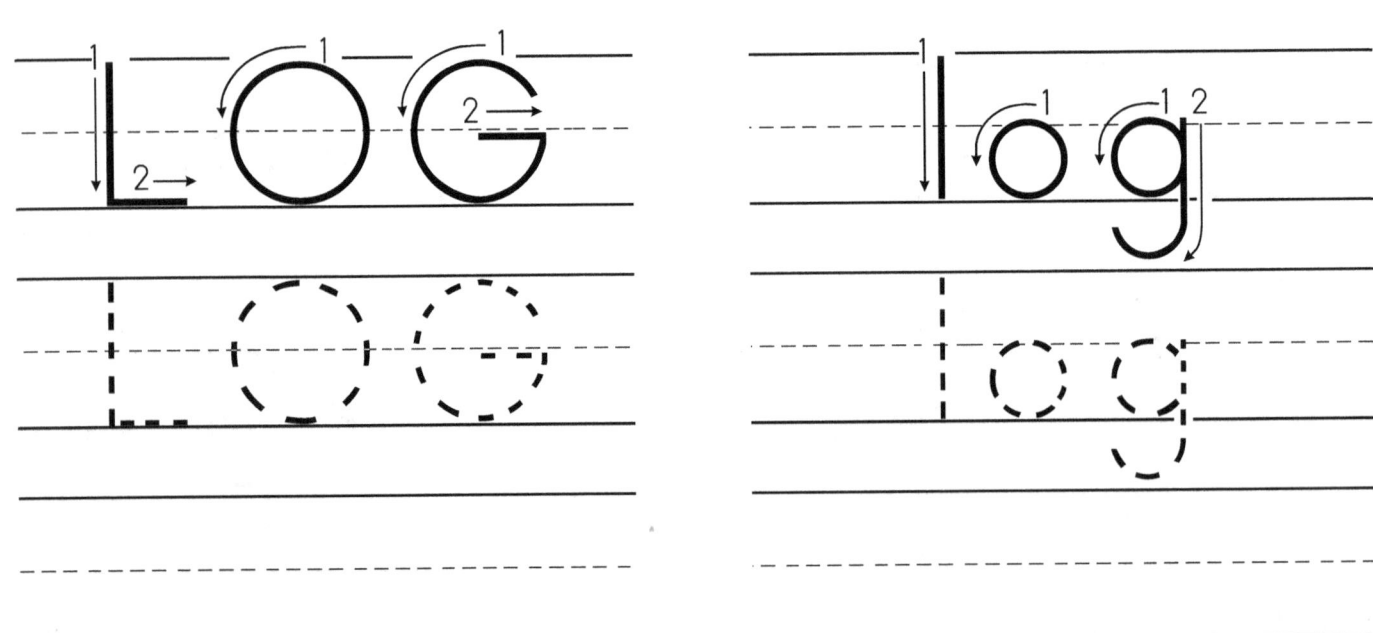

7 log

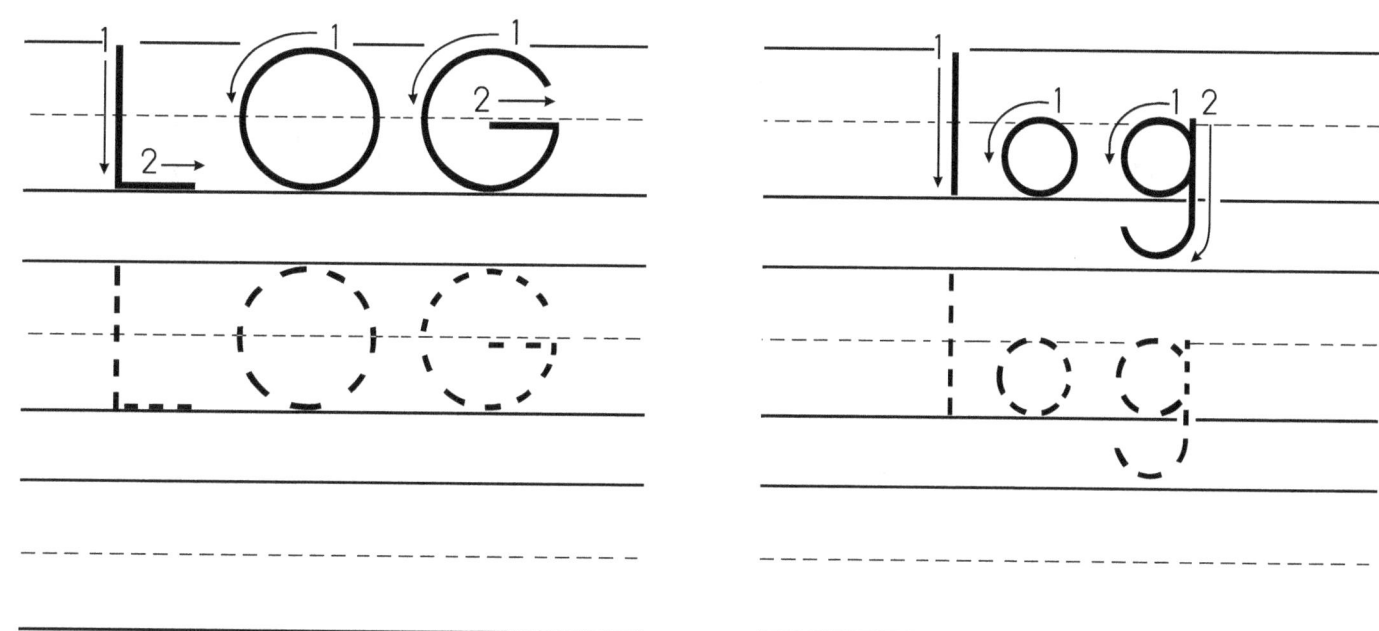

DOG

9 | dog

DOG

dog

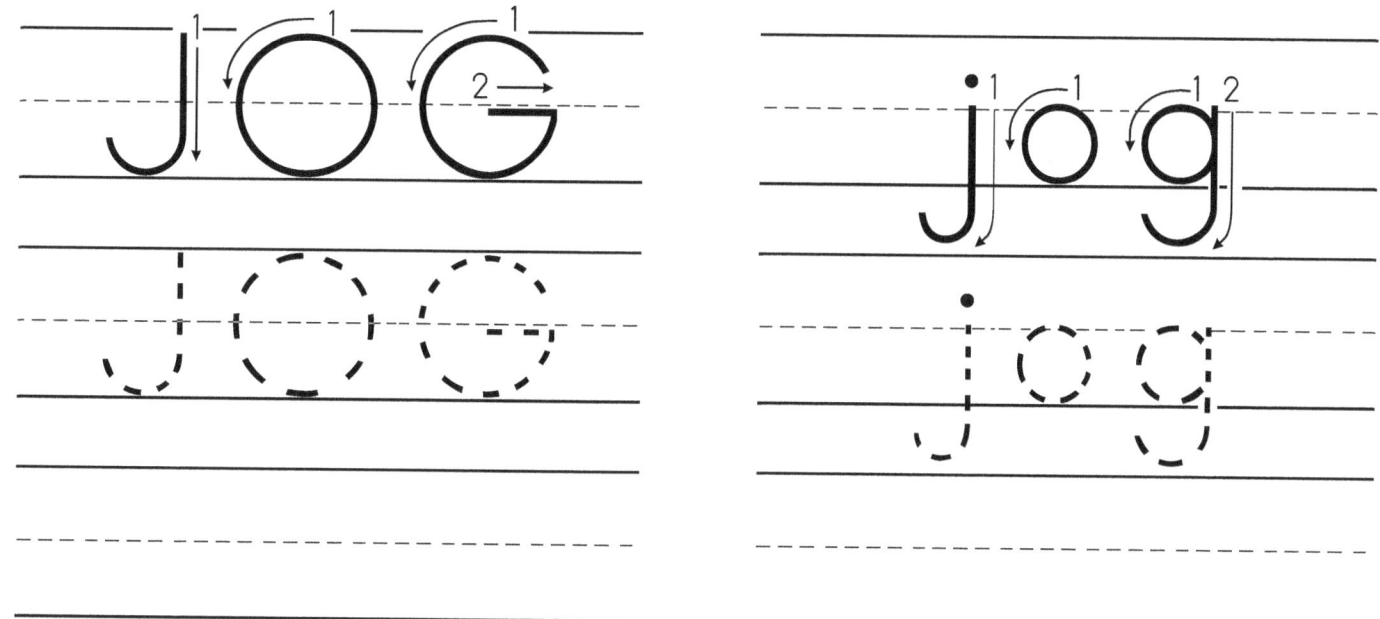

# DOG JOGS

dog     fog

jog     log

Got it!

# HUG

# 1 hug

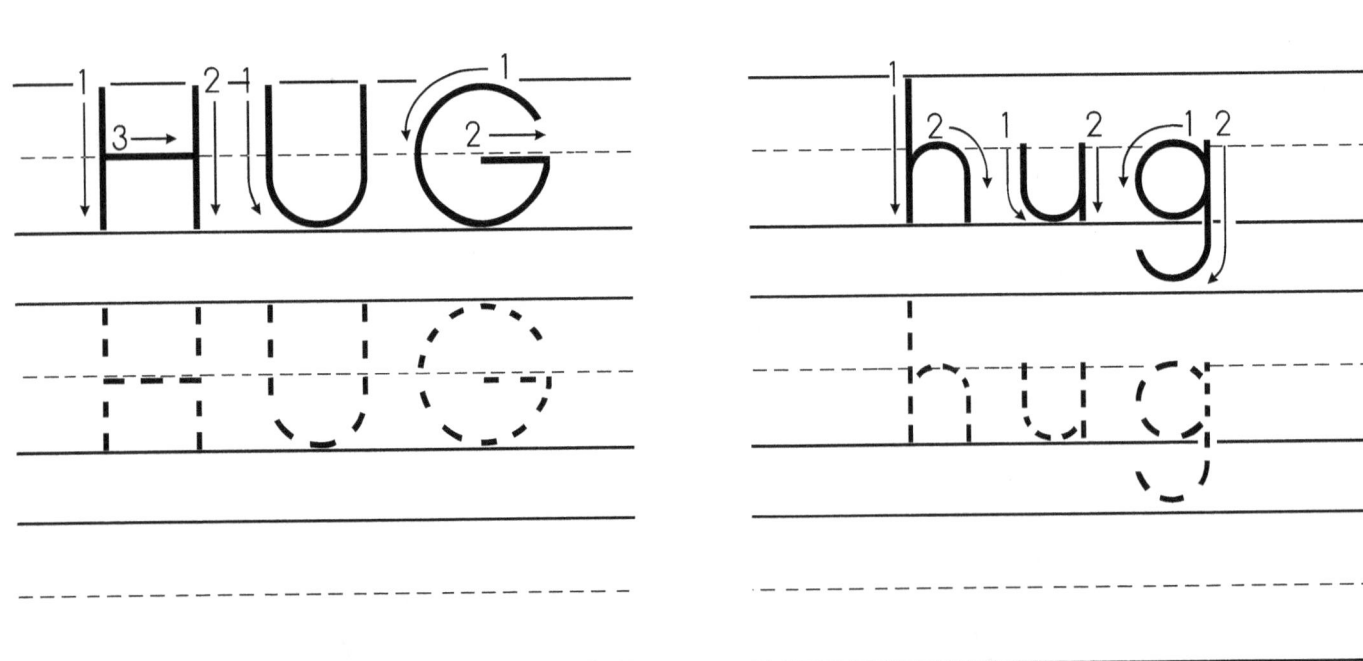

HUG

# hug

2

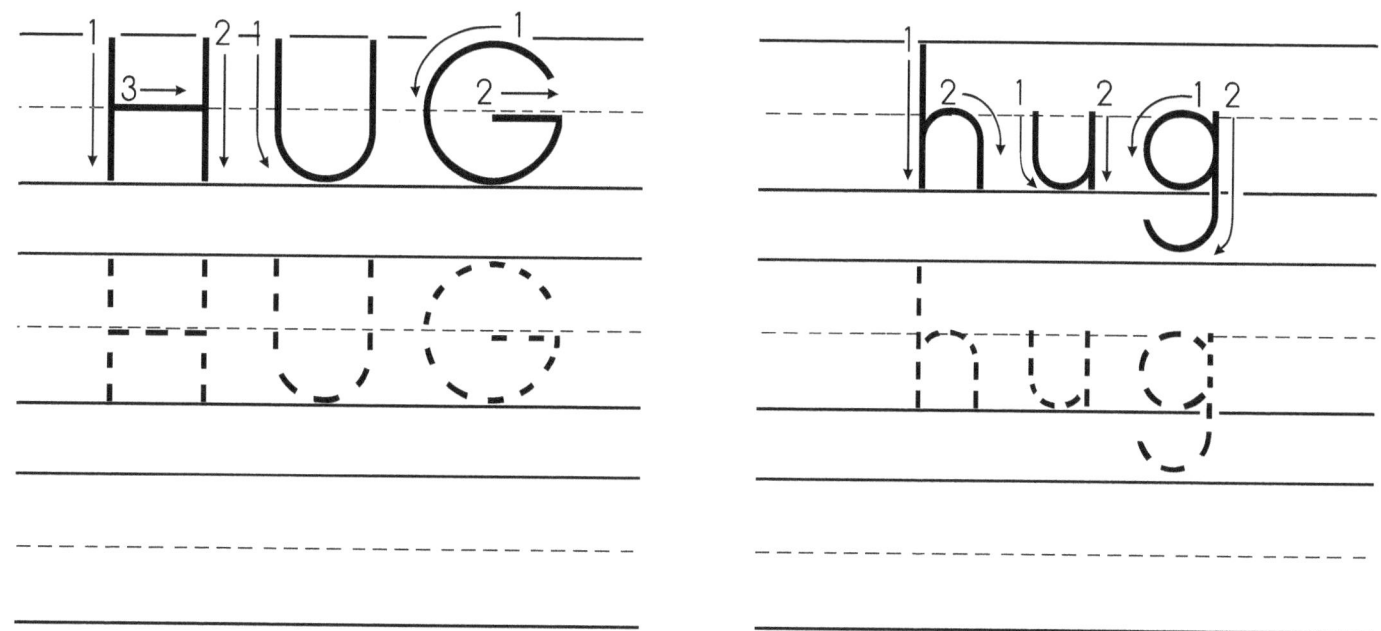

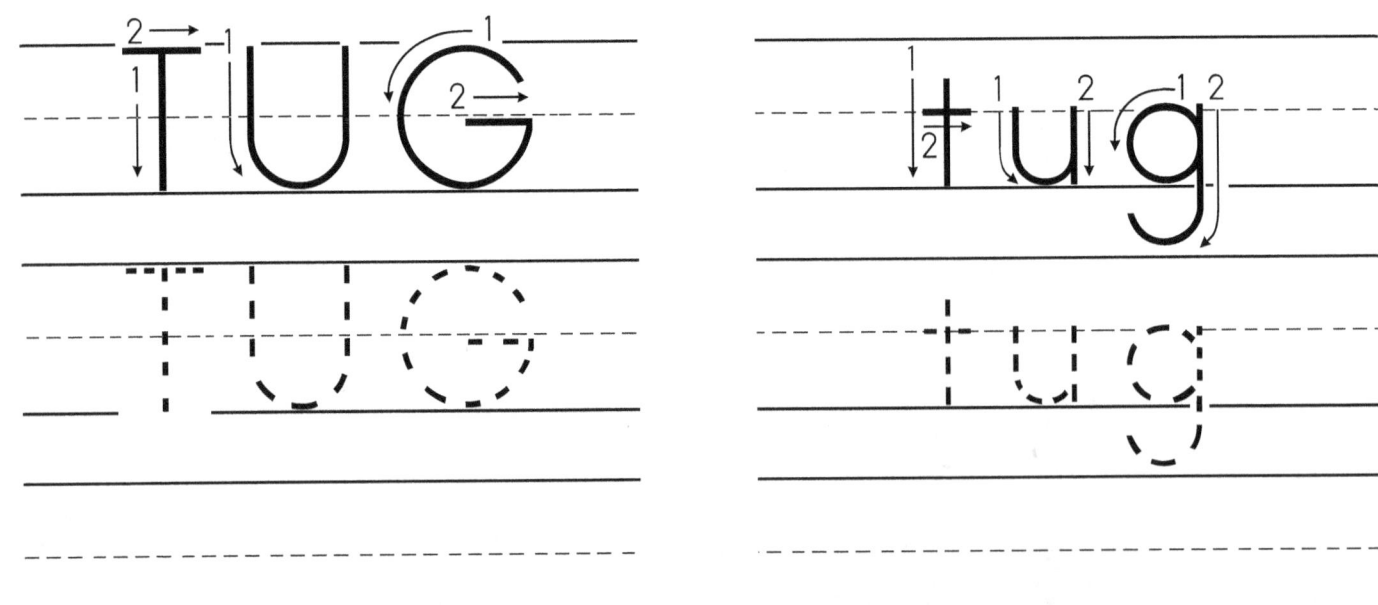

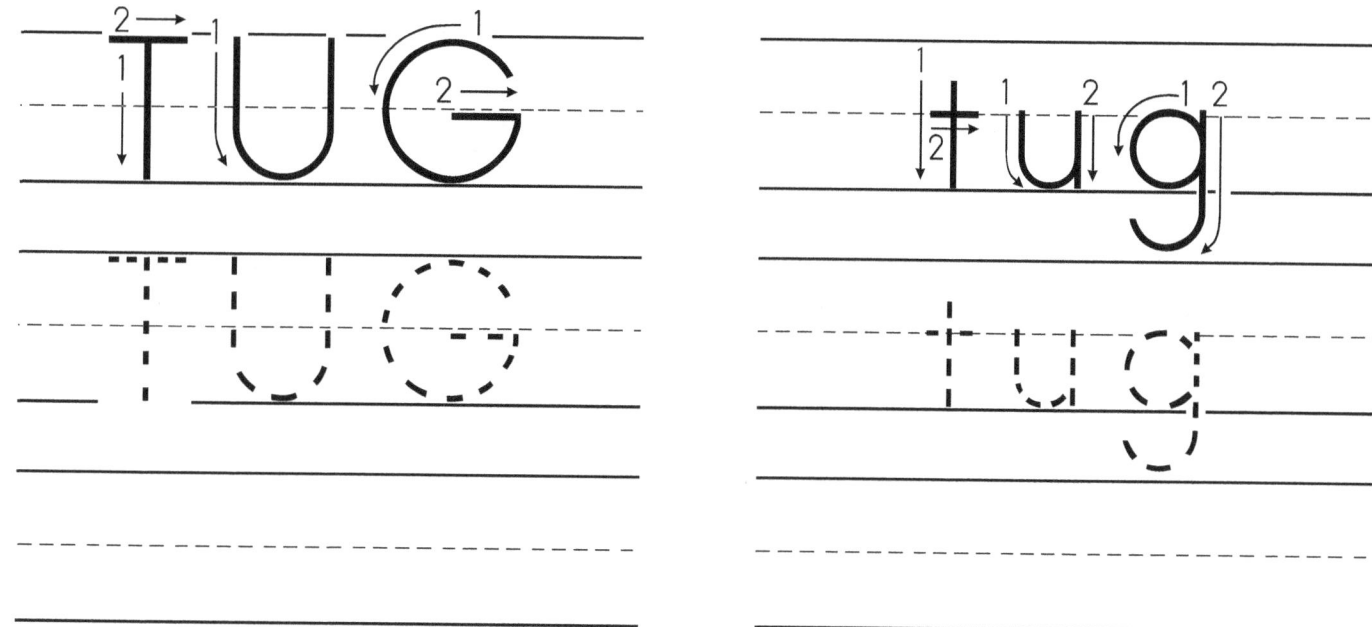

JUG

**7** jug

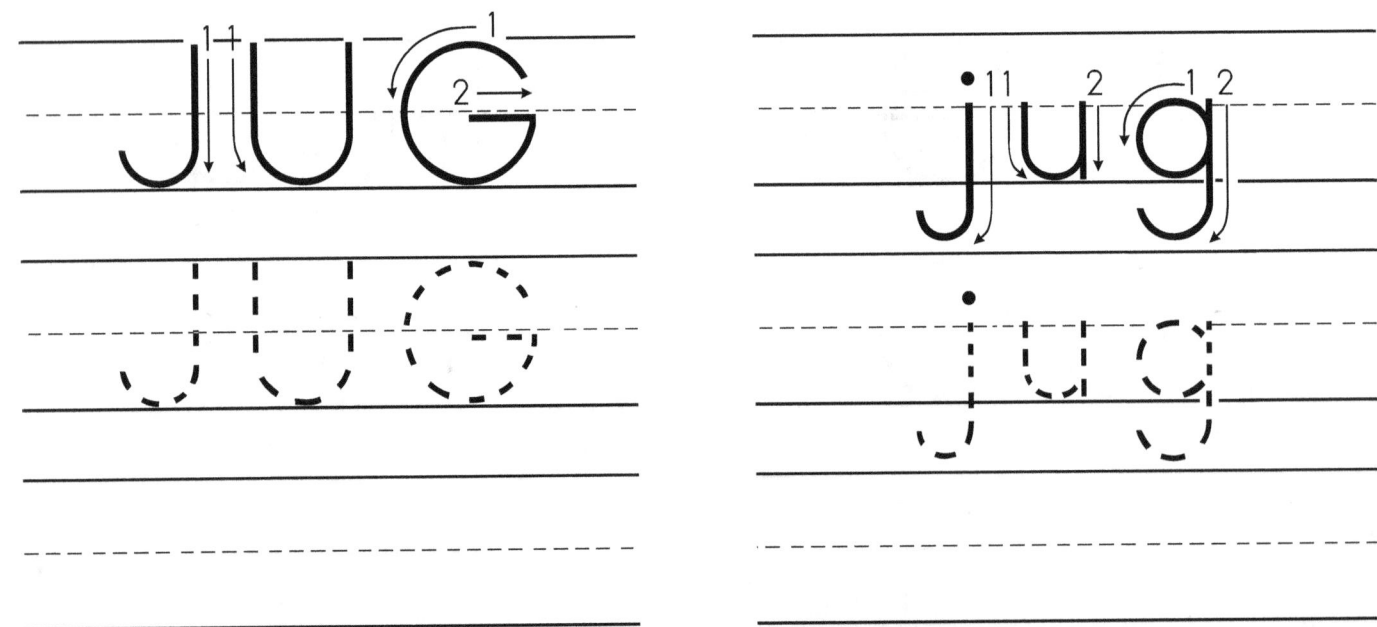

JUG

jug | 8

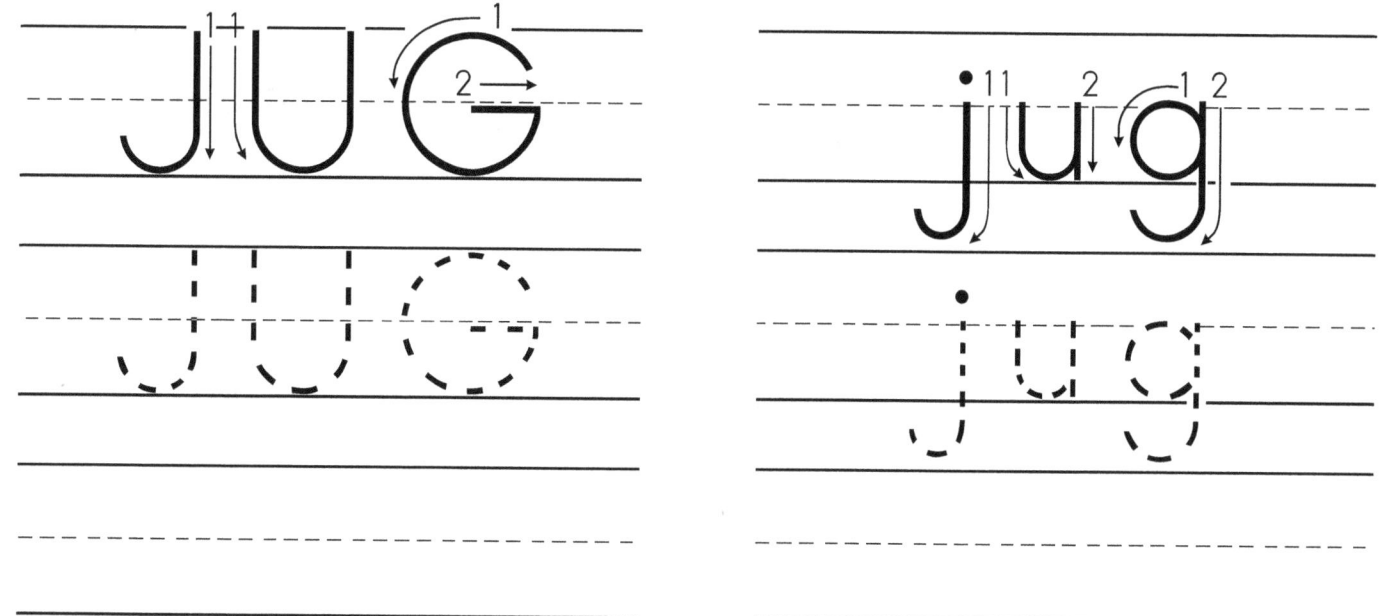

HUG

hug

10

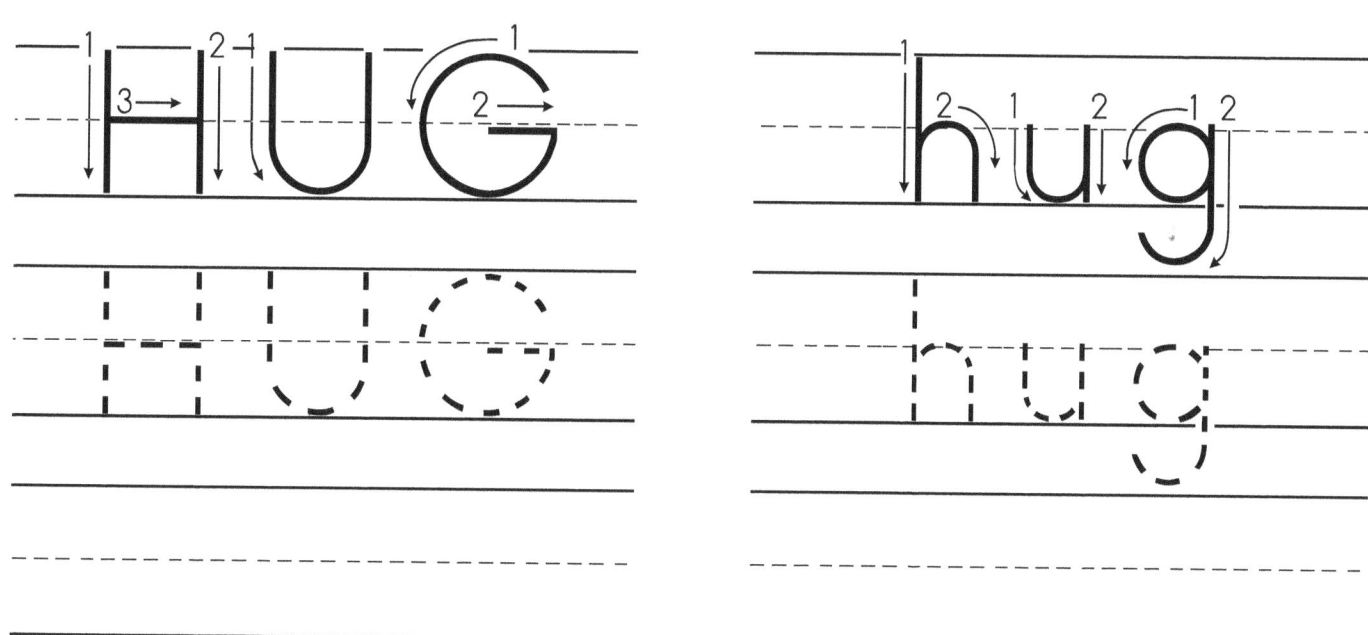

# HUG

hug    tug
mug    jug

Got it!

# FAT RAT

RAT

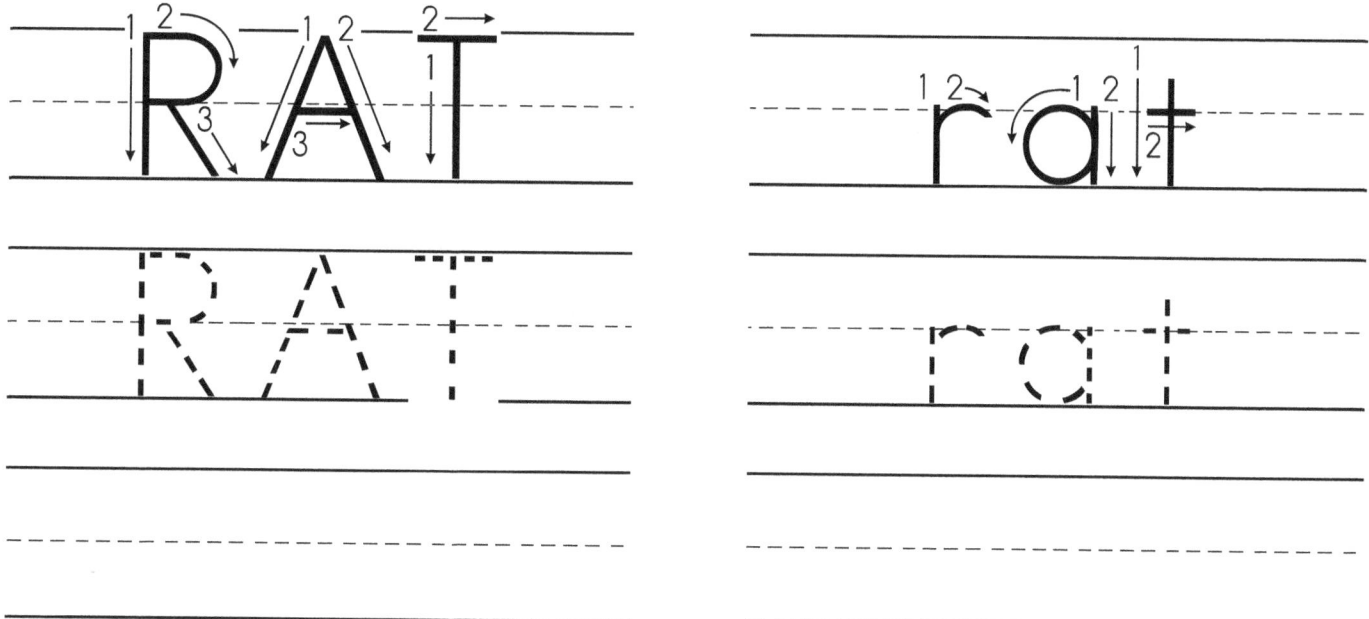

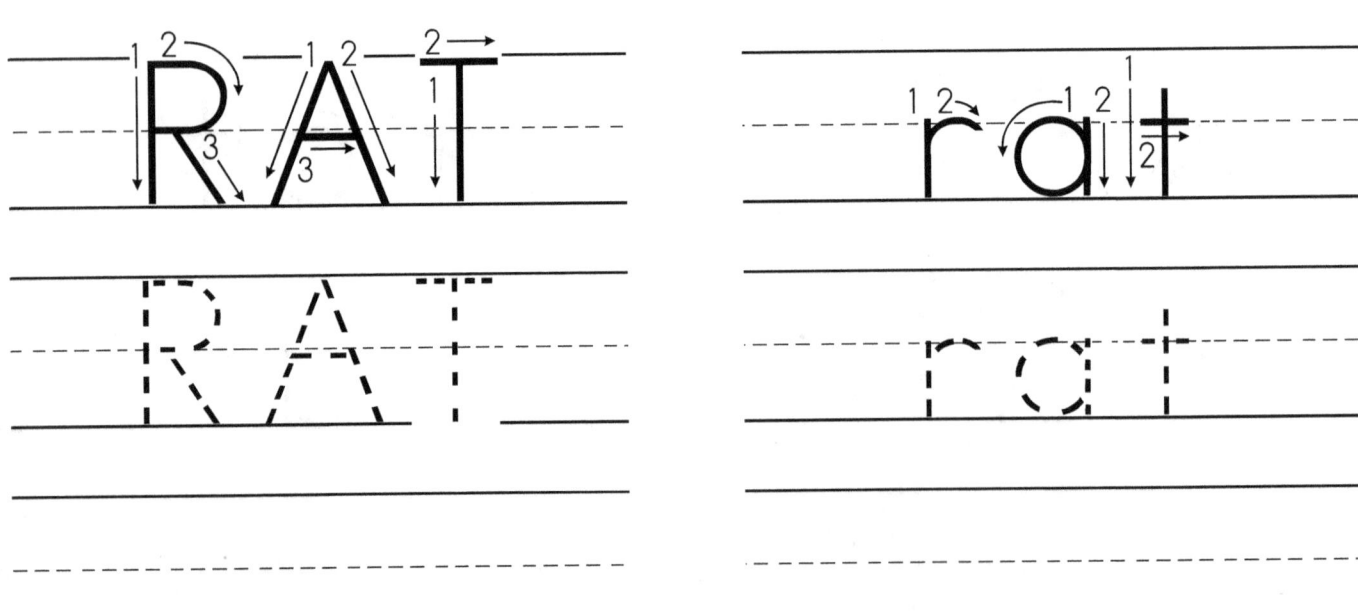

RAT

3 rat

CAT

cat | 4

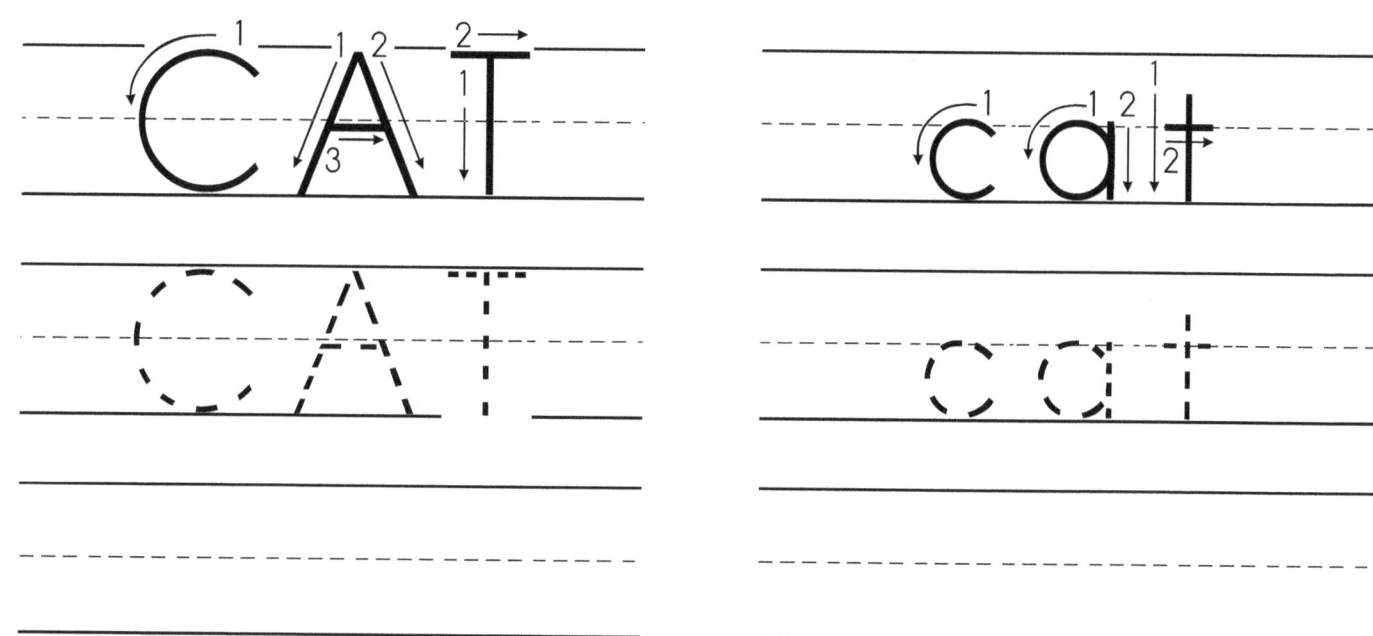

CAT

5 cat

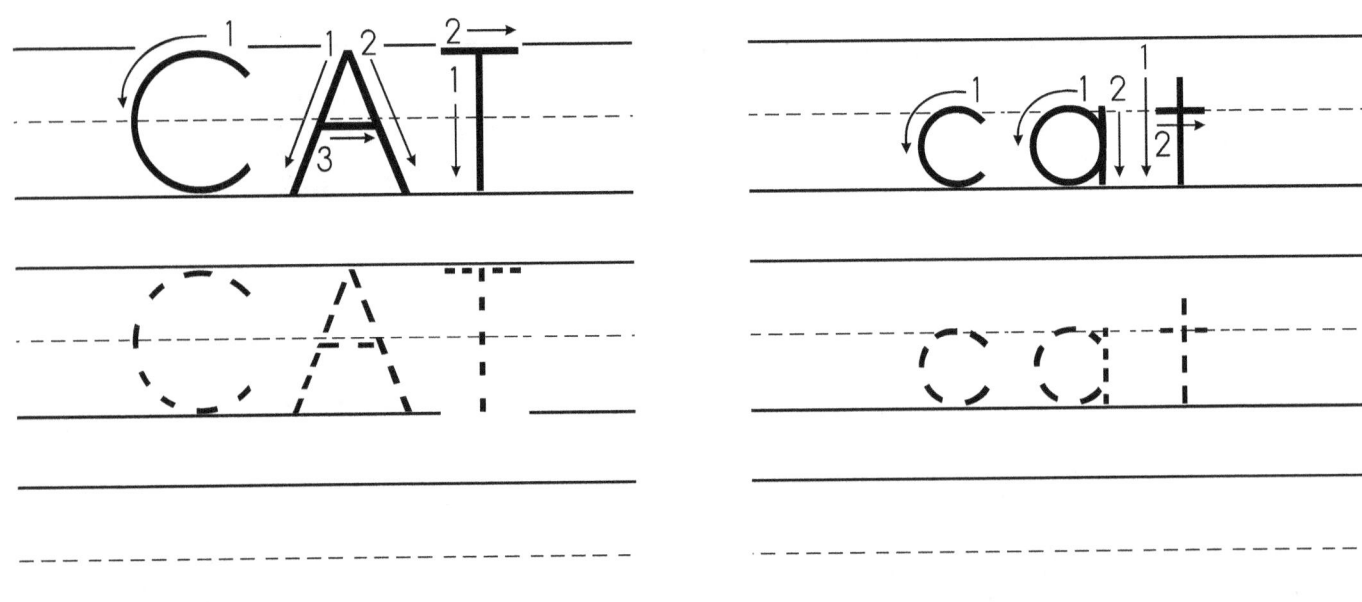

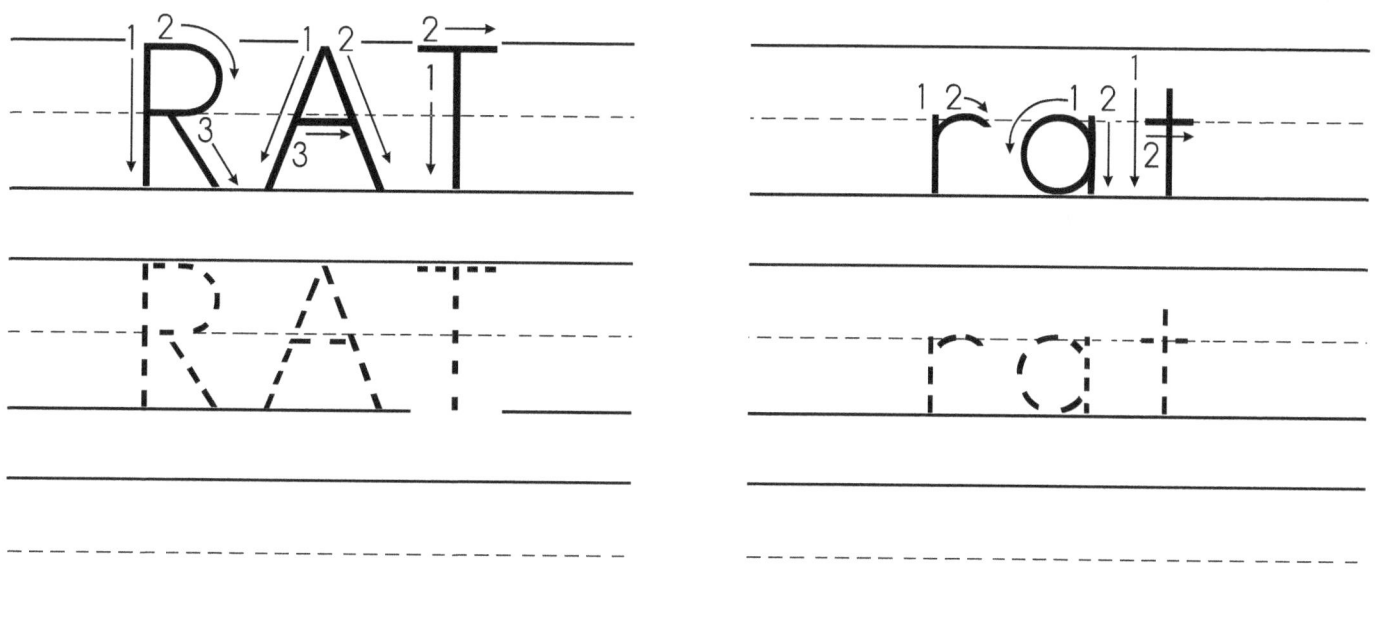

RAT

7 | rat

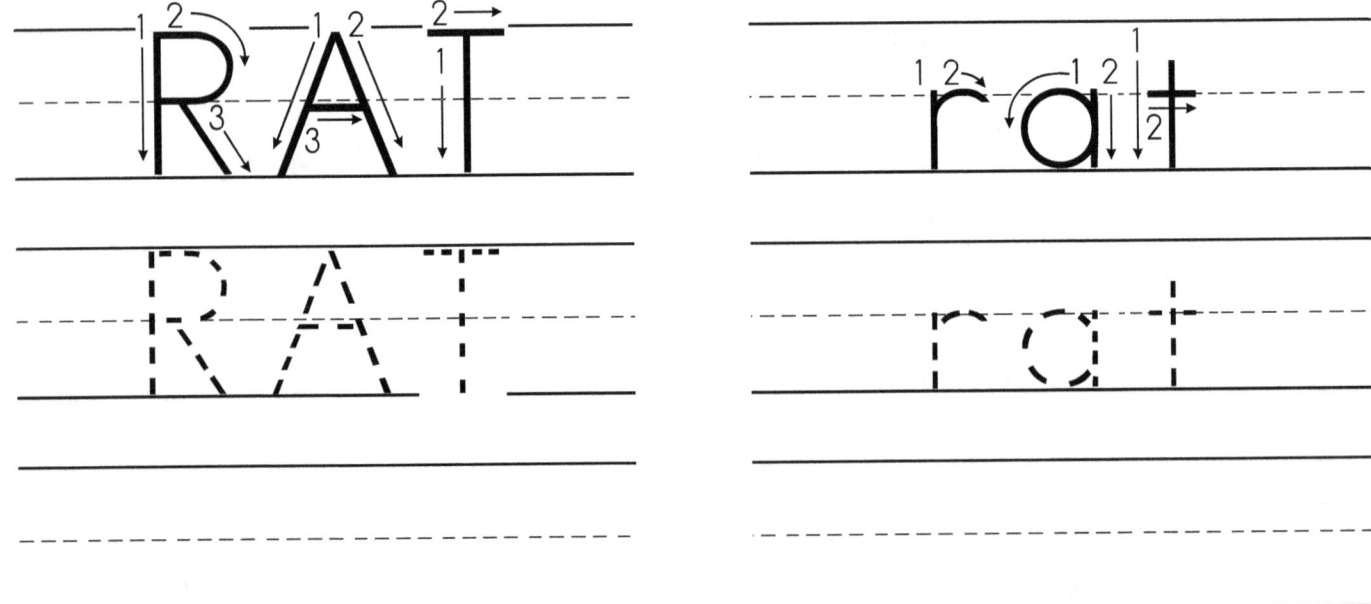

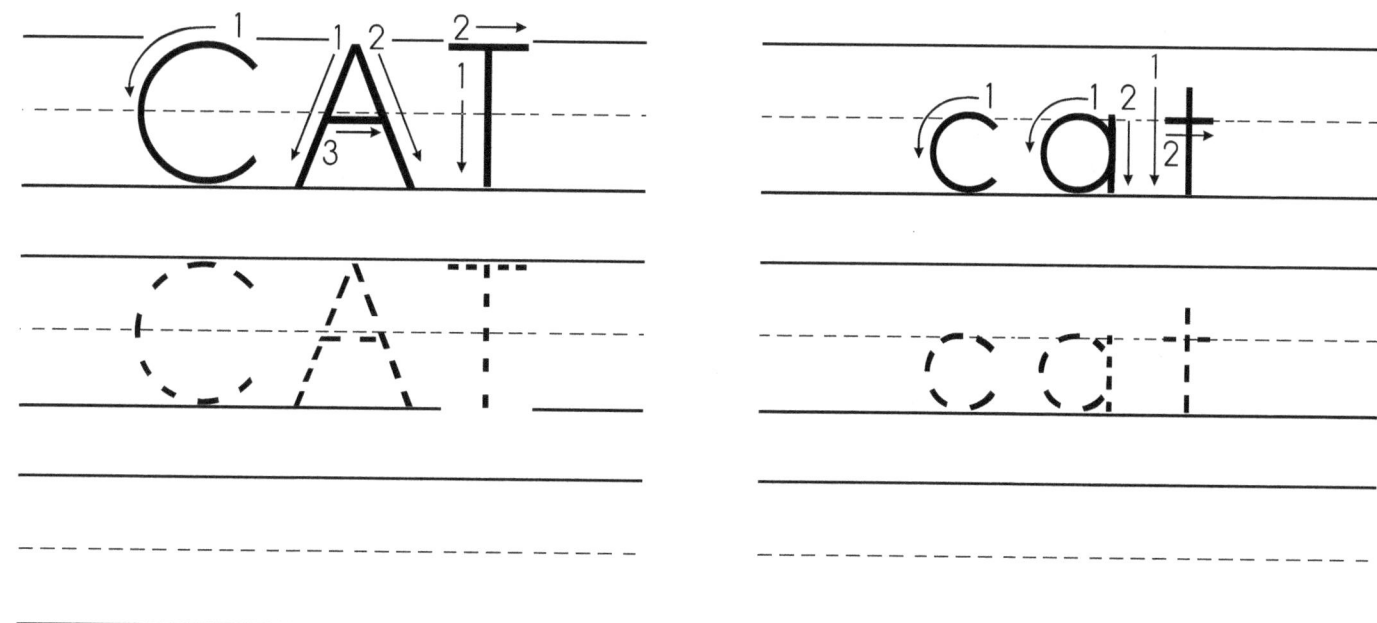

CAT

9 | cat

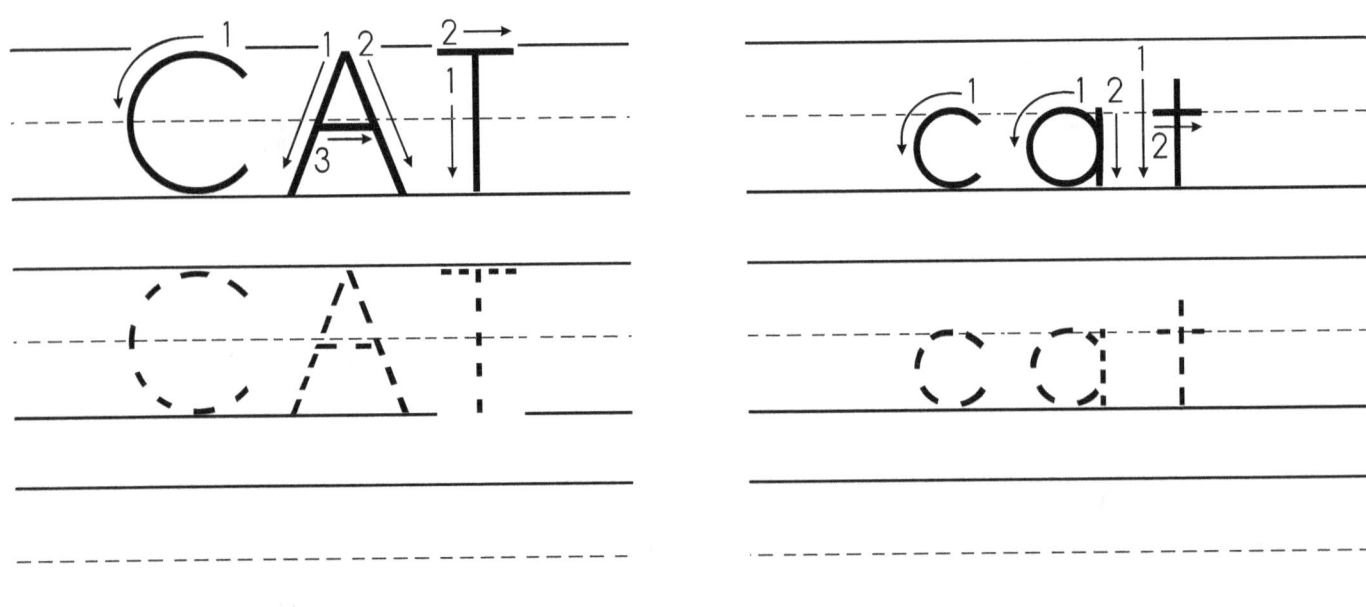

fat

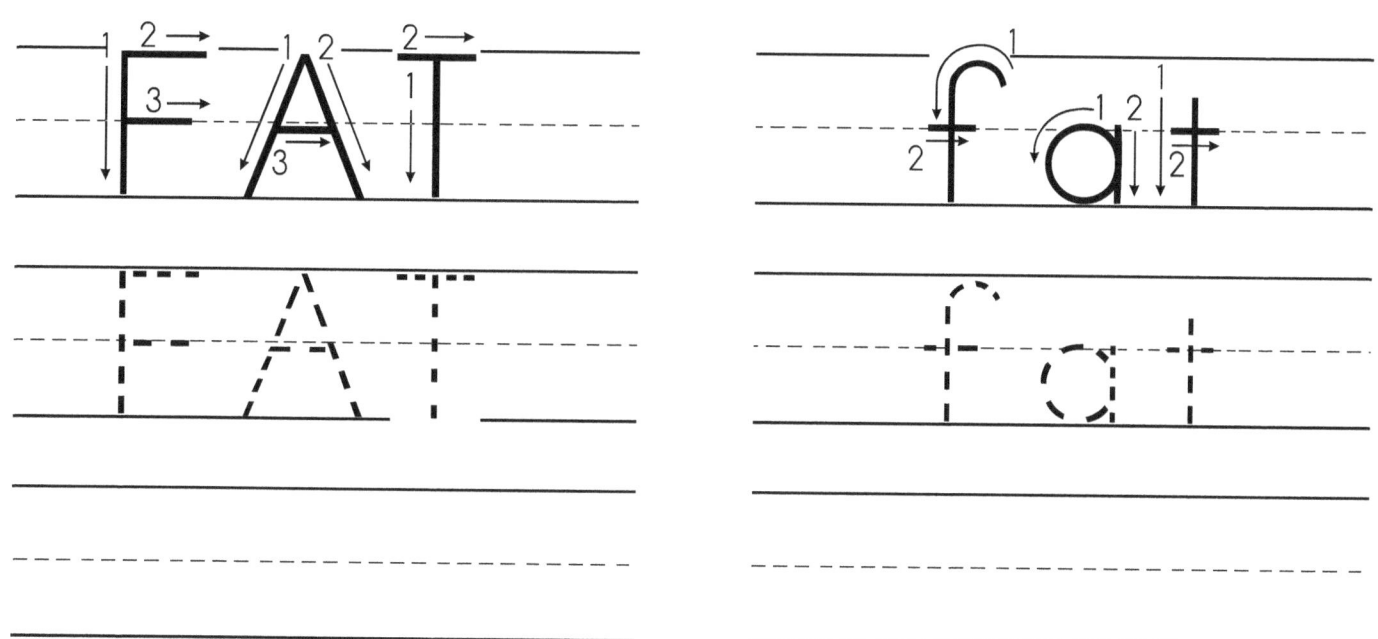

# FAT RAT

hat     cat

rat     fat

Got it!

# WET PET

PET

1 pet

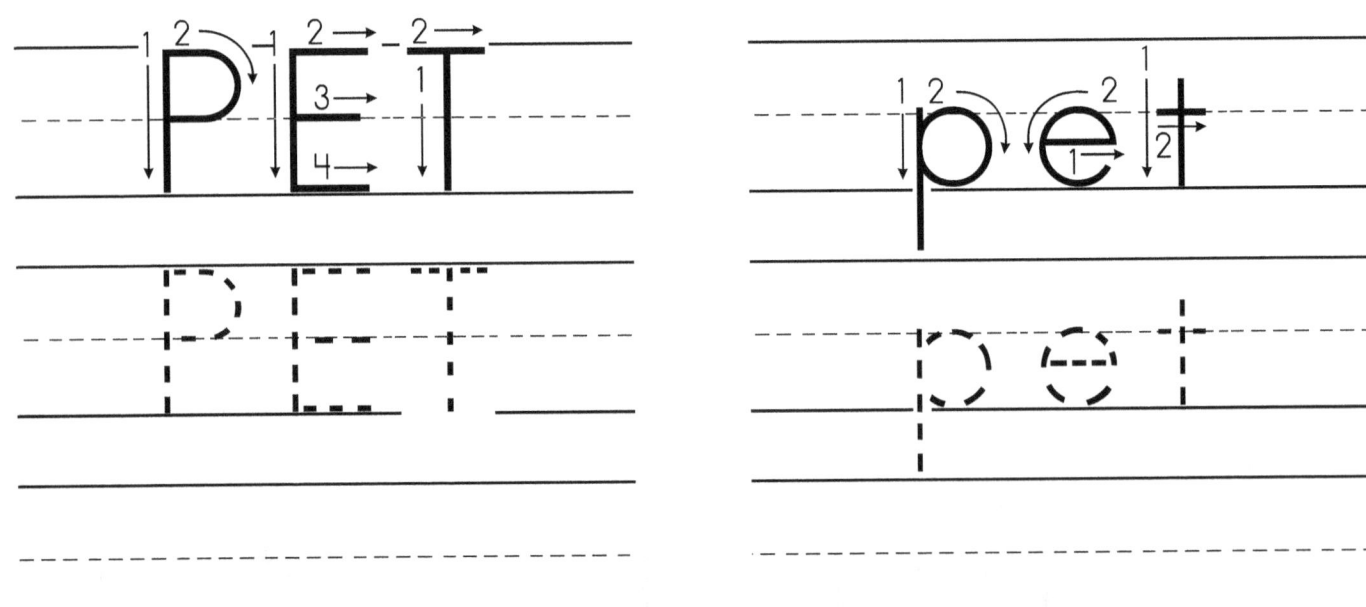

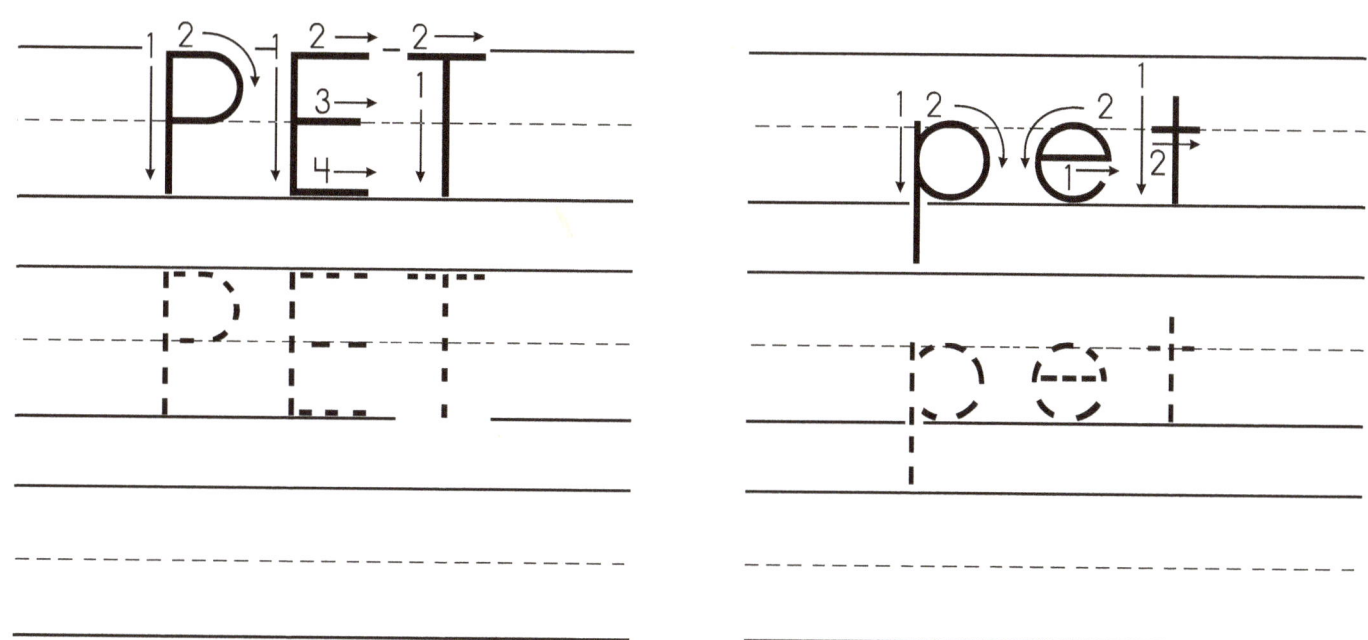

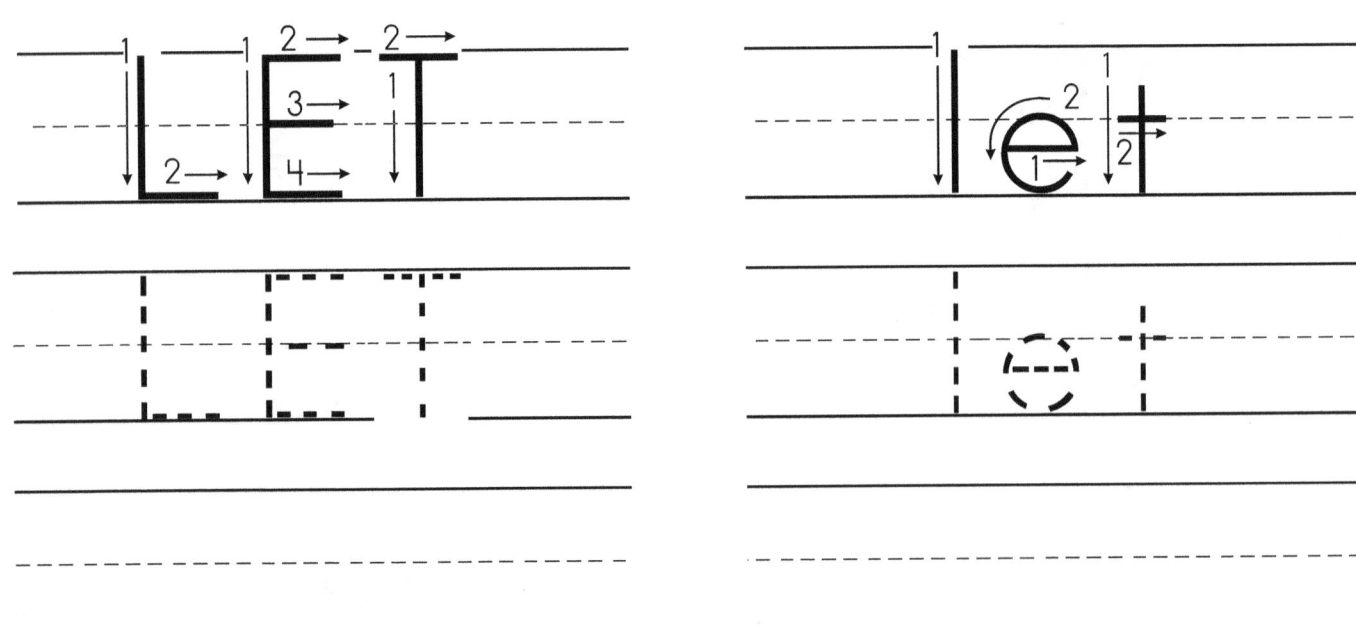

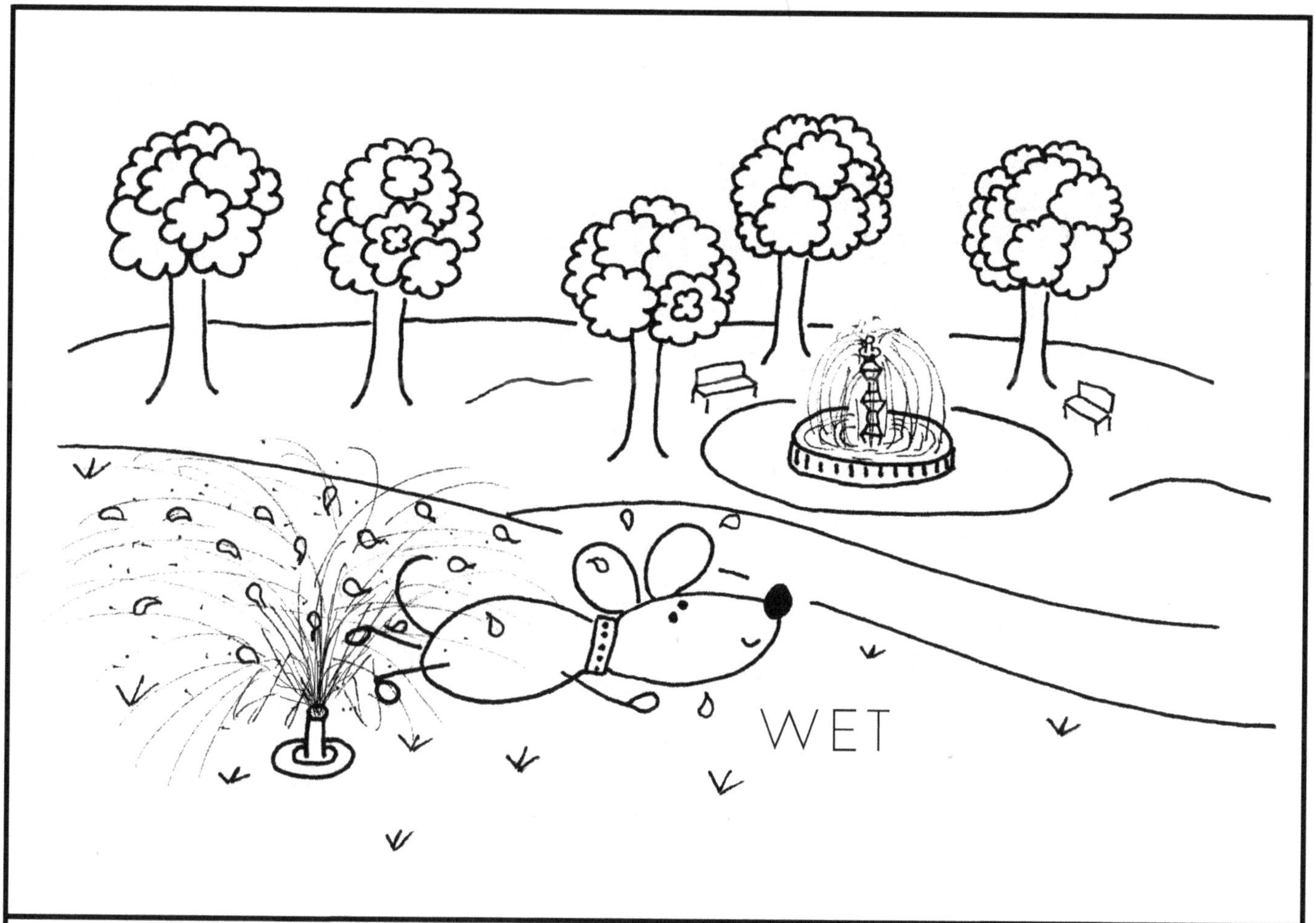

# wet

4

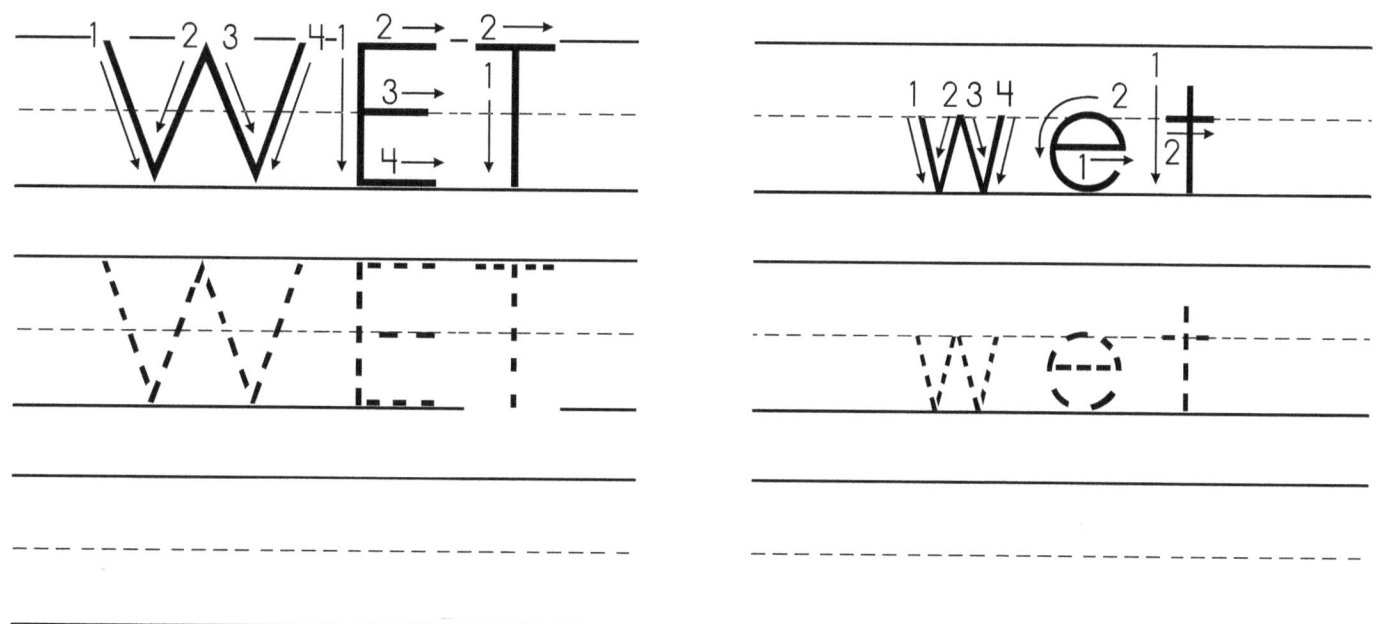

5     wet

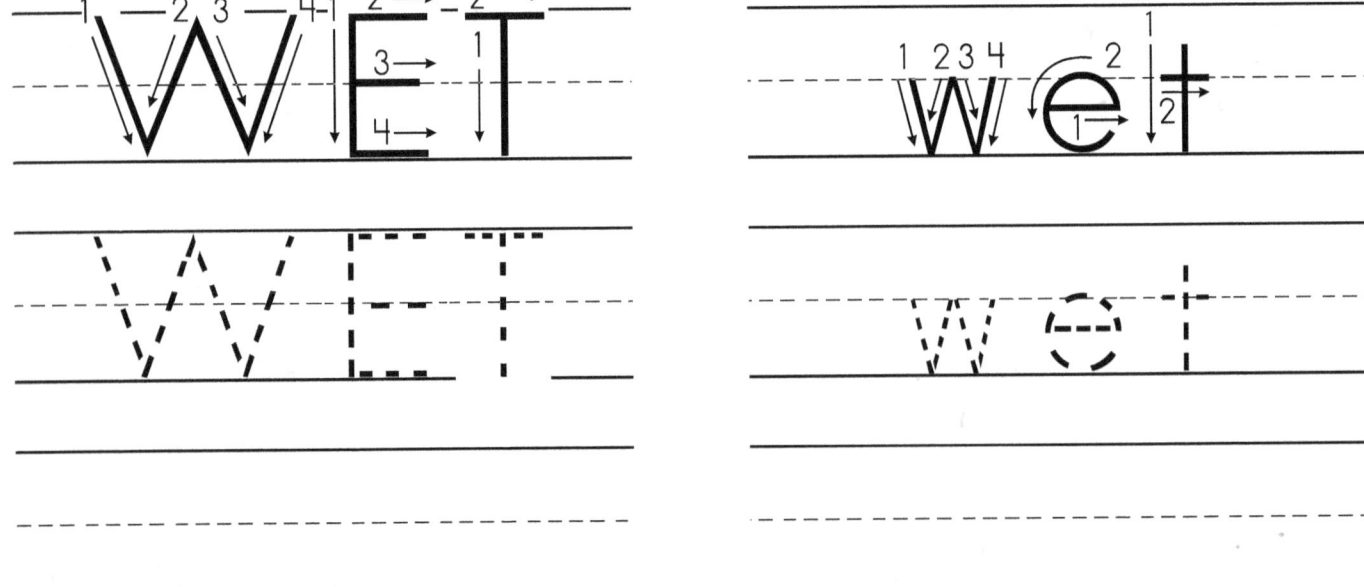

WET

wet  6

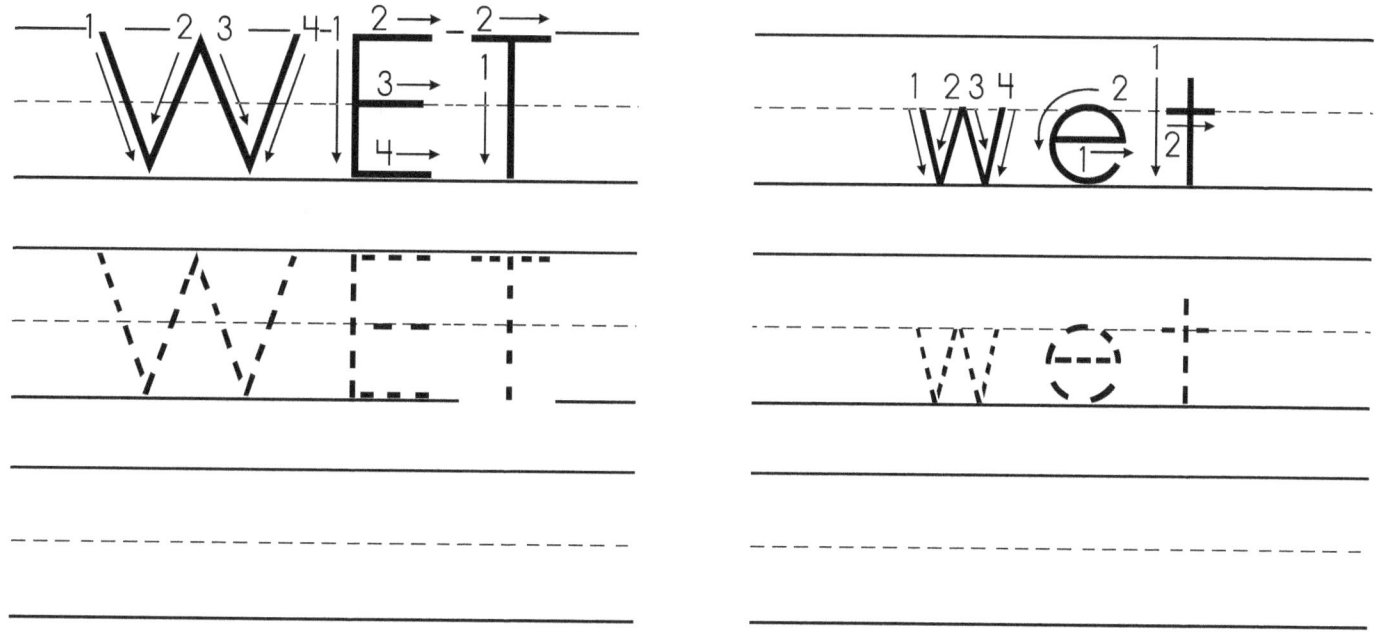

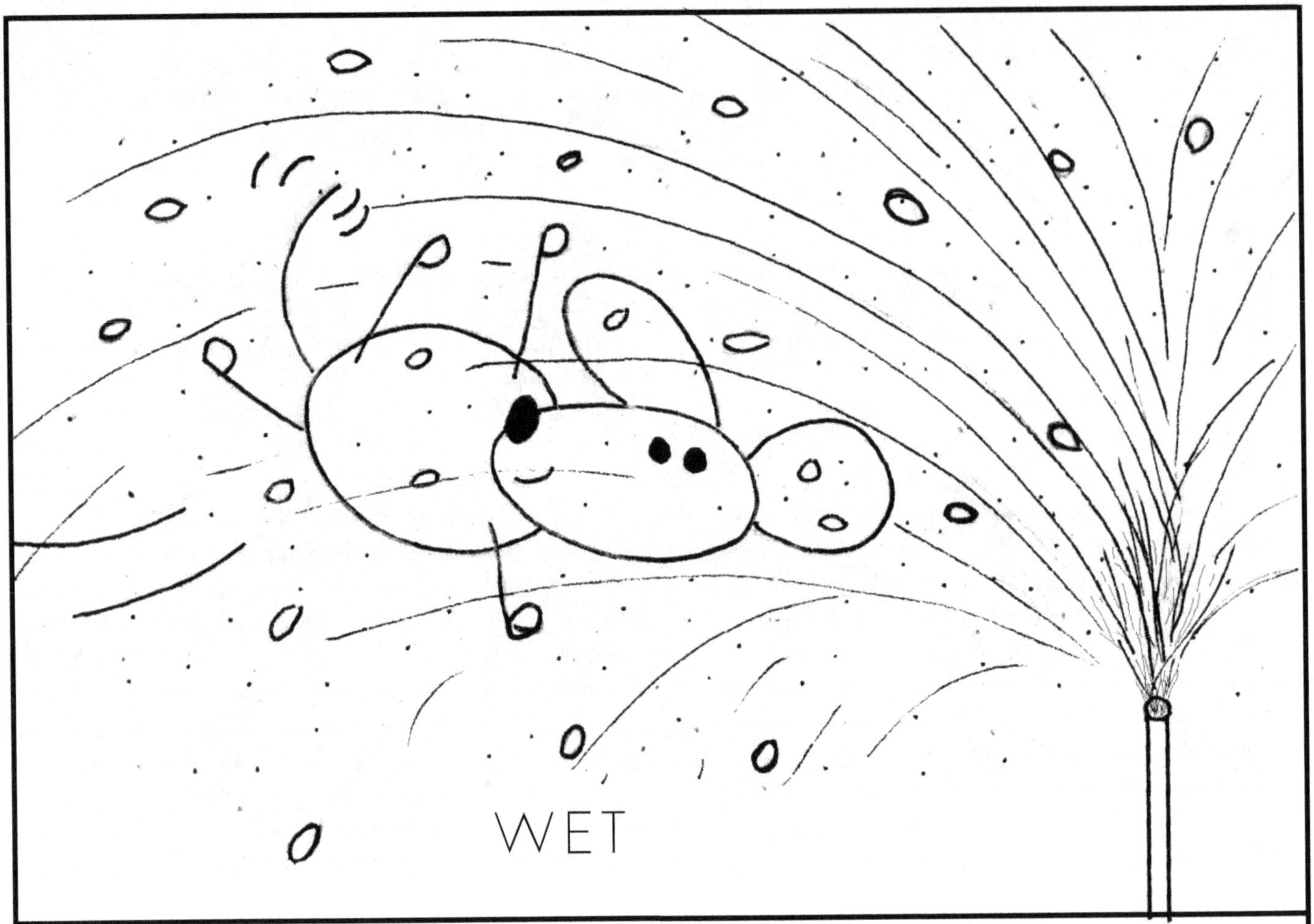

# 7 wet

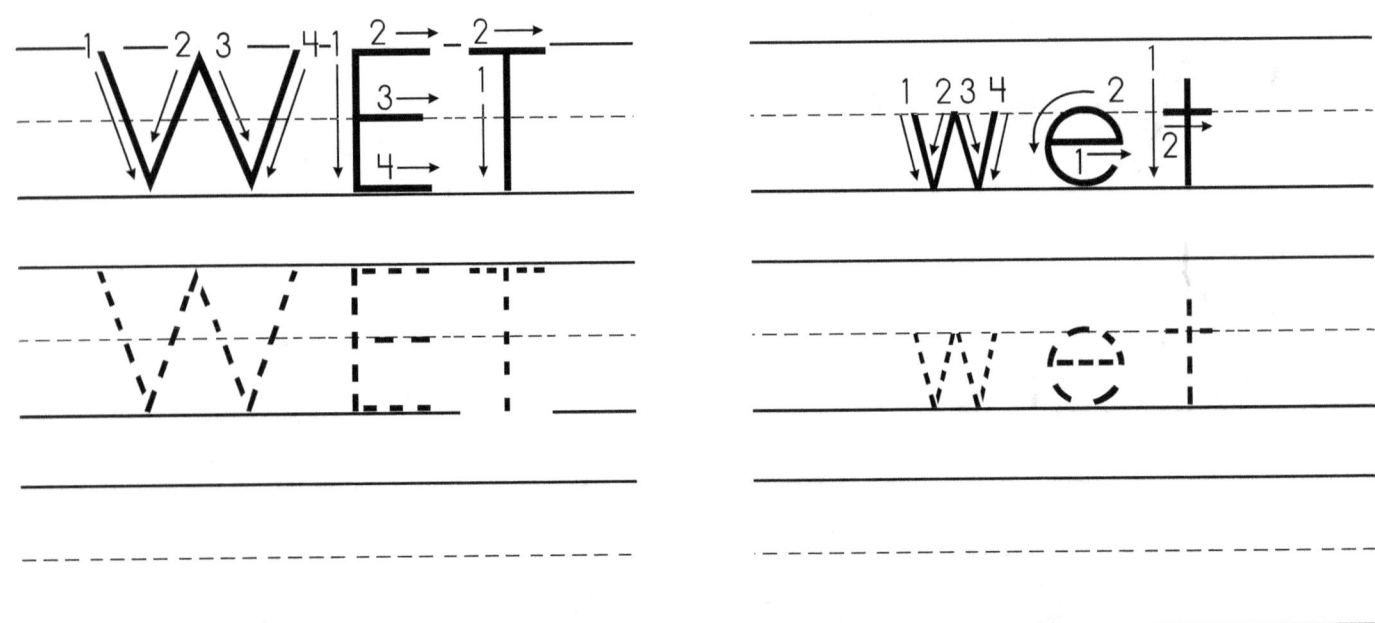

NET

net 8

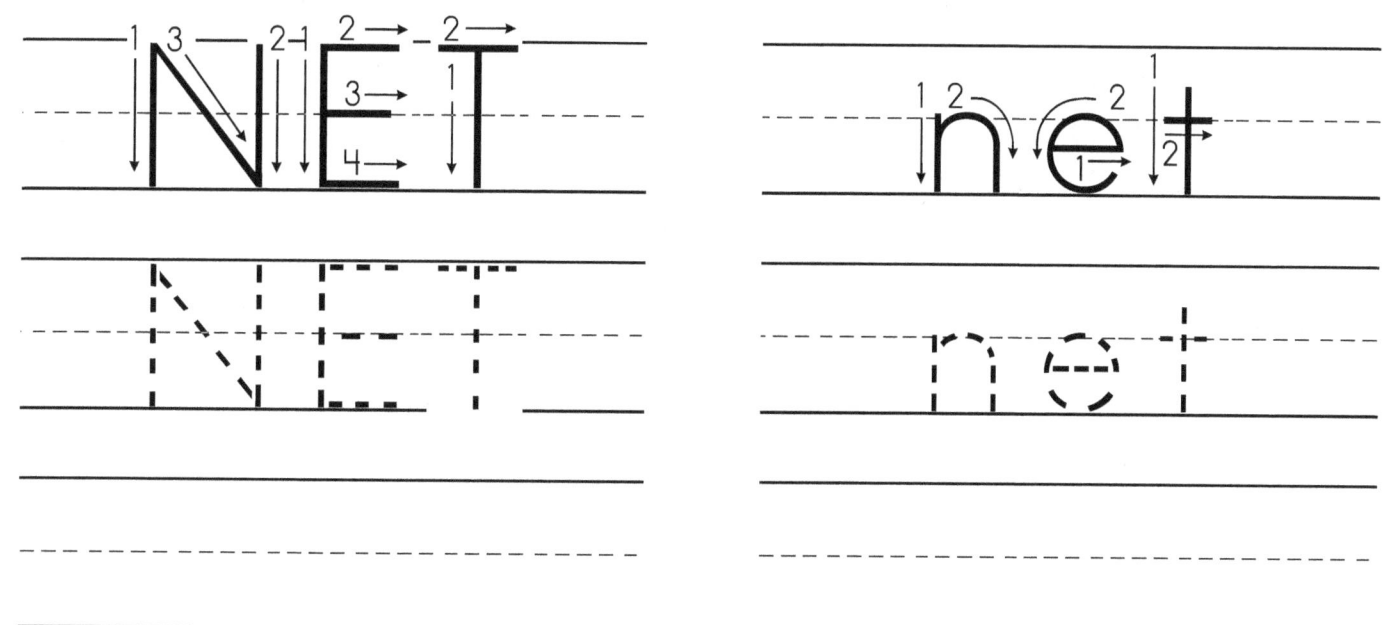

GET

**9** get

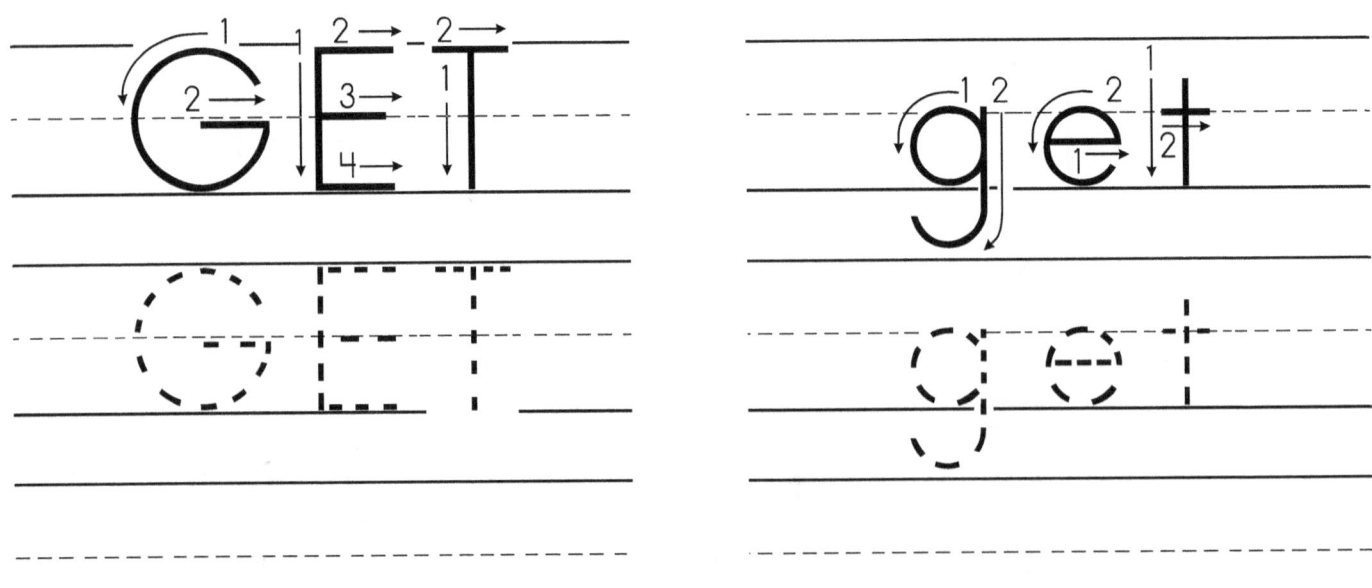

PET

pet

10

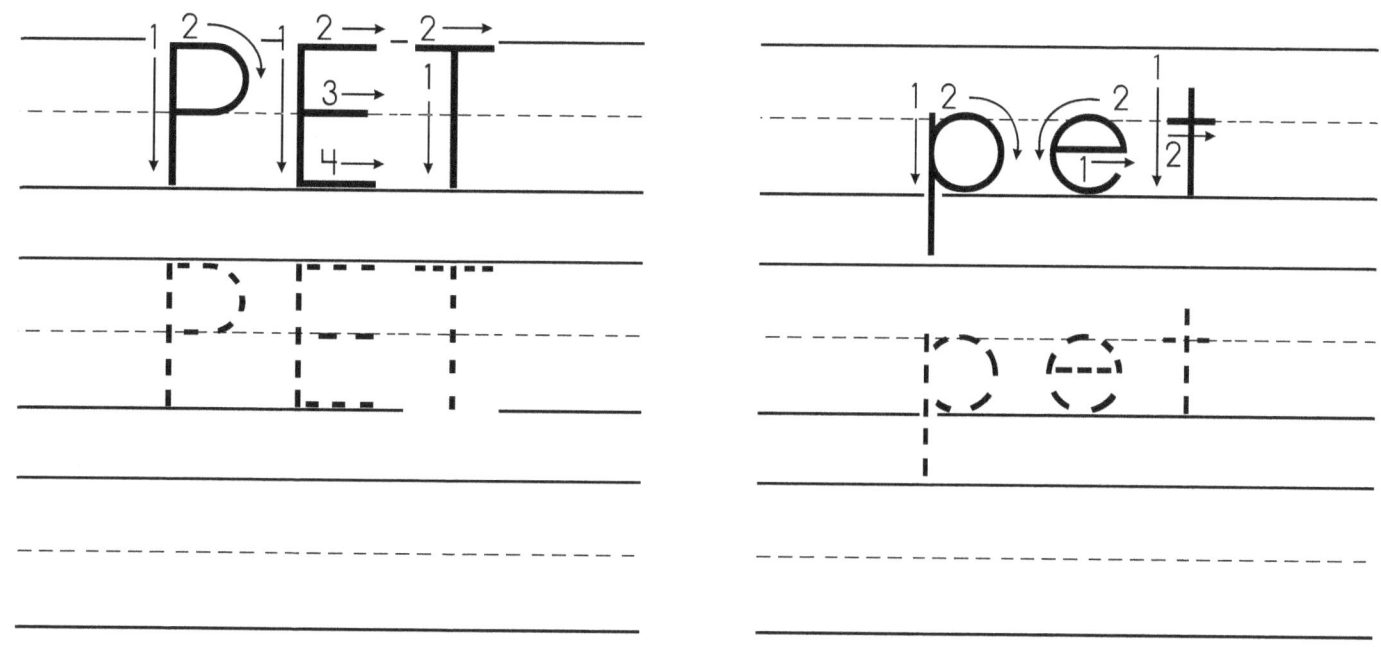

# WET PET

pet　　net
let　　get
wet

Got it!

# BIG DIG

PIG

pig

1

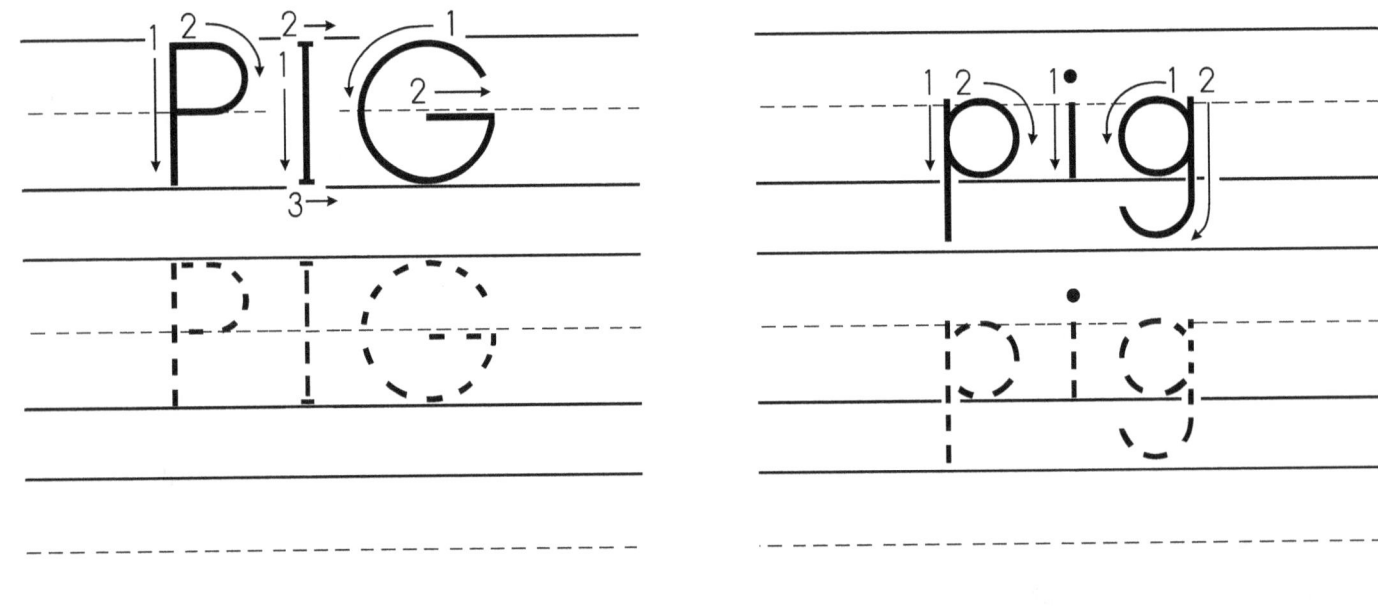

WIG

wig | 2

DIG

3 dig

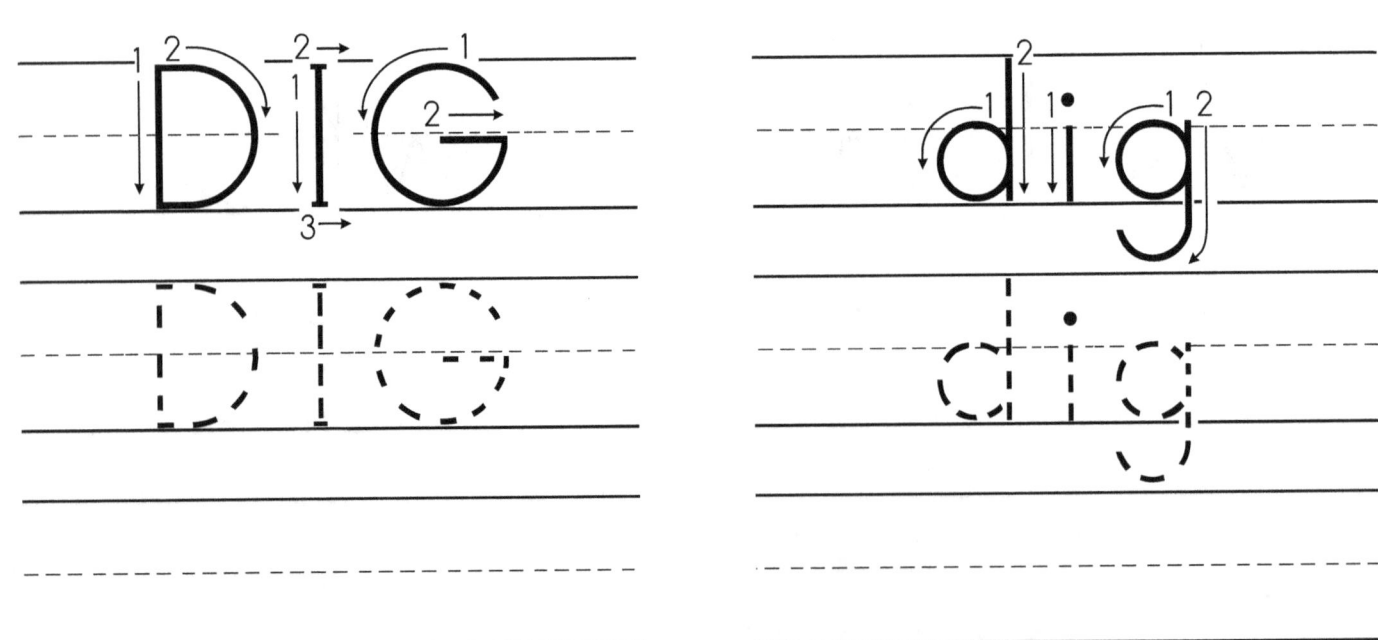

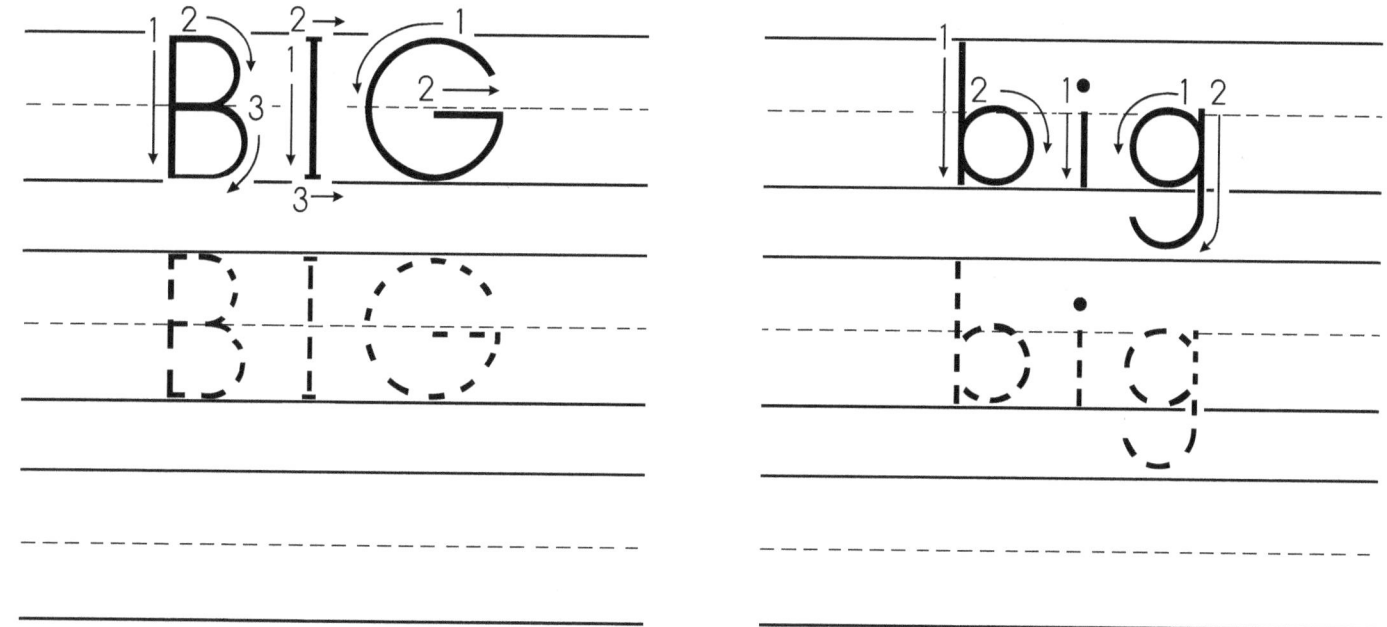

DIG

5 | dig

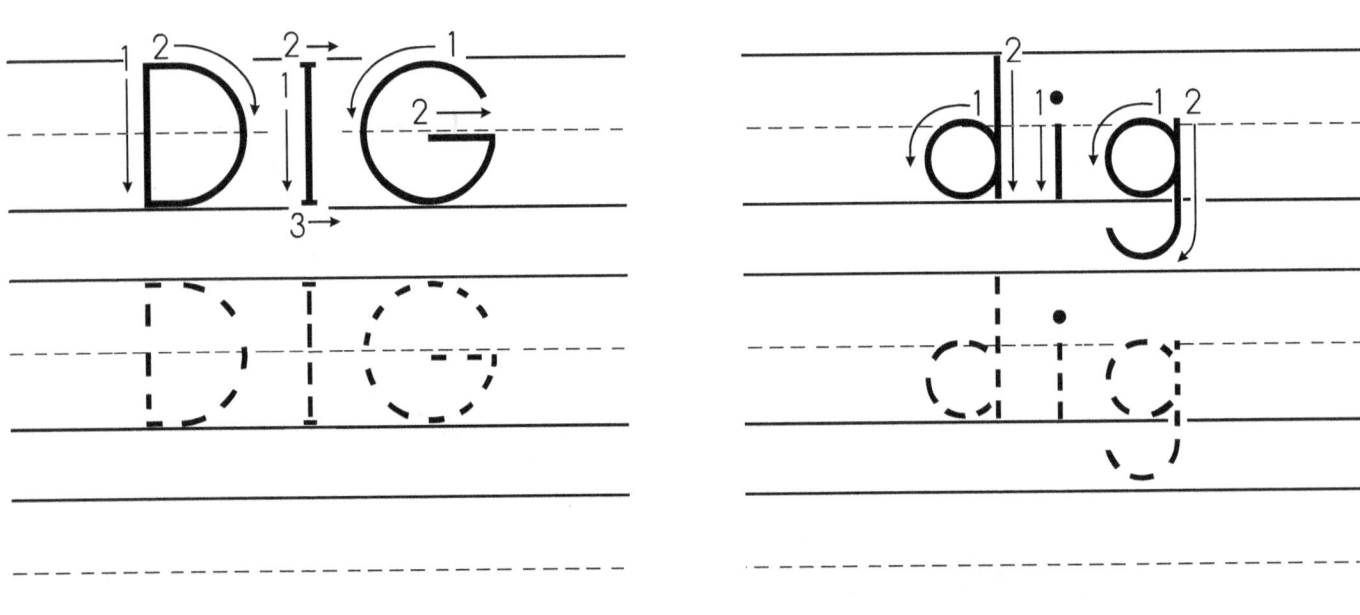

BIG

big | 6

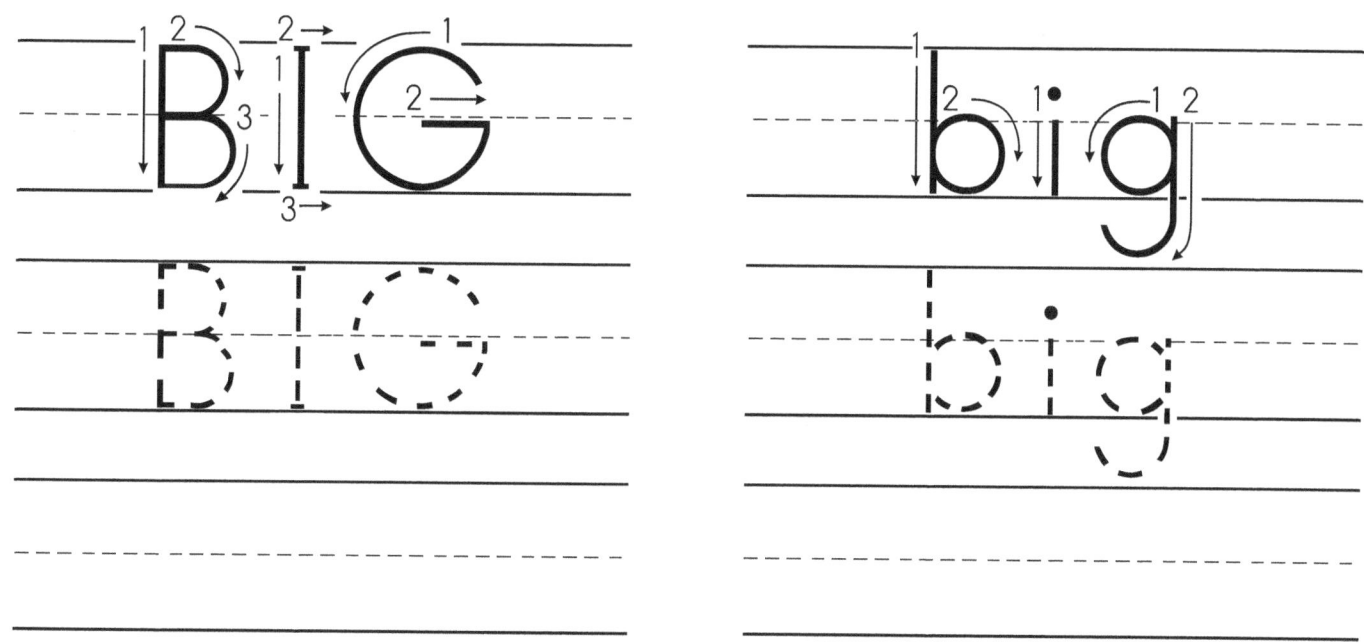

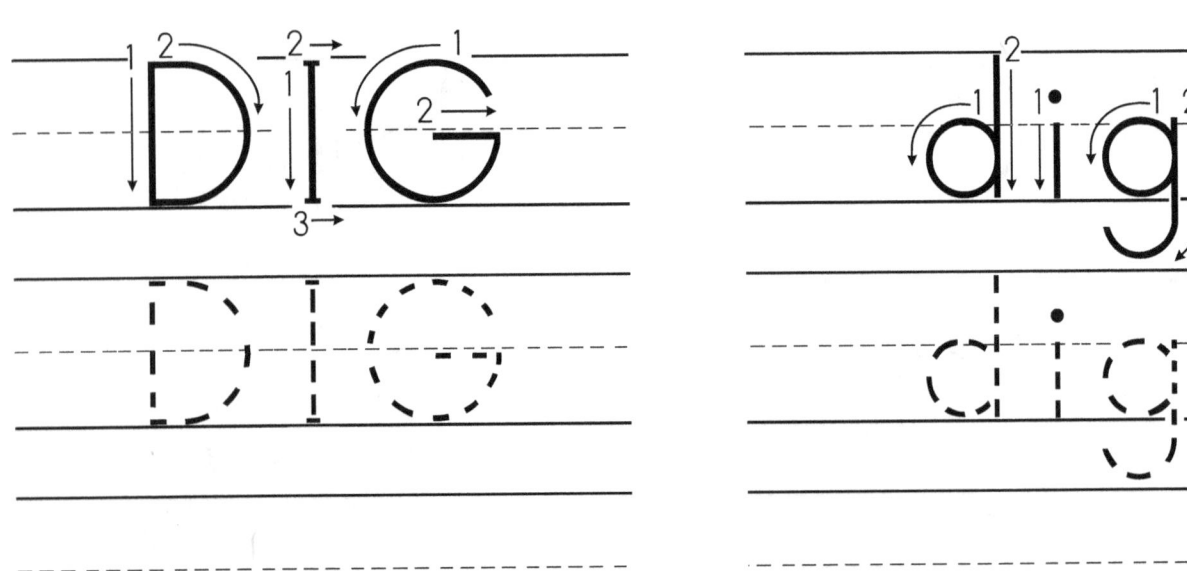

| 7 | dig |

BIG

big | 8

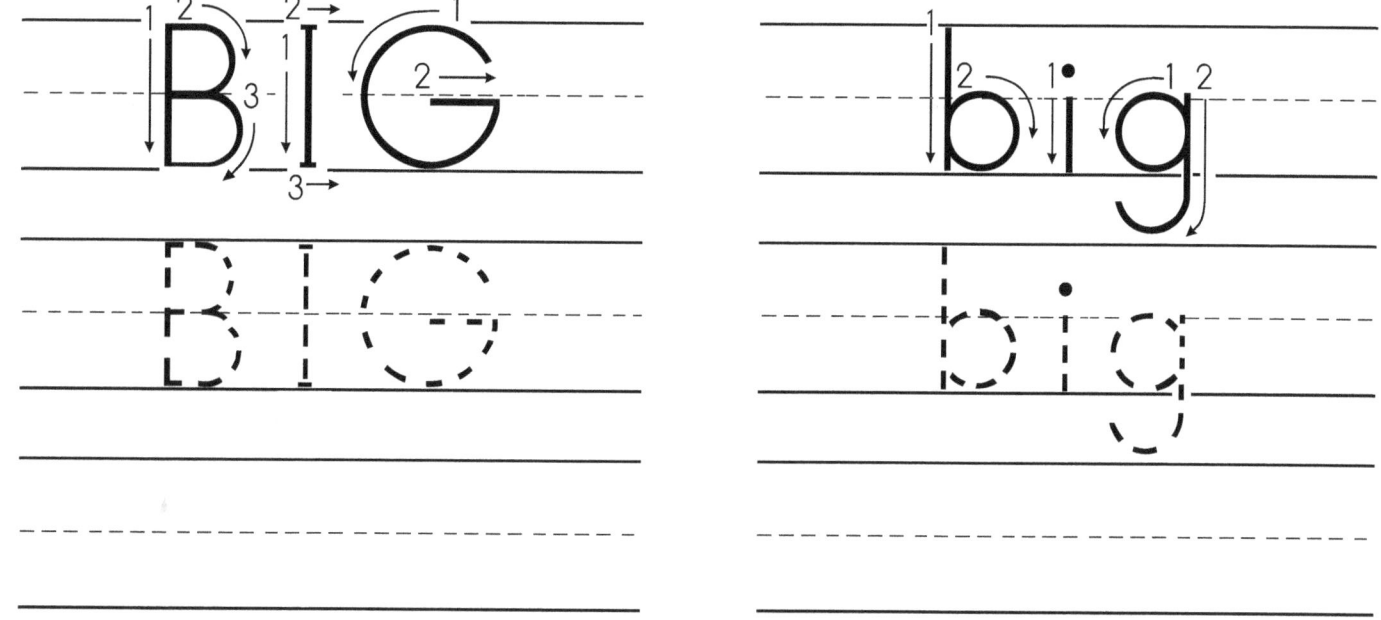

BIG

9 | big

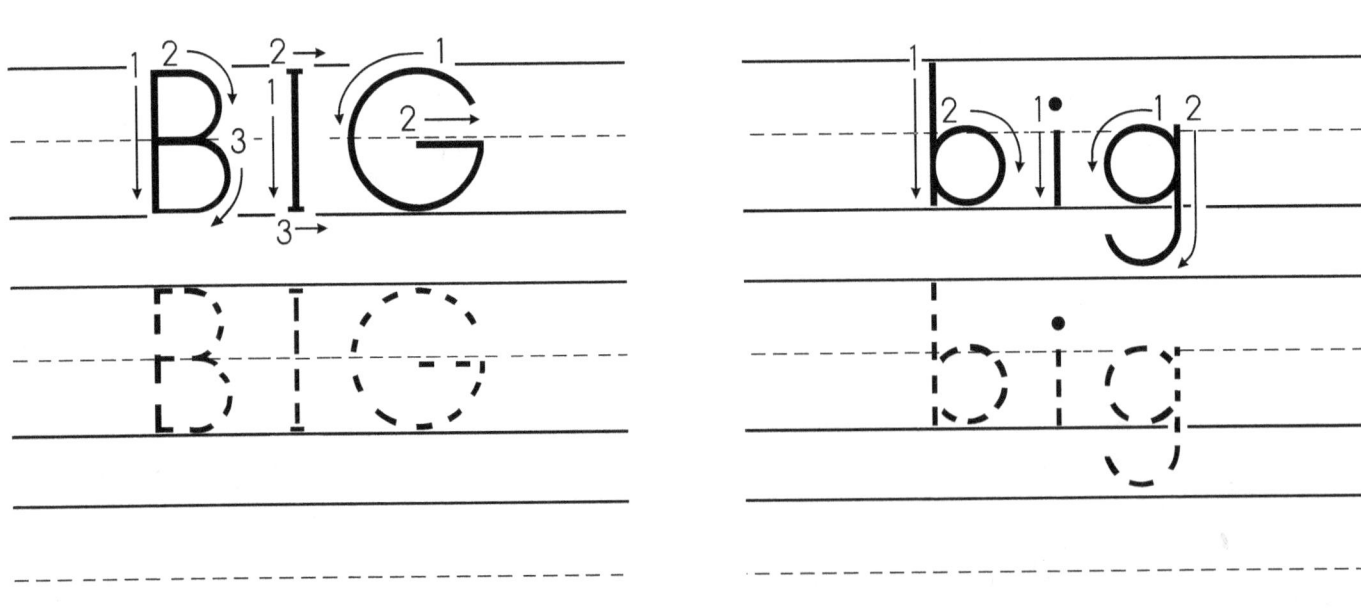

WIG

wig | 10

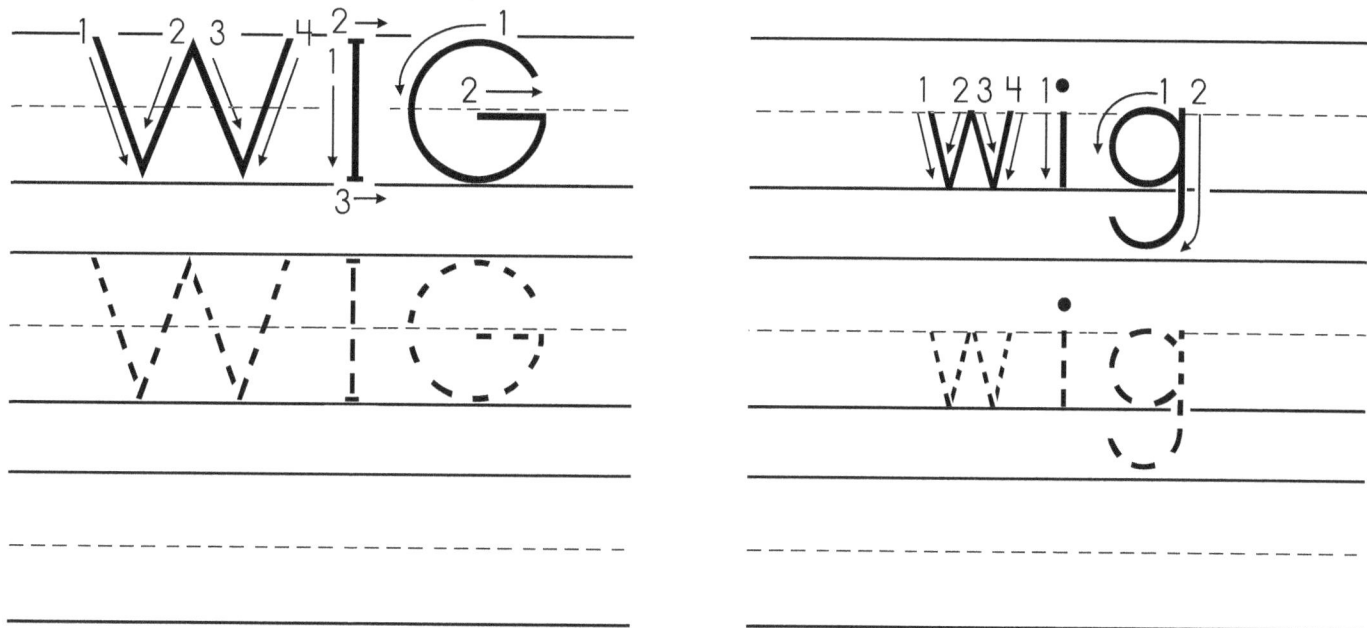

# BIG DIG

pig  dig
wig  big

Got it!

| 1 | hop |

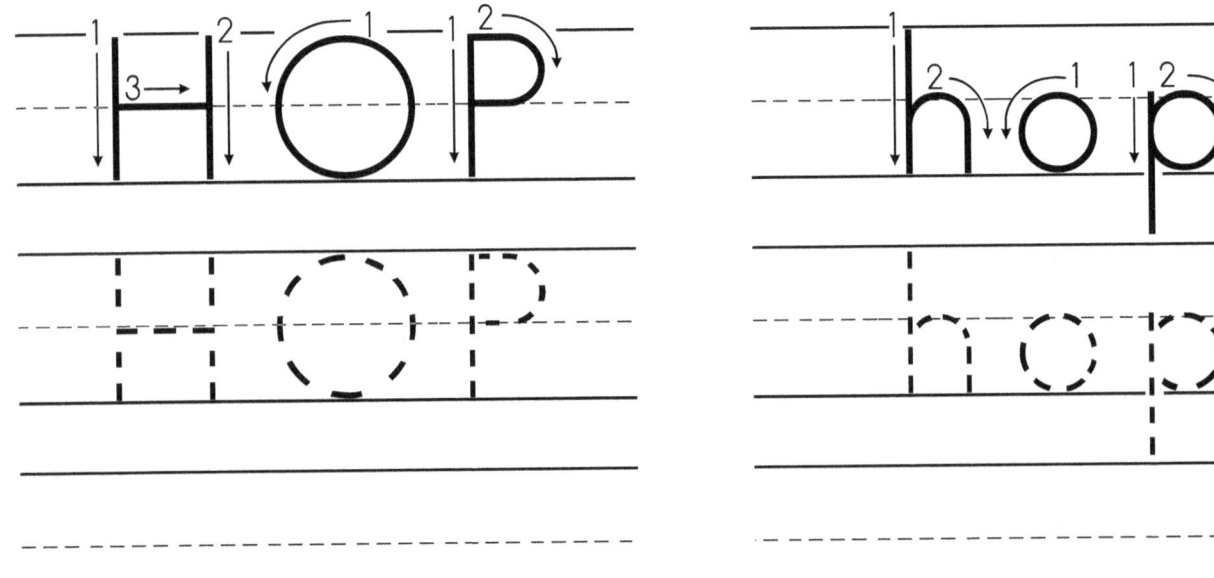

hop

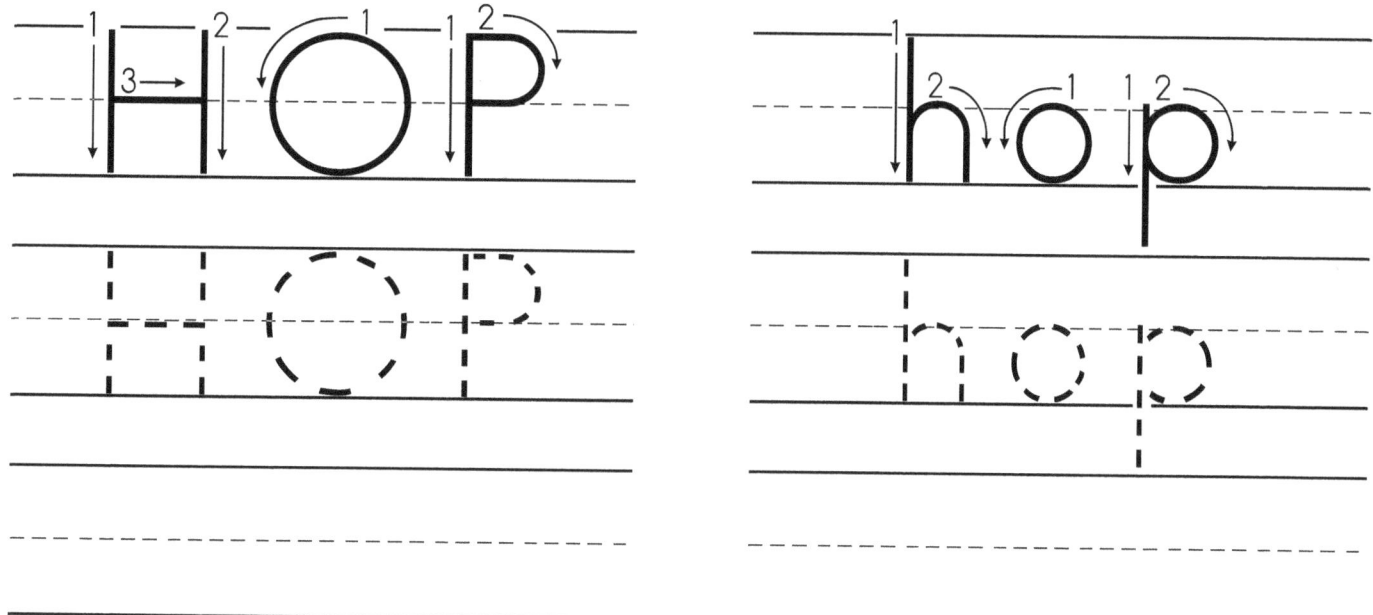

HOP

3 | hop

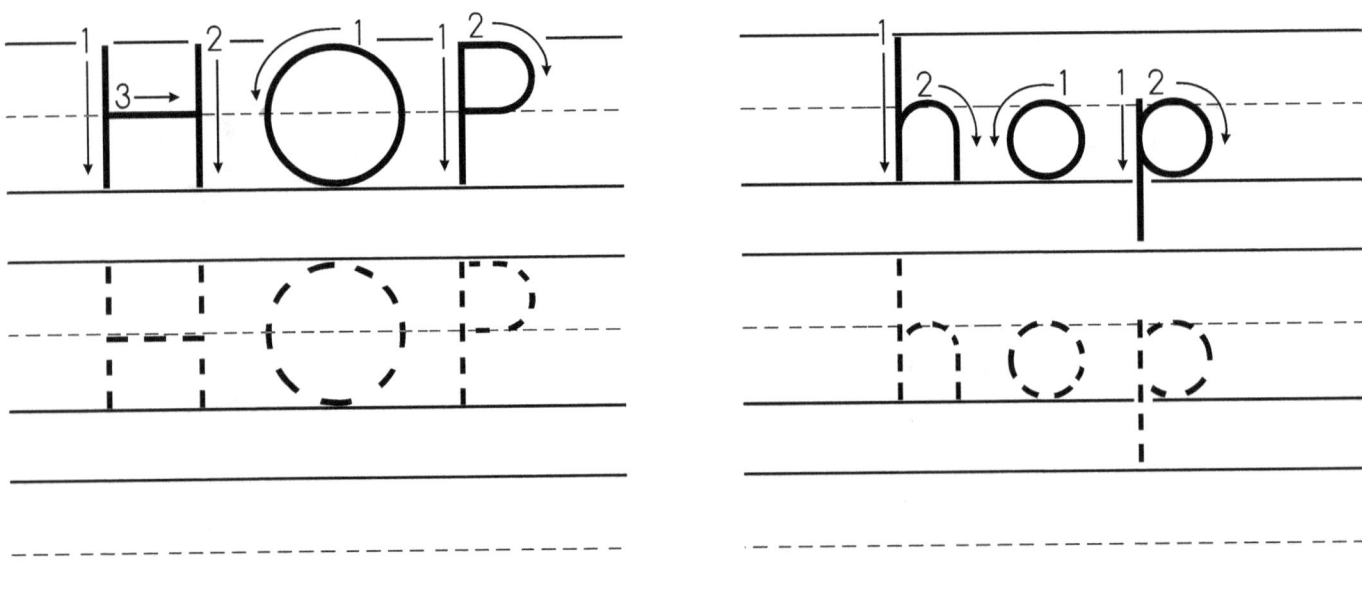

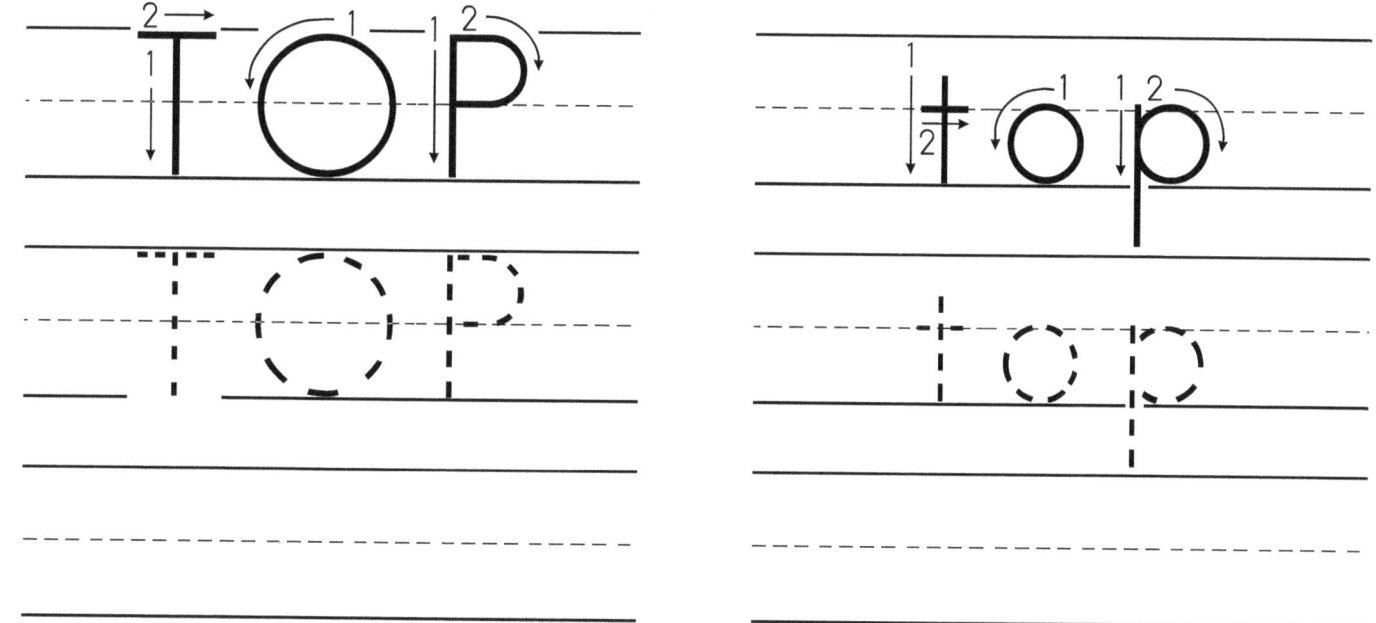

| 5 | hop |

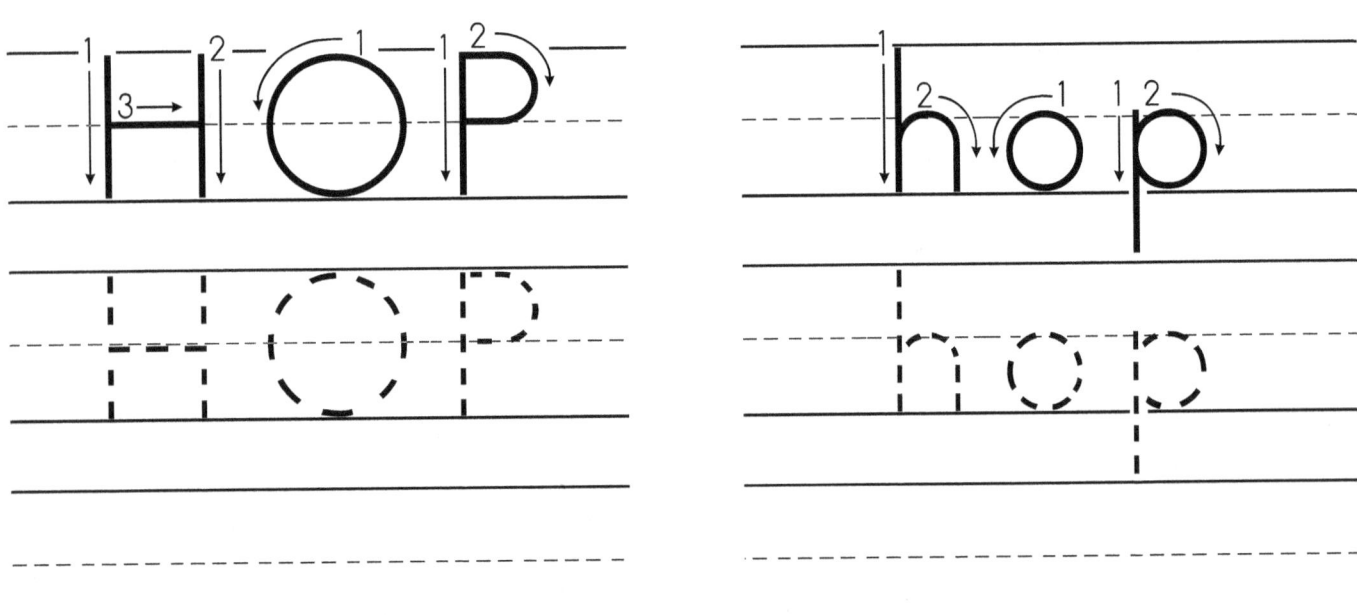

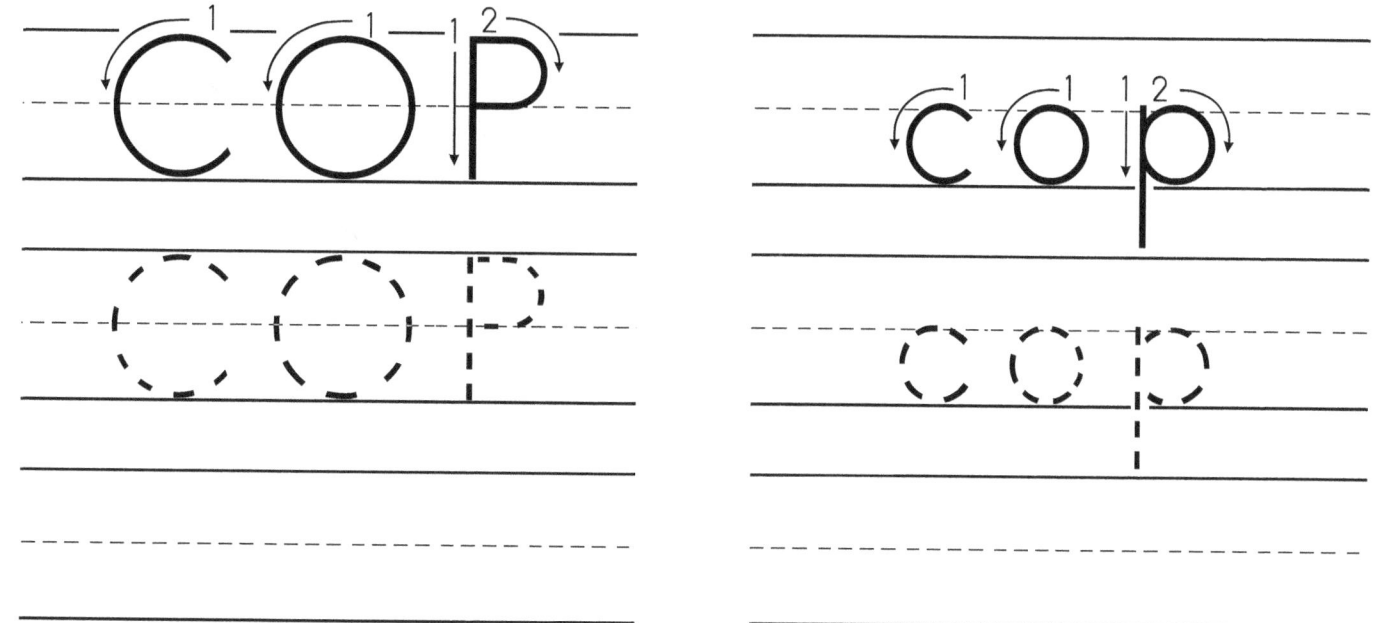

HOP

7 hop

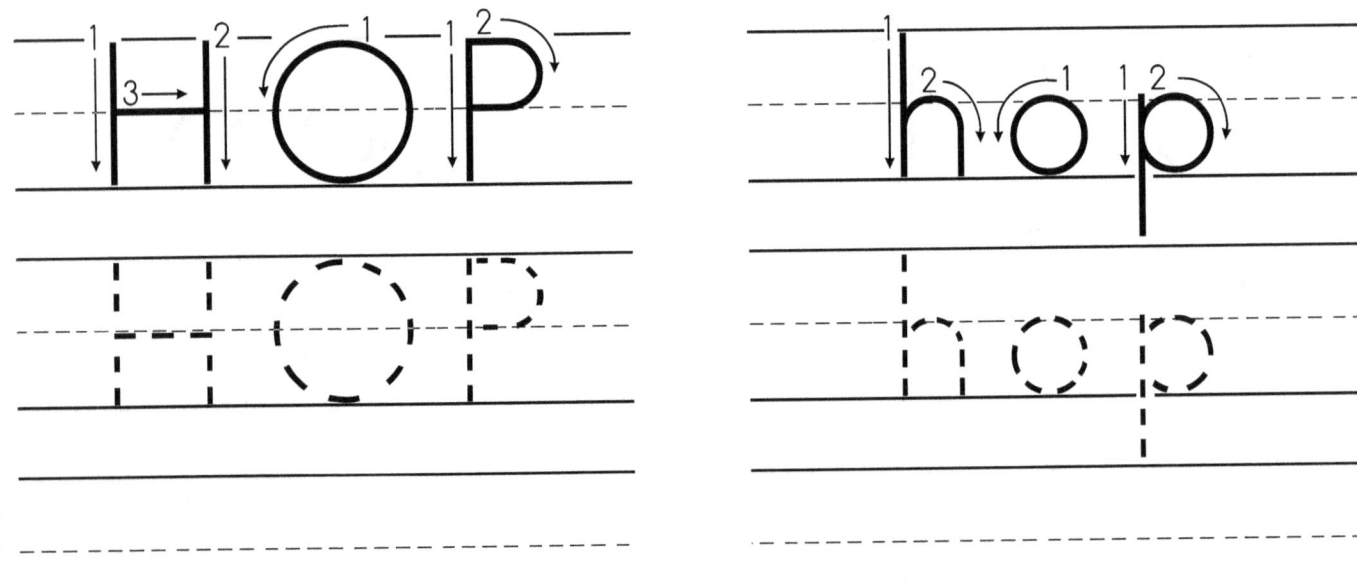

# hop | 8

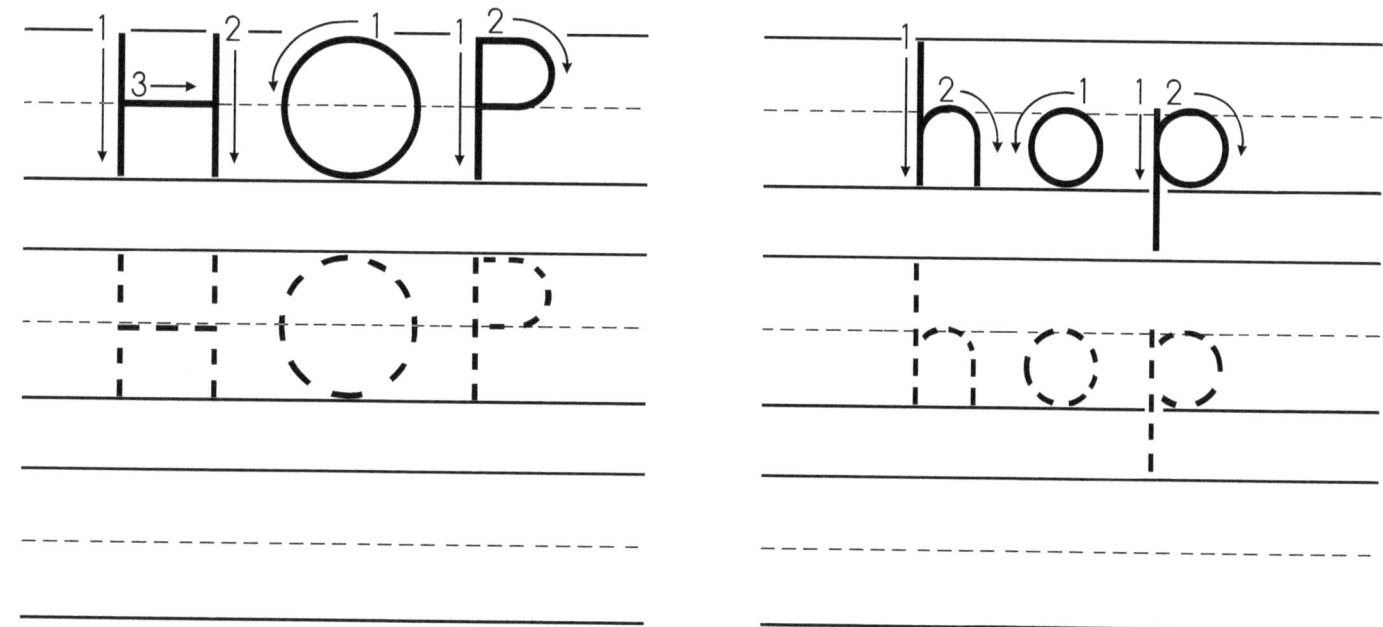

mop

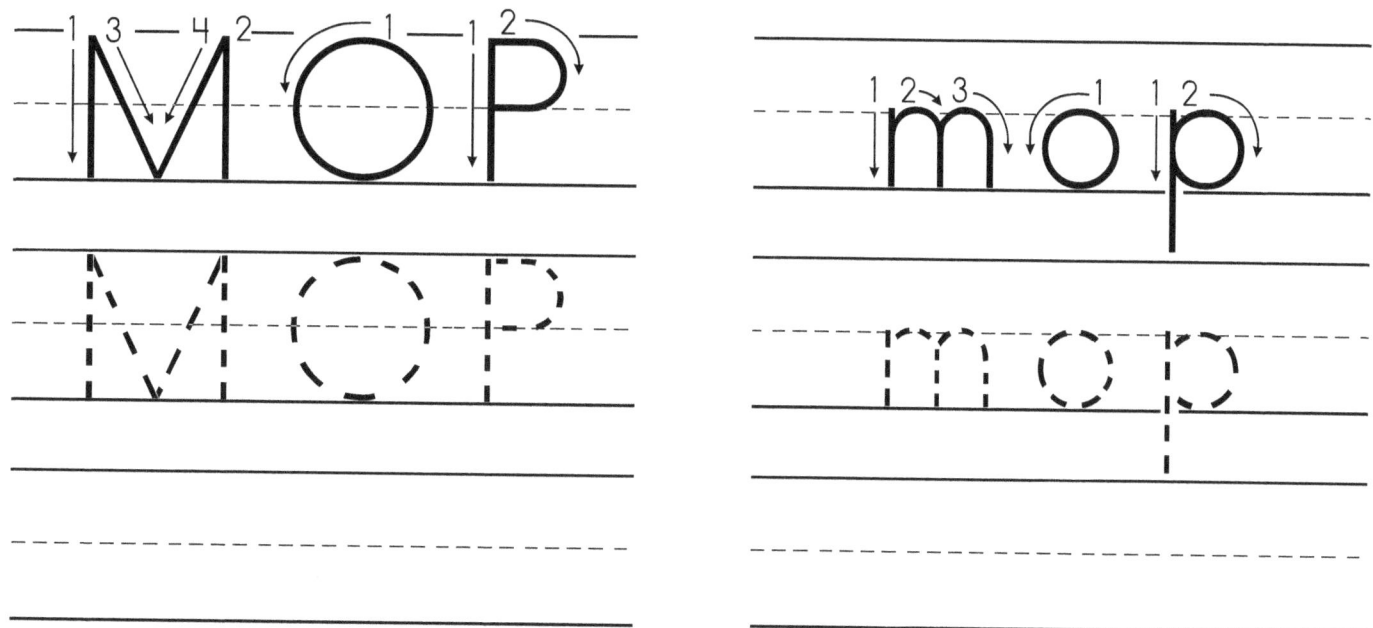

10

# HOP

hop     pop
top     mop
cop

Got it!

# GUM

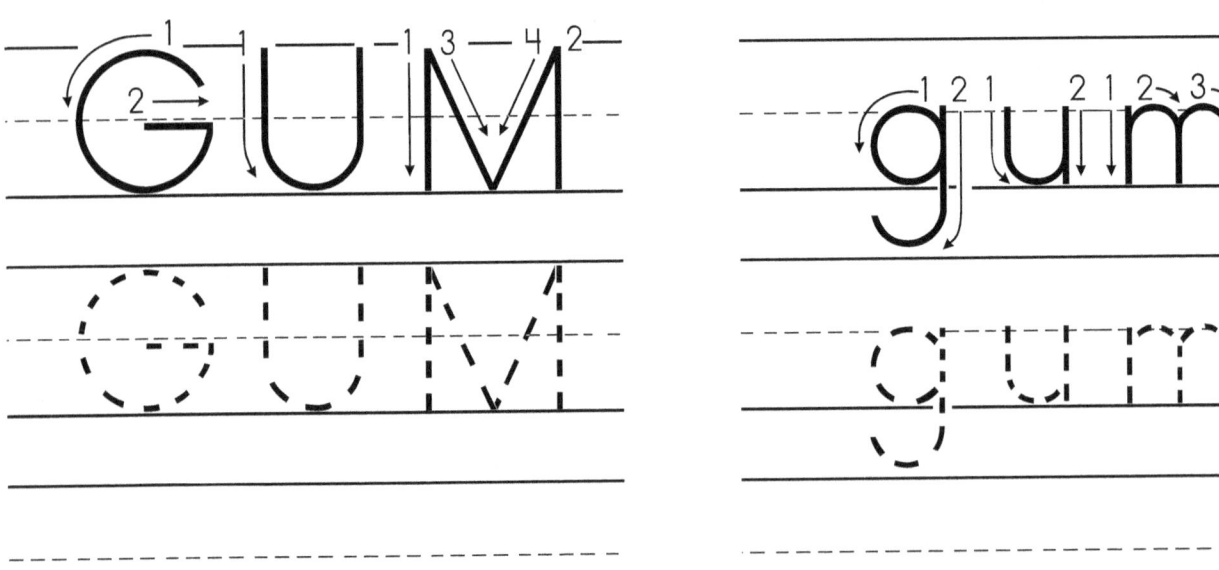

| 1 | gum |

## gum · 2

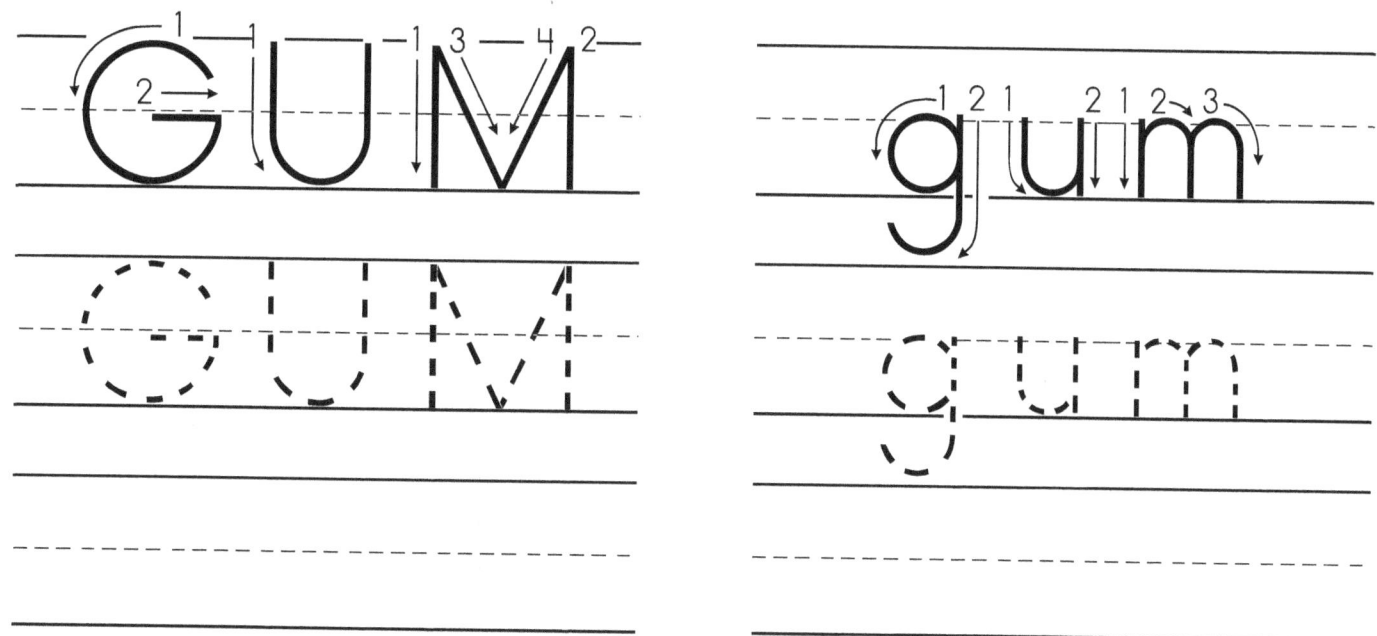

YUM

3 | yum

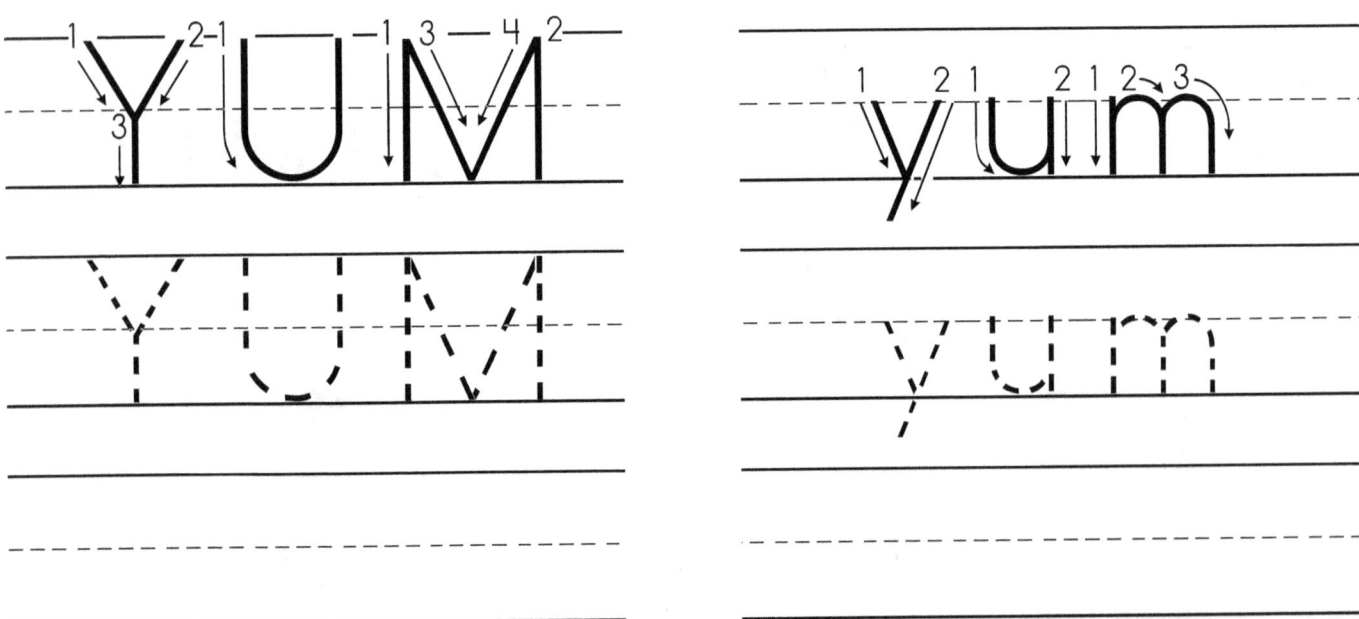

HUM

hum

4

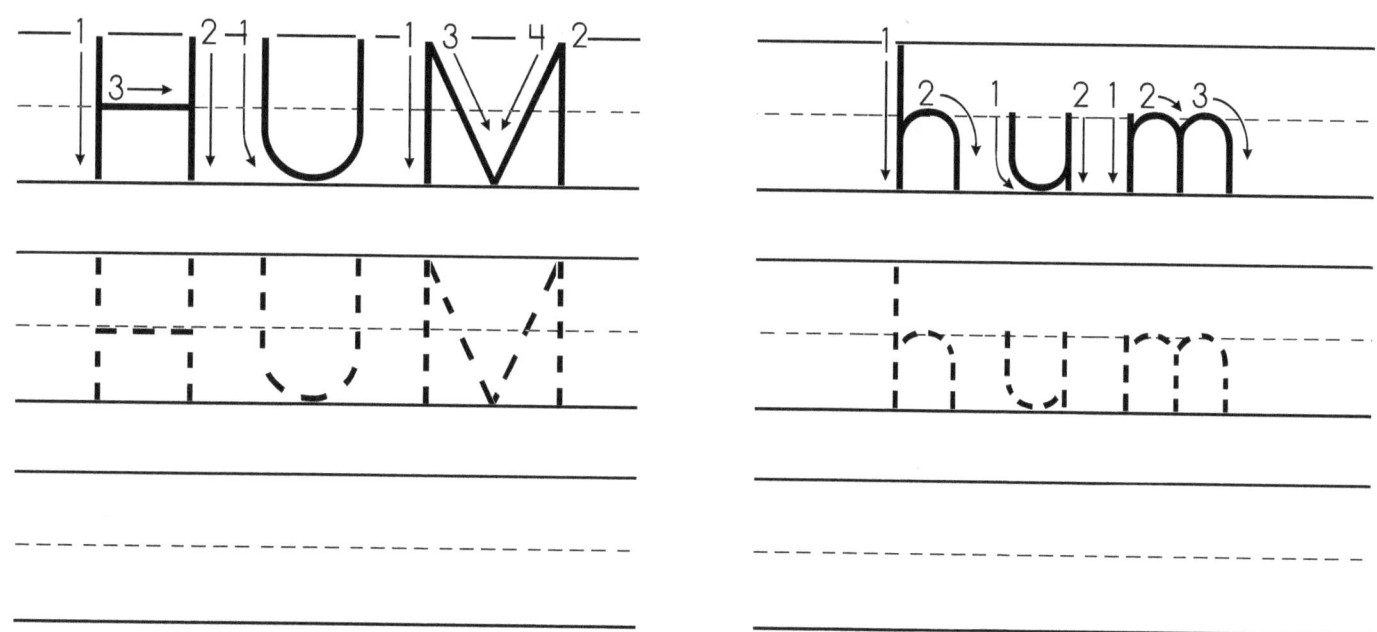

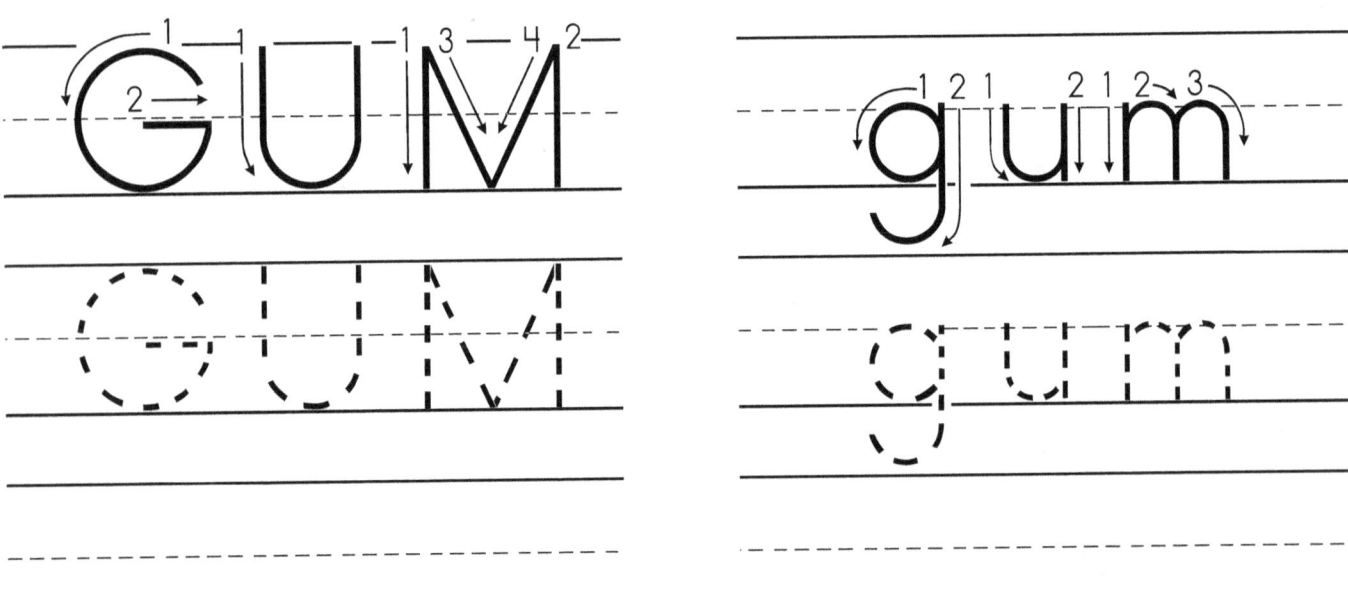

YUM

yum

6

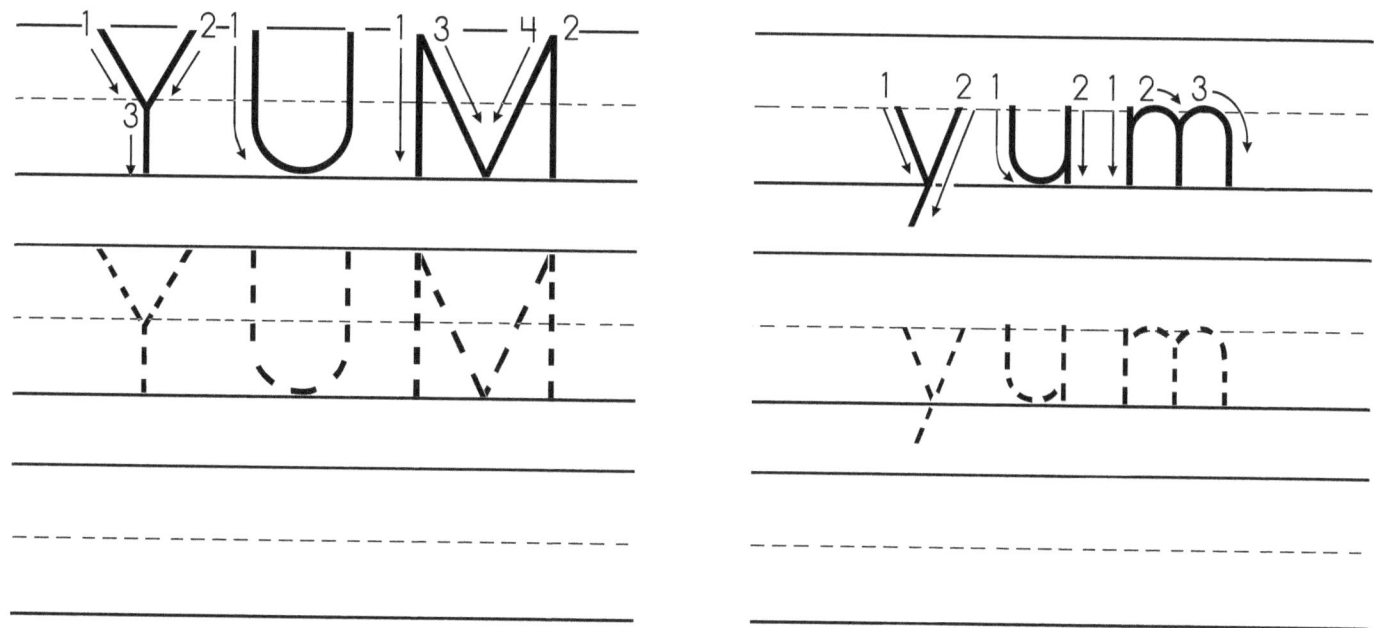

GUM

7 gum

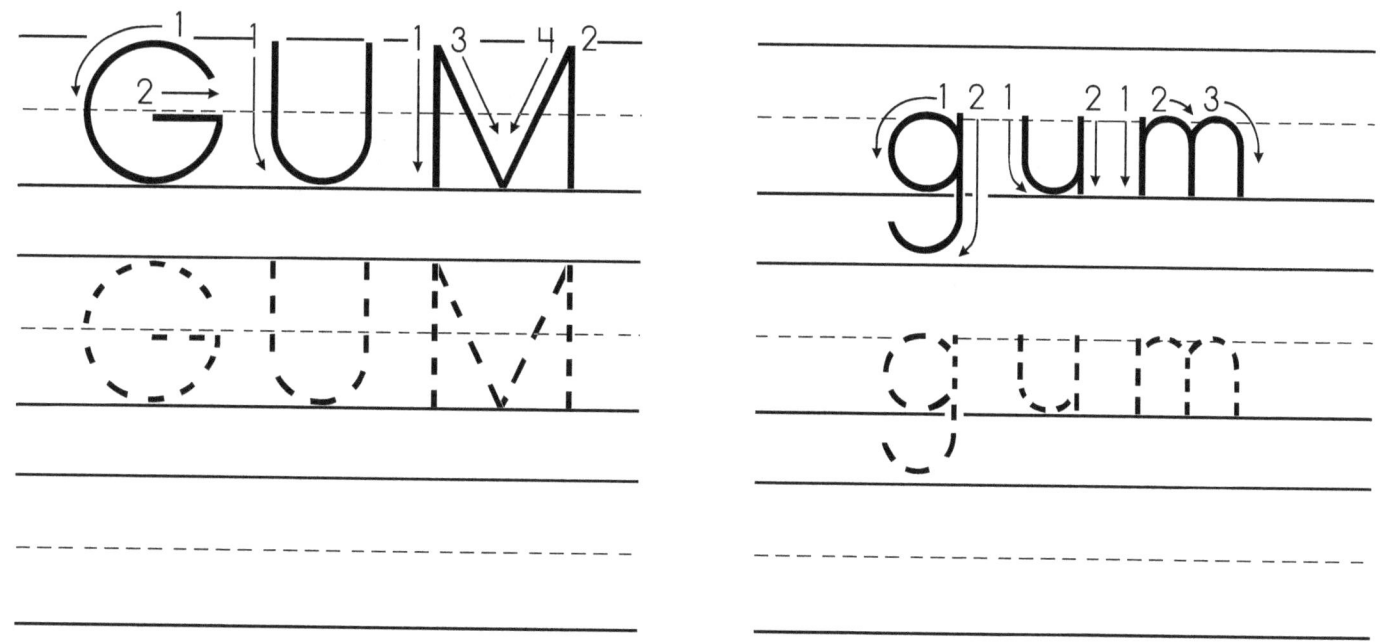

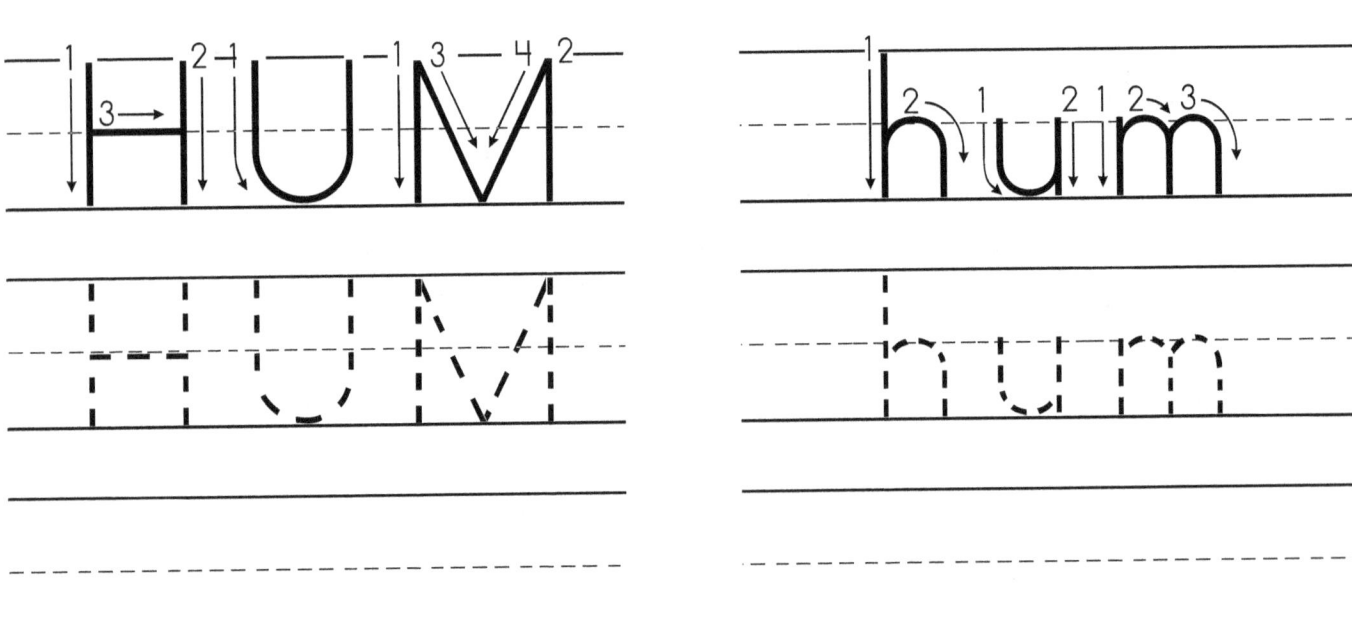

gum

10

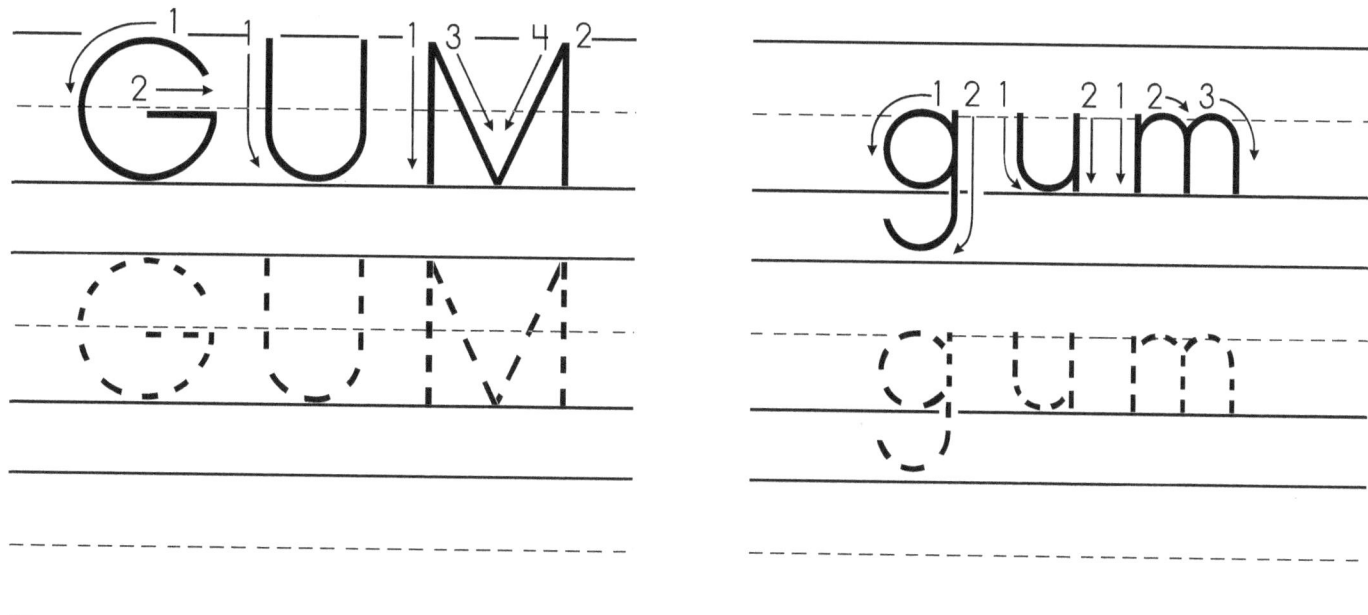

# GUM

gum   hum
yum

Got it!

# Books by Mark Linley

## About the Author

Mark Linley is a public school teacher and curriculum developer with over 20 years of experience teaching full time in the primary grades. He is the author of these and many other high quality learning materials, available on Amazon, Barnes and Noble, Teachers Pay Teachers, bartlebysbox.com, and other fine online retail establishments.

bartlebysbox.com

# Books by Mark Linley

## About the Author

Mark Linley is a public school teacher and curriculum developer with over 20 years of experience teaching full time in the primary grades. He is the author of these and many other high quality learning materials, available on Amazon, Barnes and Noble, Teachers Pay Teachers, bartlebysbox.com, and other fine online retail establishments.

bartlebysbox.com